You're nicked

Manchester University Press

series editors
JONATHAN BIGNELL
SARAH CARDWELL
STEVEN PEACOCK

already published

Paul Abbott   BETH LOUISE JOHNSON

Alan Bennett   KARA MCKECHNIE

Alan Clarke   DAVE ROLINSON

Jimmy McGovern   STEVE BLANDFORD

Andrew Davies   SARAH CARDWELL

Tony Garnett   STEPHEN LACEY

Trevor Griffiths   JOHN TULLOCH

Troy Kennedy Martin   LEZ COOKE

Terry Nation   JONATHAN BIGNELL AND ANDREW O'DAY

Jimmy Perry and David Croft   SIMON MORGAN-RUSSELL

Lynda La Plante   JULIA HALLAM

Jack Rosenthal   SUE VICE

Joss Whedon   MATTHEW PATEMAN

TV antiquity   SYLVIE MAGERSTÄDT

BEN LAMB

You're nicked

Investigating British television police series

Manchester University Press

Copyright © Ben Lamb 2020

The right of Ben Lamb to be identified as the author of this work has been asserted by him in accordance with the Copyright, Designs and Patents Act 1988.

Published by Manchester University Press
Oxford Road, Manchester M13 9PL
www.manchesteruniversitypress.co.uk

British Library Cataloguing-in-Publication Data
A catalogue record for this book is available from the British Library

ISBN   978 1 5261 2585 9   hardback
ISBN   978 1 5261 7195 5   paperback

First published 2020
Paperback published 2023

The publisher has no responsibility for the persistence or accuracy of URLs for any external or third-party internet websites referred to in this book, and does not guarantee that any content on such websites is, or will remain, accurate or appropriate.

Typeset by Newgen Publishing UK

For PC John Lamb,
Cleveland Police's finest

Contents

LIST OF FIGURES	*page* viii
GENERAL EDITORS' PREFACE	ix
ACKNOWLEDGEMENTS	xi
Introduction: defining a genre	1
1 The 1950s and 1960s: a genre comes into its own	13
2 The 1970s: an action-fuelled filmic decade?	35
3 The 1980s: emergent feminist thought and resurgent video cameras	61
4 The 1990s: transitioning from film to digital	90
5 The 2000s: looking to the past	120
6 The 2010s: looking to pastures new	149
CONCLUSION: GOOD EVENING, ALL	181
POSTSCRIPT: JED MERCURIO THRILLERS, PANDEMIC POLICING, AND POPULISM	193
REFERENCES	215
INDEX	236

Figures

1. Betty Smith looks over disapprovingly at her husband from the kitchen area, because he has not considered the social support that victims of crime require. *page* 55
2–3. Regan reminisces about Williams whilst alone in the pub on leave. The camera cuts to a shot of their previous romantic encounter from Regan's point of view to show what is occupying his mind. 57–58
4–5. Miller must learn to shun the warm sunlight and the corresponding interdependence it represents in order to thrive as a successful detective worthy of promotion. 156
6–7. Miller grows with confidence and stature as she learns how to operate independently from her colleagues. 158
8. Kevin Weatherill draws the camera into a darkened close-up as he expresses hatred of his boss to his wife Jenny Weatherill in their conservatory. 169
9. Cawood and Cartwright share the frame in a two-shot when conducting their responsive conversations whilst overlooking the neighbourhood. This starkly contrasts with the darkened close-ups of Weatherill whose enraged jealousy of Nevison Gallagher exponentially worsens when conversing with his wife Jenny in their isolated conservatory. 174

General editors' preface

Television is part of our everyday experience and is one of the most significant features of our cultural lives today. Yet its practitioners and its artistic and cultural achievements remain relatively unacknowledged. The books in this series aim to remedy this by addressing the work of major television writers and creators, and important and interesting genres of programme. Each volume provides an authoritative and accessible guide that focuses on either a particular practitioner's output or a body of related work, and assesses its contribution to television over the years. Books in the series give a carefully researched, historically based overview of the material addressed, and make a case for the importance of the work considered, by means of close textual analysis integrated with other materials. Many of the volumes draw on original sources, such as specially conducted interviews and archive material, and all of them list relevant bibliographic sources and provide full details of the programmes discussed.

In comparison with some related disciplines, television studies scholarship is still relatively young, and this series aims to contribute to this vigorous and evolving field. The series provides resources for critical thinking about television. Whilst maintaining a clear focus on writers, creators, and programmes themselves, the books in the series also take account of key critical concepts and theories in television studies. Each book is written from a particular critical or theoretical perspective, with reference to pertinent issues, and the approaches included in the series are varied and sometimes dissenting. Each author explicitly outlines the reasons for his or her particular focus, methodology, or perspective. Readers are invited to think critically about the subject matter and approach covered in each book.

Although the series is addressed primarily to students and scholars of television, the books will also appeal to the many people who are interested in how television programmes have been commissioned, made, and enjoyed. Since television has been so much a part of personal and public life in the twentieth and twenty-first centuries, we hope that the series will engage with, and sometimes challenge, a broad and diverse readership.

Jonathan Bignell
Sarah Cardwell
Steven Peacock

Acknowledgements

I am forever grateful to Stephen Lacey and Ruth McElroy for helping me overcome my imposter syndrome, through their research counsel, during the earlier stages of this book. I am indebted to Jonathan Bignell and James Chapman who, along with Stephen Lacey, created the Arts and Humanities Research Council-funded Spaces of Television research project that instigated this research. My thanks to Billy Smart and Leah Panos for their invaluable advice. Special thanks to Jeff Walden for his assistance in the location of relevant documents at the BBC Written Archives in Cavesham. I am also grateful to Alison Peirse and Charlotte Brunsdon, who encouraged me in the earlier stages of my academic career to progress to the next stage of study. Thanks to all those at the University of East Anglia, Teesside University, and Manchester University Press (Matthew Frost in particular) who took a chance on an early-career researcher. On a personal note I would like to thank Sophie Venables and our black Labrador Bagheera for their endless patience, love, and moral support. Finally, my parents have always been there to help me throughout my life. Without their encouragement to pursue my interests, none of this would have been possible. I can never thank them enough.

Introduction: defining a genre

> The uniforms will take us into parts of society that we usually don't enter.
> Tony Garnett, producer (Garnett 1998: n.p.)

The police series is a genre of British television drama that has captivated audiences for over sixty years. Its inclination to explore the more distressing aspects of British life, into which other forms of mainstream television often dare not venture, still manages to attract viewers in their millions. However, with the finale of *Broadchurch* (ITV, 2013–2017) peaking at 9.3 million viewers on Monday 17 April 2017, you could be forgiven for thinking that the genre is in decline. In comparison, *The Sweeney* (ITV, 1975–1978) regularly reached 20 million homes: that's 35 per cent of the then total British population, compared to *Broadchurch*'s 14 per cent of the public in 2017.[1] In essence, the nature of television broadcasting has changed and its audience has dispersed across a highly competitive and global, multichannel marketplace. Hundreds of channels, streaming services, and digital platforms are aggressively competing with one another, utilising algorithms to tailor entire services around our individual tastes. With the added luxury of being able to watch whatever content we want, whenever we want, on any device that we want, any programme that draws in viewers around the 10 million mark represents the most successful British television drama broadcast in the late 2010s.

Nevertheless, as a staple of British television schedules, police dramas have continuously operated as a 'Trojan horse' with the potential to influence national debate. As expressed by producer Tony Garnett (above), often the most commercially successful and critically revered police series utilise a clear iconography and set of themes. Popular with both broadcasters and audiences this recognisable format can expose the effects disenfranchised communities experience from broader socio-economic changes. Such a genre possesses the capability to reveal how national strategies employed by the Government to tackle inequality, and the perceived relationship between poverty and crime, impact upon the British public's relationship with its police force. Therefore police officer characters can be used as an incidental means of exploring transformations to traditional class identities; class relations; and the dynamics of social, economic, and gender inequality.

Following the hardship of the Second World War there was a collective belief, in light of the 1942 Beveridge Report and the writings of economist John Maynard Keynes, that the 'future of full employment, social justice, and a minimum level of welfare for all people' served as the 'ideal' to which all 'governments aspired while in office' (Kingsley Kent 1999: 335). So popular was this vision that the Beveridge Report sold over a million copies. William Beveridge became an international celebrity who regularly explained to large crowds the social principles he felt should underpin western capitalism. However, over time Beveridge's social vision has had its universalist foundations gradually stripped away by incumbent prime ministers. Harold Wilson introduced earnings-related contributions in 1966, Edward Heath introduced increased means-testing in 1973, and Margaret Thatcher removed the Government's commitment to full employment by 1986 in favour of a globalised neoliberal economy underpinned by individual entrepreneurship.[2] Analogously, the police series has maintained its position as 'a privileged site for the staging of the trauma of the breakup of the post-war settlement', given its frequent depiction of social unrest whilst Government provision for the most vulnerable continues to decline (Brunsdon 2000: 196).

This is the first study to analyse television police series produced in the UK from 1955 until the late 2010s over the course of a book. Notions of what constitutes a 'police series' can change over time. It is a genre whereby archetypal series borrow a mixture of visual and thematic tropes more readily associated with other established genres and movements. The purpose of this book is to examine how cultural understandings of what constitutes the police series have developed over each decade as the relationship between a television programme's production practices, visual style, and resultant ideology has evolved. When referring to 'production practices' I mean the authorial contribution of key practitioners to productions, the camera technologies available to them, and dominant performance styles of actors at the time. Essentially this book is a diachronic exploration of the tensions that exist between the nexus of these production choices with the subsequent style and then ideology of key texts in relation to wider socio-economic events. *You're nicked* explores how all of these factors operate in dialogue with one another and considers how they impact on the changing definitions of the UK police series genre.

Introduction   3

Reaching a definition

The police series is a genre with a number of cultural influences, including the soap opera, horror, sci-fi, western, and social realism, that are often combined in a sophisticated manner. A recurring theme repeatedly explored through this combination of influences, which prominent feminist scholars argue is intrinsic to most forms of television drama, is a sexual division of labour. This division often depicts 'the home as a space of femininity and leisure and the public world as a place of masculinity and work' (Brunsdon et al. 1997a: 19). Most existing academic studies of police series exclusively examine how police officers are portrayed in their working lives as part of the public world of work. However, academics have not always considered the extent to which the depiction of private domestic spaces can make an ideological contribution to the genre. This book is interested in how representations of gender and social class, within both public and private spaces, are articulated visually according to production practices at play within landmark series. The study will analyse how a dichotomy between the public and private spheres is reinforced, debated, or challenged by the stylistic and thematic composition of specific series. It also considers to what extent fictional television programmes can be considered 'evidence' of social change.

As hundreds of dramas broadcast from 1955 to today could fall under the umbrella term 'police series', it would be impossible to analyse them all sufficiently within a comprehensive study. Therefore, this book has undertaken a rigorous selection process. Rather than interrogating the precise boundaries that exist between the 'detective series' and the 'police procedural', I have chosen for analysis here series that regularly depict the routine work of police constables and detectives.[3] They are series grounded in the real working practices of specific constabularies at the time of broadcast. Action-based series including *Gideon's Way* (ITV, 1965–1966), *Department S* (ITV, 1969–1970), *The Professionals* (ITV, 1977–1983), *The Sandbaggers* (ITV, 1978–1980), *Spooks* (BBC, 2002–2011), and *Sherlock* (BBC, 2010–) etc. are not included. These dramas are decidedly more invested in espionage or fantasy and are less interested in the types of crime likely to be experienced by ordinary members of the public. Nor are they interested in how crime trends were being addressed by real police forces or specialist squads. Including such series could embroil this study in questions of where intelligence-gathering ends and policing begins, thus losing sight of the focus on how the representation of police procedure and its impact on the public has developed. Although such programmes may

4 You're nicked

be considered police series in another context, they are not deemed so in this instance. Similarly, the police series that have been chosen were popular at their time of transmission. I have discarded marginal series, as *You're nicked* is a study of popular police series that regularly attracted millions of viewers and so may have influenced their respective cultural and social epochs.

Current scholarship

Landmark academic studies on the stylistic composition and ideological construction of British police series often negotiate two widely believed assumptions. First, the idea that the genre traditionally abides by a masculinist discourse is treated as a truism. Second, there is an intrinsic supposition that the introduction of film cameras and then digital technology automatically updates the visual sophistication and/or ideological complexity of the genre. Alan Clarke provided the first key academic study of the British police series. His essay (Clarke 1992) maps the ideological make-up of key series in relation to the production technologies used, whilst considering what was occurring within the British police force at the time.

Clarke believes that a cluster of four ideological elements define the parameters of the British police series. These are: the threat of crime that is depicted, the type of family life the protagonist leads, whether the protagonist engages in rule-breaking, and to what extent their characteristics are individualistic. Using this guiding schema Clarke contends that *The Sweeney*'s use of 16 mm cameras provided the police series genre with a 'harder edge' compared to previous series and their 'slow moving narrative and static camerawork' (Clarke 1992: 233). However, according to Clarke, *The Sweeney* does not manage substantially to revolutionise the ordering of the genre's ideological components. Protagonist Jack Regan (John Thaw) is still an honest and incorruptible police official who works tirelessly 'to protect the public from villains who prey on society' like his predecessor George Dixon (Jack Warner) of *Dixon of Dock Green* (BBC, 1955–1976) (Clarke 1992: 243). Following this analysis Clarke argues that the BBC's later series *Juliet Bravo* (BBC, 1980–1985), in comparison to *The Sweeney*, 'provides a transformation in the genre through the reordering of ideological elements' (Clarke 1992: 248). Both series were created by Ian Kennedy Martin but now the threat of crime is reduced in scale; protagonist Jean Darblay's (Stephanie Turner) family life is given more script time; there is no rule breaking; and the emphasis on individual traits, domestic situations, and career progression of the main character paint a different picture of individualism. Because 'the transformation of the genre is a product of social forces of production shaping these ideological parameters', Clarke also maintains that it is important 'not to isolate moments of fictional representation from the rest of the lived world' (Clarke 1992: 252). In particular he considers *The Sweeney*'s depiction of individualism in part as a response to the appointment of Robert Mark as Metropolitan Police Commissioner.

Clarke's study proved to be pivotal to the academic study of police series. His focus on the leading protagonist as the principal site for discerning how a series' style, ideology, and relationship to the real world intersect has dictated subsequent studies of the genre. For example, Lez Cooke's *British Television Drama: A History* (2015a), and his contribution to the *Television Genre Book* (2015b), situate the development of the police series in relation to the stylistic tendencies of British television drama at the time of production. Both studies reiterate Clarke's narrative by characterising key technological developments, such as the rise of film-camera technology and then digital handheld cameras, as updating the verisimilitude and ideological reordering of the genre. Cooke's brief readings of *Z Cars*, *The Sweeney*, and *The Cops* (BBC, 1998–2001) continue to represent an accessible basis for studying this genre that still has yet to be substantially challenged. Each analysis considers how changes in production technologies and their resulting visual discourse can impact upon a protagonist's characterisation in relation to what was happening within the British police force at the time.

Analysing the rich lineage of British police series requires watching hundreds of hours of content. Therefore academic works often focus on the representation of police officer characters within a very specific time period over the course of a book. This ensures that a more nuanced account of the genre's developments can be excavated. Susan Sydney-Smith's *Beyond 'Dixon of Dock Green'* (2002) begins with Robert Barr's *Telecrimes* documentary series (BBC, 1946) and concludes with *Softly, Softly* (BBC, 1966–1976) to consider how overlooked texts influenced better-known series from 1946 up until 1966. Her analysis of the six-part *Pilgrim Street* (BBC, 1952), for example, ascertains that all the 'germinal ideas' of *Dixon of Dock Green* and *Z Cars* (BBC, 1962–1978) can be traced back to this particular series and its depiction of 'ordinary everyday crime' (Sydney-Smith 2002: 79). Similarly, Helen Piper's *The TV Detective* (2015) examines British detective series broadcast from 1992 to 2012 to chart the detective genre's 'aesthetic directions' as a means of categorising the types of dissident protagonists that are central to the genre (Piper 2015: 2). In so doing, Piper's genealogical study considers how the development process within different television production contexts can impact upon the narrative and stylistic form of detective subgenres. Both authors concentrate on a twenty-year period in order to provide a more detailed account of development within a specific era that cannot be achieved by books operating within a larger timeframe.

Correspondingly, the BFI TV Classics series takes an even more concentrated approach. Each book devotes itself to one television series to draw out links between the drama in question and its social context. Mark Duguid's *Cracker* (2009) traces the origins and development of ITV's series in the context of early 1990s television and places it in its contemporary social and political landscape. Meanwhile, Charlotte Brunsdon's *Law and Order* (2010) analyses the controversial BBC serial in relation to contemporary criminal justice scandals of the 1970s to explore the outrage that the broadcasts caused.

Another approach to studying the police series, adopted by other contributions to the Manchester University Press Television Series, involves focusing on the career of a particular screenwriter or producer. Stephen Lacey's *Tony Garnett* (2007), Julia Hallam's *Lynda La Plante* (2005), Lez Cooke's *Troy Kennedy Martin* (2012), and Steve Blandford's *Jimmy McGovern* (2013) each analyse one television auteur. Each book examines how a television practitioner develops their authorial signature and to what extent their contributions may have impacted upon the visual, verisimilar, and ideological development of UK police series.

Lastly, Sue Turnbull's comprehensive *TV Crime Drama* (2014) contains a chapter that examines the developments, in the form and style, of the British procedural series from its inception up until 2014. It considers what has been valued within the British context of production in relation to America. Similarly, her later chapter entitled 'Women and crime' examines the representation of women police officers in UK, US, and Scandinavian crime drama. Whilst the strength of Turnbull's book is that it manages succinctly to cover the entire history of the genre and open up a dialogue among different countries' practices, she still largely conforms to the oft-repeated narrative of the genre's development in the UK. Whilst Turnbull has instigated a well-needed reassessment of the genre, it scrapes the surface in terms of the precise class and gender politics that are at work in pivotal series.

Rationale and methodology

In response to this scholarship, *You're nicked* is the first study to examine British police series from 1955 until the present day in a way that

Introduction 7

conceptualises the importance of the genre's position within the wider socio-political context. It considers the unique insight the genre may be able to provide the postwar settlement's disassembly and the ways in which television drama may have intervened in the debates that led to this process. At the time of writing, television scholarship on the British police series has made little attempt to engage with criminological theory largely because each study, following Clarke's schema, primarily analyses the representation of police-officer characters as a measure of a given programme's ideology. To change the academic landscape this research analyses the depiction of the recurring civilian character types and their reasons for committing crime. It asks to what extent the crimes committed can be ascribed to social inequality, fracturing class relations, the dissolution of class identities, a lack of employment opportunities, or inadequate social justice. Where appropriate this representation of crime is mapped on to key criminological theories of the time and historical accounts of changes that were enacted within the British police force in response to public fears surrounding certain crime trends.

The diachronic methodological approach adopted here, usually synonymous with feminist studies of television drama, is particularly interested in how the representation of public and domestic spaces, and the differences that exist between them, can metonymically contribute to broader discussions regarding the public's understanding of class identity and gender roles.[4] Centring this discussion on the nature of the tension that exists among the production methods used, visual style produced, and resultant ideological composition created, in relation to cultural influences as well as socio-economic happenings, will reassess how understandings of what constitutes a police series have changed over time. Examining the nature of this interplay both through 'landmark', and critically overlooked but commercially popular police series, will further complicate the police series canon.

To examine this interplay, and deduce how the style produced by specific production technologies contributed to the ideological composition and development of the police series, my textual analysis is informed by Keir Elam's semiotics: a mode of analysis referred to as a 'science dedicated to the study of production of meaning in society' (Elam 1980: 1). Like Helen Wheatley's (2005) pivotal analysis of *Upstairs, Downstairs* (ITV, 1971–1975), my semiotic approach also pays particular attention to Elam's interest in the relationship shared between a character's attitudinal markers (gesturing) and their illocutionary markers (dialogue). I employ the approach pioneered by Wheatley because it has a refined ability to uncover the disjuncture that can exist between a character's

8 You're nicked

immediate dialogue and their gesturing. By paying particular attention to a character's framing, movement, positioning, and interaction with their set design, i.e. reading a scene 'spatially', one can deduce how dominant social issues of the time were being addressed (Wheatley 2005: 155).[5] Like Wheatley I subscribe to the view that 'the rhetoric of television drama is a rhetoric of discussion' because 'television does not present firm ideological conclusions – despite its formal conclusions – so much as it comments on ideological problems' (Newcomb and Hirsch 2000: 566, 565). Therefore I apply this form of textual analysis to the way specific social concerns are discussed in public and private spaces whilst keeping attuned to a programme's production practices and the social changes occurring in British society at that time. My analyses consider to what extent the police series genre can be treated as evidence of social change and what its contribution to that social change might be.

Structure of the book

To revaluate the development of the British police series each chapter is structured into three sections. The first section analyses how the visual style of the production mode in question frames the police-station space. It examines how the camerawork and set design are used to depict the police force's institutional politics, its inner rivalries, and its ideological stance towards preventing and solving crimes. The second section of each chapter then examines how these stylistic tropes are used to frame the domestic settings of civilian characters. It considers to what extent a series can intervene in national debate by paying specific attention to the economic anxiety and social pressures families were experiencing in relation to the fracturing postwar settlement and its impact on class and gendered identities. Lastly, the third section of each chapter examines what happens when the spatial composition of the police station and civilian home are combined within the homes of police officials. A police officer's, or detective's, domestic space must strike a balance between the sense of order featured in the police station with the socio-economic pressures occurring in the other civilian homes within their community. Therefore methodically studying the relationship among production technologies, style, and ideology within three different types of space in each chapter, in relation to socio-economic and criminological developments in British society, will reformulate dominant understandings of a genre that has been central to British television's development as a communicative medium.

Chapter 1 initially examines how *Z Cars* negotiates modernity in relation to the BBC's previous hit *Dixon of Dock Green*. Shot in real time by six simultaneously recording video cameras within a television studio, *Z Cars* weekly attracted 14 million viewers and is widely considered to have helped establish the founding conventions of the British police series genre. Set in the fictional Liverpool estates Newtown and Seaport, *Z Cars* has a distinctive regional flavour. Here, in terms of criminology, deviant subculture theories are particularly prevalent given the distinction repeatedly made between working class men's cultural goals and the institutional means by which they cannot achieve them. Essentially this first chapter argues that *Z Cars* instigated a shift in social-realist culture away from the inherent nostalgia of soap operas towards a more sobering assessment of alienated men who have slipped through the cracks of the postwar settlement.

Chapter 2 challenges traditional genre studies that grant too much significance to *The Sweeney* when looking at the 1970s. 'The 1970s: an action-fuelled filmic decade?' redresses such a balance by comparing *The Sweeney*'s use of film cameras on location, utilised to capture the cut-and-thrust working practices of the Flying Squad, in relation to *Hunter's Walk* (ITV, 1973–1976). The latter is a series that uses video cameras in the studio to undertake lengthy ethical discussions on how to keep the fictional Northamptonshire town of Broadstone at peace. Whilst *Hunter's Walk* invites a viewer to draw on their own conclusions, there is no such autonomy in *The Sweeney* as the camera becomes primarily interested in identifying with a principal protagonist and conforming to their perspective. Rather than being narratively focused on the act of pursuing criminals, *Hunter's Walk* concerns itself with the repercussions of crime and the suffering of victims within the home from a somewhat feminist perspective.

Chapter 3 brings the very popular 1980s series *Juliet Bravo*, *The Gentle Touch* (ITV, 1980–1984), and *The Bill* (ITV, 1984–2010) back into academic consciousness to argue that the gender politics of each programme are actually more intricate than previously realised when analysed spatially. *Juliet Bravo* uses the dimensions of Hartley station, a fictional Yorkshire-based police force, to echo the Scarman Report, that stated the priorities of the police and public had diverged. Meanwhile *The Gentle Touch*'s use of the close-up, as part of a melodramatic discourse, occupies a sceptical stance towards the additional paperwork that was being introduced in anticipation of the 1984 Police and Criminal Evidence Act as a response to Scarman's criticisms. Building on this reading, 'emergent feminist thought and resurgent video cameras' explores how both series explore the ideological inconsistencies of Margaret Thatcher's reassertion of the Victorian two-parent family unit through the representation of civilians' and police officials' private lives. Following this comparative analysis, *The Bill*'s use of Outside Broadcasting (OB) units is considered. I argue that this production technique, which brought video cameras and the studio method of recording drama to real outside locations, actually depoliticises the domestic space as part of a wider postfeminist discourse.

Chapter 4 first examines *Prime Suspect* (ITV, 1991–2006), *A Touch of Frost* (ITV, 1992–2010), and *Cracker* (ITV, 1993–2006). Each programme shares a stylistic and thematic affinity with the horror film, as the psychology of barbarous murderers are investigated in relation to larger socio-political anxieties. By utilising different stylistic traditions of the horror genre, each series captures an increasing dissatisfaction with the Home Office's 'rational actor model' approach towards tackling crime, which had dominated political discourse since 1970. From *Prime Suspect*'s fear of a growing underclass, to *Frost*'s criticisms of an increasingly sexually promiscuous middle class, and *Cracker*'s concerns surrounding an emerging working-class 'masculinity in crisis', 'The 1990s: transitioning from film to digital' considers the different ideological implications that arise from each series' exploration of British society's apparent social decline. 1998's *The Cops* is subsequently analysed for ushering the use of handheld digital cameras into the genre in a manner similar to the then-popular docusoap format. Set within Manchester in the fictional council estate of Skeetsmore, the series uses the digital cameras to frame both police officers and civilians. The resultant unstable aesthetic mimics the precariousness of sociologist Anthony Giddens's new individualism whilst critiquing the New Labour Government's use of 'left realism' criminology, adopted to tackle the disproportionate number of personal crimes suffered by the so-called 'underclass'.

Chapter 5 focuses on how police series of the 2000s use digital effects, particularly colour saturation, to access a nostalgia for the past as a means of addressing contemporary uncertainties. *Waking the Dead* (BBC, 2000–2011), *New Tricks* (BBC, 2003–2015), and *Life on Mars* (BBC, 2006–2007) all borrow visual elements from the sci-fi genre to examine how the nature, role, and difference between public and private spaces have changed over the past thirty years. Each series assesses the impact an increasing use of technology has on the police force and civilian life in relation to the past with varying ideological results. Accordingly, all three programmes are at odds with one another when considering how traditional detective work should be integrated with new, intelligence-led policing directives to combat increasingly complex forms of crime.

Introduction   11

Chapter 6 considers how the most successful police series broadcast since 2010 have marketed themselves as 'quality' television drama through their use of high-definition cameras and aerial photography. 'The 2010s: looking to pastures new' examines how such a stylistic direction has enabled *Broadchurch* and *Happy Valley* (BBC, 2014–) to draw connections between character and landscape in a manner similar to the recent Nordic Noir television crime genre, but in a way that merges the visual discourse of British landscape television documentaries with British new-wave social-realist cinema. Each series presents a different view of the way in which the 'squeezed middle' class can cope with austerity. *Broadchurch* advocates pro-social conservatism and postfeminism's 'new traditionalism' as a means of enduring the suffocating and erosive community pressures of its southern coastal town. Meanwhile, the West Yorkshire-based *Happy Valley* employs Raymond Williams's common culture to guarantee its lower-middle-class community's survival.

Lastly, the conclusion builds on the main developments uncovered by the book to provide a new framework for studying British television genre. Having focused on the use of space to challenge inherent assumptions repeatedly made about different production techniques, modes of realism, narrative formats, and ideologies, *You're nicked* provides a revisionist history of British television, British society, and British culture.

Notes

1. Figures obtained from ITV (2017); and Gambaccini and Taylor (1993). The percentage of the overall population these viewers encompassed was then worked out through the Office for National Statistics (2017).
2. These actions were implemented by the 1966 Supplementary Benefit Act, the 1973 Social Security Act, the 1982 Social Security and Housing Benefit Act, and the 1986 Social Security Act.
3. For a consideration of the differences that exist among the detective series, police procedural, and action series see Creeber (2015b).
4. See the analysis of soap operas, sitcoms, and daytime television conducted by Carole Lopate (1977), Tania Modleski (1979), Richard Dyer *et al.* (1980), Ellen Seiter (1982), and Patricia Mellencamp (1986), who collectively broaden the meaning of the term 'political' in television studies and wider culture to 'include a general interest in everyday life, especially the female-associated spheres of domesticity and consumerism' (Brunsdon *et al.* 1997a: 5).
5. Wheatley argues that reading Lady Marjorie (Rachel Gurney) spatially reveals a character who, despite voicing anti-feminist sentiments, is struggling with repressed desires. Marjorie wears a high collar and heavy corsetry, and is positioned behind her desk when expressing such opinions to provide her character with 'a sense of containment' (Wheatley 2005: 154). This contrasts starkly

with her relaxed demeanour and kimono dress on a visit to the opera with a man who is not her husband. Taken together these elements signify Marjorie's longing for the 'exotic outside to which she has no access' (Wheatley 2005: 154), and so address feminist debates concerning the clash between societal expectations of housewives in relation to their personal aspirations.

The 1950s and 1960s: a genre comes into its own

1

> We would concentrate on smaller everyday type of crime ... we set out to show a part of police work and I think we were right to stick to an approach which, within its self-imposed limits, is the true one.
>
> *Dixon of Dock Green* creator Ted Willis (Willis 1964)

> Cops were incidental – they were the means of finding out about people's lives.
>
> *Z Cars* producer John McGrath (quoted in Laing (1991): 127)

My study begins with an analysis of *Z Cars* (BBC, 1962–1978). I unearth the circumstances that led to *Z Cars*' commissioning and its transformative production practices. I then examine how the programme's resultant visual discourse upholds a humanitarian approach to policing in spite of Newtown station's institutional obstacles. Lastly, I consider how this benevolent view of police work is complicated by the way characters who fall outside welfare-state provision in relation to 'deviant subculture' criminology are addressed by representations of working-class men's private lives. The chapter explores how *Z Cars*' mobile camerawork, compared to *Dixon of Dock Green*'s (BBC, 1955–1976) conservative visuals and ideology, enabled the programme to uncover the emerging cracks in the postwar consensus. Although, given the clear dichotomy presented between public and private spaces, I argue that establishing the British police series as a permanent fixture of the television schedule was underscored by a new candid form of social realism devoted to the stresses of working-class men's experiences.

A genre is born

The unflinching mode of social realism implemented by *Z Cars* was, in part, a response to the arrival of commercial television. Following the UK Government's 1954 Television Act an Independent Television

Authority (ITA) awarded licences to production companies throughout the UK. Each company, or franchise, was tasked with providing programming for the region in which it was based. Launching the Independent Television (ITV) channel shook the BBC to its very core, as its comfortable twenty-year monopoly was now over. Whilst ITV was still obliged by the same public-service broadcasting legalities, it managed to revolutionise the production and reception of drama productions. The Manchester-based Associated British Corporation (ABC) produced the hugely successful *Armchair Theatre* (ITV, 1956–1974), which broadcast weekly plays written especially for television. These plays injected a new type of realism into television drama as they were anchored in a distinctly northern working-class experience. Broadcasting now had a 'new sensitivity towards popular culture in its class, regional, and generational variety' (Corner 1991: 9). Such television overshadowed the BBC's drama output and ensured ITV 'considerably surpassed the BBC's audience share' by 1960 (Cooke 2015a: 33). In comparison, the BBC's first head of drama, Michael Barry, heavily relied on theatre material and the classics. The BBC was still governed by the belief of its first director general, John Reith (1927–1938), that as a public-service broadcaster its drama must not be for entertainment purposes alone. Drama should inform, educate, and then entertain because 'he who prides himself on giving what he thinks the public want is often creating a fictitious demand for lower standards' (Reith 1925: 3). Such a disposition would oversee BBC drama until Barry's departure in 1961.

Whilst viewers were migrating to ITV in large numbers, one police series was standing firm. *Dixon of Dock Green* represented one of the BBC's few drama successes of the late 1950s and early 1960s, attracting audiences of '10 million by the middle of 1957' (Cooke 2015a: 52). By the first quarter of 1961 *Dixon* was the second most popular programme of the BBC's schedule with a viewing average of 13.85 million viewers (Sydney-Smith 2002: 104). The format of the programme, as devised by scriptwriter Ted Willis, fitted perfectly with the BBC's Reithian public-service ethos. *Dixon* was not drama for entertainment's sake. Based on the experiences of its police consultants, Dixon informed the British public of its police force's working practices. London-based police constable George Dixon (Jack Warner) was a character who initially appeared in Ealing Studio's cinematic release *The Blue Lamp* (1950), co-scripted by Willis. Like Reith, Dixon operates as a paternal guardian of public decency, directly instructing viewers at the start and end of each episode to take care of their own family, 'in the interests of state and country' (Sydney-Smith 2002: 109). *Dixon* embodies what is deemed to be 'a conservative attitude', as criminality is viewed as a problem 'endemic to all classes' rather than a product of society's failings (Sydney-Smith 2002: 114). In 'The rotten apple' (11 August 1956), the corrupt policeman Tom Carr (Paul Eddington) thieves 'just for the hell of it'. This ideological framework portrays criminals as 'pathologically evil' because they are solely responsible for having chosen to be 'apart from, rather than a part of, society' (Sydney-Smith 2002: 114). Following the arrest Dixon comforts viewers by concluding that Carr 'was the only bad copper I ever met'.

Such a simplistic representation of crime and comforting view of the law are informed by a conservative approach towards character, given the production practices that dictated *Dixon*'s broadcast. A minimally designed *mise-en-scène* was largely due to the infrastructure of the BBC. *Dixon* was produced by the BBC Light Entertainment Department and so shared personnel with other programmes, including the sitcom *Handcock's Half Hour* (BBC, 1956–1960) and various children's programming. In these light-entertainment productions set designs were subservient to spoken dialogue. This is because 'the obsessive circularity of the dominant narrative model, in which the situation that gives each series its peculiar identity must be returned to unaltered' (Bignell and Lacey 2005b: 13). This approach towards character and situation, leaving actors somewhat displaced from their surrounding *mise-en-scène*, was highly different from the practices employed by ITV. In contrast, ABC set designer, Voytek, was given licence to create 'a dramatic frame which by its influence on the actors and the audience will project the inner life of the play' (quoted in Taylor 1962: 27). Set designers on *Dixon* had no such impact. Designer Richard Wilmot's biggest concern was that 'the stock sets are beginning to look decidedly shabby after nine episodes', and so he requested 'extra man hours' to refurbish them (Moodie 1957: n.p.). Operating as a functional backdrop meant the sets had no influence on *Dixon*'s characters.

Furthermore, camerawork in *Dixon* is mostly observant. The camera is not an inherent part of the performance and it does not undercut the spoken word. Again, whilst this visual discourse fits with Willis's conservative ideology, it can also be attributed to the compromises producer/director Douglas Moodie had to make with BBC management. Moodie had to submit a 'special request' to use a fourth camera, and it was not until 1958 that he was given permission to use four cameras on a regular basis (Sampson 1958: n.p.). Even then only one camera was motorised, meaning the other three were pedestal-mounted and immobile. Also, the use of a fourth camera was only agreed under the condition it was used 'in the event of a breakdown of one camera', as *Dixon* would continue to be shot by 'three cameras' (Sampson 1958). Meanwhile, ITV's *Armchair Theatre* was using six mobile cameras per production. According to producer Leonard White, pedestal cameras at ABC were used 'as travelling hand-held units, covering endless shot-cards, pushing and pulling to the next position, selecting the lens from four alternatives on the turret while being encouraged by the director ... to "get in closer"' (White 2003: 57). *Dixon*'s static camerawork possesses no such visual expression in presenting characters and situations.

The results of these compromises made during *Dixon*'s production are apparent in the opening to 'Father in law' (1 September 1956). Dixon stands in his front room talking to a host of characters the day before his daughter's wedding. The characters are positioned in 'frontal' compositions where they stand together shoulder to shoulder as they look out to the camera, unable to interact with the set behind them (Cooke 2005: 84). Framing the actors in two mid-shots throughout the scene leaves characters unnaturally grouped together, unable to move around freely as they would in real life. Then an exchange of close-ups ensues between Dixon and each character as he talks to them one at a time in preparation for the wedding. The focus here is on the spoken word, as the surrounding set design is largely out of view. There is no visual discourse to undermine or complicate the spoken dialogue as was being achieved at ITV. The head of drama at ABC, Sydney Newman, believed 'I love good talk in plays, but ... individuals should be communicated to the audience by what they are doing and how they are reacting. Story, character delineation, all these things: you demonstrate them' (Newman 1962: 4). In *Dixon*, attitude, story, character, and delineation are spoken in a literal manner.

Characters function as archetypes in *Dixon*, partially because the actors all occupy the foreground and cannot make use of the set's depth or disturb the placement of objects. Dixon is a father in a literal and symbolic sense as communicated throughout this scene. Usually placed centrally within each shot, he is father to his daughter Mary (Jeanette Hutchinson), father to his son-in-law Andy Crawford (Peter Byrne); he fathers the younger policemen who ask for advice and he is also father to the nation watching at home, as episodes are guided by his paternal recollection and perspective of events. Therefore *Dixon* creates a 'patriarchal ideology' where the feminine is fixed to 'the heart of the domestic sphere' (Sydney-Smith 2002: 110). *Dixon*'s conservative ideology manifests as a combined result of Willis's deliberate intention only to 'show a part of police work' and the strict Reithian principles under which BBC drama was operating (Willis 1964: 7). This ideological outlook is matched by an equally conservative and literal visual aesthetic that was a consequence of the compromises reached between producer/director Douglas Moodie and the BBC's

Light Entertainment Department's working practices, resources, and management.

Nevertheless, this reassuring patriarchal archetype struck a chord with audiences. In 1957, after *Dixon*'s 100th episode, a *Radio Times* feature stated that 'the police service could trace an increase in recruitment due to the series', which should therefore be 'strongly applauded' (Sydney-Smith 2002: 108). To this day George Dixon remains an indefatigable figure firmly ingrained within national consciousness. Whenever the working practices of the police force are scrutinised often the press refers to Dixon as the wholesome, community-oriented bobby on the beat as the standard to which all police officers should aspire.[1]

Z Cars enters production

Dixon of Dock Green alone could not save the BBC from its mass exodus of viewers. In 1960 Hugh Carleton Greene took over as director general, stating that he would 'throw open the windows and let in a breath of fresh air' (Sydney-Smith 2002: 157). Under Greene's premiership Michael Barry resigned as head of drama in 1961 and ABC's head of drama Sydney Newman would replace him in 1963. Essentially the BBC's new strategy was to beat ITV at its own game. It would now produce 'popular programmes of sufficient quality' in forms of 'continuing drama that could build up a regular and committed following' (Laing 1991: 126). Norman Rutherford was appointed the BBC's acting head of drama, and Elwyn Jones, who had previously been in charge of documentary drama, was appointed as his assistant. During this transitionary period scriptwriter Troy Kennedy Martin pitched his idea to Jones about a series that would follow a Lancashire-based constabulary and its use of patrol cars. Given an increasing appetite at the BBC to feature more drama in the northern regions, Jones commissioned *Z Cars* and teamed up Kennedy Martin with established documentarian Robert Barr.[2] According to Barr, *Z Cars*' quality 'comes from a constant war between me who wants it to be documentary and Troy, who wants to write fiction' (quoted in Lewis 1962: 310). *Z Cars* was then produced by the BBC's Documentary Department, and so inaugurated a documentary approach to character. Producer John McGrath spent a week with the actors 'discussing the complete social background of every character ... we filled it all in, in great detail. Not one of these blokes would say a line without knowing why he was saying it' (quoted in Lewis 1962: 309). This practice could not have been any further from ITV's *Armchair Theatre*, where it was uncommon for actors to have a say, even if, as Anthony Quinn claims, a director's understanding was 'totally at odds' with an actor's conception of their own role (quoted in Taylor 1962: 33). *Z Cars* proved immediately successful. Pulling in audiences of 14 million per episode by its eighth week of transmission it would receive peak audiences of 16.65 million: 3 million more viewers than *Dixon* (Laing 1991: 129–135).

Social realism

Such treatment of character can now be recognised as social-realist: a form of drama that often requires actors to be attuned to how 'environmental factors' impact 'on the development of character' to provide 'gritty character studies of the underbelly of urban life' (Hallam and Marshment 2000: 184). However, in 1962 televisual social realism that 'reveals the situation of the working class at the level of its culture and everyday practices' had a rather nostalgic flavour (Lacey 2007: 5). Social-realist discourse in the early 1960s was wary of commercialism and its perceived ability to eradicate traditional cultures. This was first stated in Richard Hoggart's *Uses of Literacy* (2009 [1957]) and was repeated by the 1960 Pilkington Committee on Broadcasting, of which Hoggart was a member. The Pilkington Report criticised ITV for debasing culture, believing there was a need for 'a greater proportion of the more thoughtful and challenging types of programme' (Pilkington Committee 1962: 11). The first types of series-drama arising from this climate included the melodramatic series, or 'glossies', *Emergency Ward 10* (ITV, 1957–1967), *Coronation Street* (ITV, 1960–), *Compact* (BBC, 1962–1965), and *Dr Finlay's Casebook* (BBC, 1962–1971). *Coronation Street* shared a particular affinity with Hoggart's writings, as the series nostalgically depicts a self-contained type of working-class community that was in reality amidst the process of disappearing. *Z Cars* instigated a shift from *Dixon*'s nostalgically Hoggartian depiction of working-class life to a society where a sense of community has been severely diminished. Now there were 'no reassuring endings where decency and family life triumphed' (McGrath 2005 [1976]: 71). *Z Cars* provided a new social realism revealing 'a dry-eyed lament for life as it is messily lived in Britain in affluent 1962' (Lewis 1962: 310).

This sobering sensibility made *Z Cars* the first police series to recognise that the police were becoming increasingly vulnerable to attack. In their attempts to combat physical harm the British Police developed new, more technologically developed tactics. The constable patrolling a beat was increasingly replaced by constables in cars responding to crime rather than just seeking to prevent it. Technology 'fundamentally altered the role of the policeman' (Hall *et al.* 1978: 46). The unit-beat policing

The 1950s and 1960s 19

system utilised patrol cars and personal radios, meaning a policeman was no longer seen as 'the friendly helpful bobby, keeping the peace and thereby preventing crime'. He was no longer 'knowledgeable about his community and sharing some of its values'. Instead 'contact with the people he polices became minimal' (Hall et al.: 46). The impact such changes had on the nature of police work, and the police's relationship to the public, are explored in scenes that occur within Newtown station.

Newtown station

On average *Z Cars* devotes ten minutes of an episode to scenes that unfold in the Newtown or Seaport station. With the mean duration of a typical station scene lasting one-and-a-half minutes, such scenes might seem inconsequential.[3] However, *Z Cars* has a high-octane pace that was inspired by popular American series *Highway Patrol* (ITV, 1955–1959). With the programme transmitted live from Studios 3 and 4 of BBC's new Television Centre, six mobile video cameras would use a range of shot scales over fifteen different sets per episode to engender a rapid editing speed that had not yet been experienced by the BBC. Following the introduction of Ampex video recording technology in 1958, *Z Cars* was able to fuse filmed inserts of outdoor scenes previously recorded at Ealing Studios with live-transmitted drama to provide 'a faster pace than was usual in live studio drama of the time' (Cooke 2012: 103). Producer John McGrath had one rigid rule: 'no camera move, no cut, until the next piece of story was to be revealed. But the stories unfolded very quickly, so there were a lot of cuts' (McGrath 2005 [1976]: 40). With an average shot length lasting 12 seconds – i.e. 5 shot changes per minute and 250 shots an episode – *Z Cars* is able to disclose visually a lot of ancillary narrative information through its station scenes (Laing 1991: 128). The frequent editing and repositioning of the six cameras makes the repeated exclusion and inclusion of characters within the frame an important part of the visual discourse. Usually these relatively short station scenes depict the power dynamic at play between the uniformed division and the Criminal Investigation Department (CID) in relation to the public. Such exchanges provide the audience with an insight into the politics supposedly occurring behind the scenes of the British police force.

Compared to Dock Green station, Newtown station is a far less paternal and cooperative environment, as it is pervaded by disputes, bickering, and rivalry. Housed together in a relatively small space, Newtown CID repeatedly discipline their uniformed colleagues for failing to keep focused on what they see as more pressing cases, including large scale theft. Often it is the plain-clothed CID detectives who challenge the PCs' humanitarian concerns. Contrary to the dominant reading of *Z Cars* that characterises the 'professionalism of the police' being 'wearied by the nastiness of human nature' (Lewis 1962: 310), a sense of community exists between the officers and the public. Rather than the increasing use of technology displacing officers from their community, it is often CID who threaten the uniformed division's relationship with its citizens.

This reading is exemplified in 'Found abandoned' (2 April 1962). An elderly lady, Annie (Elizabeth Begley), rescues an abandoned baby. Although uniformed officers PC Weir (Joseph Brady) and PC Smith (Brian Blessed) are determined to find and arrest the parents responsible, Detective Inspector Dunn (Dudley Foster) orders them to work on a case involving stolen goods instead. These priorities are articulated spatially when Smith and Weir enter Newtown station having failed to apprehend a gang of thieves at the railway goods yard. As Smith begins to walk away from the front of the desk to log the stolen items, Annie taps him on his back to enquire about the baby's health. Before Smith can answer her, Dunn interrupts him. Dunn walks behind the police desk instructing Smith not to 'sit about gossiping'. The camera pans with Dunn as he walks behind the police desk and proceeds to discipline Smith for not making a single arrest at the yard. This indexical camera movement changes one's focus to a new dialogue exchange as the camera pushes Smith and Annie off-screen. When the camera cuts to a reaction shot of Smith he is now framed alone, omitting Annie from view. As the dialogue intensifies and Dunn tells Smith to wipe the smile from his face, a quick succession of close-ups between Smith and Dunn focuses on Smith's sullen expression whilst he is being disciplined. When this dialogue exchange finishes the same long shot used to establish the interior of the station reveals that Annie has disappeared from the station altogether without anybody noticing.

Despite this indexical camera movement, which draws a viewer's attention to the conflict between Smith and Dunn, the key action here is Annie's disappearance. Usually camerawork within station scenes responds to authority by following the officer of senior rank. This time the camera's point of interest displaces Annie's query. Here Annie's caring nature in wanting to check on the baby's health goes unnoticed and is deemed insignificant. As the camera realigns itself in reaction to Dunn's entrance he excludes a woman from his station space and ignores her compassion in favour of disciplining his staff. What the cameras choose to include and exclude in the frame, owing to actors' frequent repositioning and fast-paced editing, provides an insight into the series' view of police work. Repeatedly, CID exploit the station's small size frequently to impose their rank, whilst often excluding 'the feminine', which 'disappears from what subsequently becomes a primarily masculinist discourse' (Sydney-Smith 2002: 168).

However, the station scenes are not necessarily advocating this masculinist discourse. Troy Kennedy Martin identified 'a gap between the uniformed constable and the plain clothes detective' where 'one is dedicated to keeping the peace, the other to fighting crime' (Kennedy Martin 1961: n.p.). In line with Kennedy Martin's research into the Lancashire Constabulary, Z Cars frequently depicts a rift between the uniformed branch and CID. Such a rift reflects how 'CID was formed as a totally autonomous force with a structure and hierarchy bearing little resemblance to the uniform branch' (Hobbs 1988: 41). Repeatedly, CID intervenes in cases to fracture further the uniformed division's relationship with its public. In 'Hi jack!' (22 May 1962), PC Bob Steele (Jeremy Kemp) is pressured by Dunn and Detective Chief Inspector Barlow (Stratford Johns) to deceive his old friend Les Fielding (Glyn Houston). Steele is forced to visit Fielding under the guise of friendship to inspect his flat for stolen goods and extract a confession. Fielding served alongside Steele in the army, but CID ignores Steele's personal reservations. Similarly, in 'The whizzers' (26 June 1963), Weir finds that one of his shifts has been altered so that he is obliged to play rugby for his police team rather than for his preferred hometown side. Despite the reservations of its uniformed colleagues, CID is portrayed as having a detached and callous pragmatism that does not care for community relations where the law is concerned.

Conversely, the public reach out to the uniformed branch for help and are met with a sympathetic response to personal crises. In 'Four of a kind' (2 January 1962), middle-aged Mrs Jones (Anna Wing) manoeuvres behind the police desk without being instructed and without hesitation. She is able to do so because there is little barrier to speak of between the space behind the police desk, where the uniformed officers work, and the space the public occupy in front of it. Once behind the desk Mrs Jones is able to lean into Steele and grip his hand as she explains her predicament. Immediately, having listened to her enquiry, Steele rushes to Mrs Jones's home to dissuade her son from assaulting her family and home with an axe. Compared to the CID personnel who secretively operate in their offices behind closed doors there is a reliance on the uniformed police and their understanding of such matters. Elderly people and women can often be found entering the station to ask the uniform branch for help. In this regard police work appears to be presented as an extension of social work. Consequently a lot of physical contact is shared between the public and the police in Newtown station. As well as Mrs Jones's clutching of Steele's hand and Annie's tapping on Smith's back in 'Found abandoned', 'Contraband' (26 June 1962) features Mr Stansfield (Frederick Peisley) giving Smith and Weir gifts to thank them for convincing a shop manager not to press charges against his shoplifting daughter. Whilst dispensing his gifts Stansfield puts his hand on PC Sweet's (Terence Edmond) arm as he leans over the police desk and slides a cigar into Sweet's pocket. Gesturing plays a key part in demonstrating the extent of the close relationship between the public and police. However, Stansfield is made to feel like a criminal by CID as Barlow ensures all the gifts are returned, thus fracturing the mutual bond between the public and uniformed officers.

Relations between the public and the police at the time of *Z Cars* are considered by some historians as 'harmonious with the majority of the population (including most of the working class)' (Ascoli 1979: 79). Despite the technological advancements that had limited a policeman's amount of regular contact with the public, *Z Cars* appears to agree with this view. Kennedy Martin was keen to make a clean break with the Hoggartian brand of social realism by holding 'a mirror up to English life as it is at the moment' in a way that had not previously been achieved on television (quoted in Lewis 1962: 311). However, there is still an underlying sense of community shared between vulnerable members of society and the uniformed police. When analysing the camerawork, positioning, and gesturing of characters, a reading of the station emerges that can be taken as a possible critique of the pressures CID impose on the uniformed policemen who are trying to maintain a rapport and respect with their community. Whilst the general public are regularly forthcoming with physical contact when seeking help, the camerawork and positioning of CID personnel undermines this mutual understanding as detectives further stigmatise vulnerable members of the public. Therefore Newtown station scenes echo the divisions unearthed by criminologist John Mays, whose study of a constabulary in Liverpool found that just over 40 per cent of police personnel were content believing that they were 'verging on being social workers' (Mays 1954: 181).[4]

In response to the nostalgic social realism of soaps and 'glossies', *Z Cars* does not depict the public's appetite for a shared sense of community as being irrefutably dead. Rather, *Z Cars*' visual discourse reveals that community feeling exists but has become more fragmented; is displayed in a more subtle manner; and proves to be divisive, given the varying priorities that exist between CID, who fight crime, and the uniformed branch, who keep the peace. *Z Cars* portrays a key aspect of the uniformed division's role as being able to assist vulnerable people, from abandoned babies to distressed elderly women, with an understanding that CID lacks. Despite the social work of PCs being threatened by CID's opposing priorities, uniformed police workers are presented as a compassionate arm of the State that citizens can reach out to for the necessary security and assistance promised to them by the postwar consensus.

Working-class men

With ten minutes of an average *Z Cars* episode capturing scenes that unfold in the police station, the remaining thirty-five minutes depict civilians residing in their homes within the fictional Newtown and Seaport areas. By far the largest proportion of character types that feature are working-class men who commit crimes as a means of grappling with their changing social status in 1960s Britain. In line with *Z Cars'* commitment to a less nostalgic mode of social realism, the programme does not have a clear-cut ideology towards criminality like its predecessor series *Dixon of Dock Green*. Rather than the criminals simply being pathologically evil they work through a number of issues prevalent to working-class men in relation to criminological theory of the time as part of 'a rhetoric of discussion' (Newcomb and Hirsch 2000: 566).

The framework of criminological debate had significantly shifted in the late 1950s and early 1960s. Up until this point biological or psychological versions of a 'predestined actor' model had been developed by criminologists to explain how factors internal to a human being could determine that they act in ways they had little or no control over. Conversely, by 1962 'deviant subculture' theories from America were being increasingly adopted to understand how crime may be driven by the conditions of a person's social environment. Such approaches were underpinned by Robert Merton's anomie theory, with its primary aim to discover 'how some social structures exert a definite pressure upon certain persons in the society to engage in nonconformist conduct' (Merton 1938: 672). Merton proposed that a distinction between cultural goals and institutionalised means must be achieved. 'Cultural goals' refers to the 'material possessions' and 'symbols of status, accomplishment and esteem that established norms and values encourage us to aspire to, and are, therefore, socially learned' (Hopkins Burke 2013: 140). 'Institutionalised means' refers to the 'distribution of opportunities to achieve these goals in socially acceptable ways' (Hopkins Burke 2013: 140). Whilst Merton's theory had little impact when it was first published in 1938, the 1950s and 1960s experienced a golden age of anomie theory where criminologists built upon Merton's findings. Merton's perspective provided the most 'influential sociological interpretation of deviance' during the mid twentieth century (Messner and Rosenfeld 2013: 13). *Z Cars*, through its depiction of working-class men, explores a number of prominent strands of anomie thought.

Retreating young men

The use of props and their inherent symbolism play a significant part in addressing the cultural anxiety felt by working-class men and how this intersects with criminology. 'Stab in the dark' (23 January 1962) sees Sadie Arnot (Jeanne Hepple) stabbed on her doorstop by Tom O'Connor (Tony Calvin) with a large fish knife. After Detective Chief Superintendent Robins (John Phillips) detains O'Connor, Robins rationalises the situation. He claims O'Connor was so resentful of Arnot's 'quiet comfortable home' in relation to O'Connor's own alcoholic father and inability to hold down a job that O'Connor decided to 'take it out' on Arnot. Similarly, in 'Four of a kind' Rodney Jones (Peter Anderson) holds his mother's baby hostage with an axe as he is 'frightened of being at home with the kids'. Jones has become mentally unstable after falling off a crane at a building site and suffers from headaches. Jones tells PC Steele that all he wanted to do was 'chop some wood'. O'Conner's fish knife, stolen from a fish-and-chip takeaway, and Jones's axe are used to attack signifiers of the domestic spaces the men feel confined by, whilst symbolising their repressed desire to contribute to the labour market and provide for a family.

Initially these characters appear similar to the angry young men of literature, theatre, and new-wave cinema who attack signifiers of an 'affluent society' or a more generalised 'cultural anxiety around the question of male identity' (Hill 1986: 25). However, what sets the men of *Z Cars* apart from Jimmy Porter (Richard Burton) of *Look Back in Anger* (1959), Arthur Seaton (Albert Finney) of *Saturday Night and Sunday Morning* (1960), and Frank Machin (Richard Harris) of *This Sporting Life* (1963) is that they are amidst a process of retreating from society. O'Connor and Jones are young men on the cusp of entering Merton's 'retreatism'. They are rejecting both the cultural goals and their means of acquisition (including all illegal methods), which leads them to drop out of the social order completely. Whilst the angry young men of cinema, theatre, and literature childishly rebel against a future of being tied down to a job, wife, and subsequent middle-class values, they inevitably conform to the social order. The men of *Z Cars* attack these signifiers because they are unable to attain a comfortable and materialistic life and so are frustrated. Rather than assault being used to seize 'upon the manipulation of violence as a route to status', as was being discussed by prominent criminologists, these acts of violence inaugurate the men's retreat pattern of behaviour (Cloward and Ohlin 1998 [1960]: 175).[5] Jones and O'Connor are the young people who have fallen through the cracks of the postwar social contract as their circumstances sit outside Beveridge's 'uniform society', i.e. they have not been able to assume the role of patriarchal breadwinner to a family (Fraser 2009: 306). Full employment was understood, following Beveridge's recommendation, as a rate of unemployment that could stand at 3 per cent to cater for people in between jobs looking for work. Z Cars accesses the types of people who fall into this pool and the crises they can face.

Disillusioned old men

Significantly this retreatism is not exclusive to adolescents. In the episode 'Friday night' (8 June 1962), a drunken man, George (Robin Wentworth), is escorted home after throwing a brick through a window. It transpires George was walking home after his retirement party. He took it upon himself to commit this act of vandalism when discovering that the retirement clock presented to him by his employers after twenty-five years of service does not work. Therefore Z Cars can be seen to bring a new perspective to anomie theory and its various explanations of crime. Deviant subculture theories, as were being discussed in the 1960s, predominantly rationalise why adolescent delinquents resorted to achieving cultural goals through unlawful means within gangs. In contrast, Z Cars focuses on the resentment displayed by older men who have conformed to the social order and yet still resort to criminal acts because they have few cultural goals to show for abiding by the socially acceptable means of achieving status, possessions, and wealth. One reason for this shift in focus on the sorts of crimes being committed, and the types of people committing them, could be that both British new-wave films and British criminological studies of deviant subcultures were made outside the class they focused on as they romanticised the Other. In contrast, television drama firmly 'rooted itself in a particular experience of class from the inside', given its working-class actors, writers, directors, and producers (Caughie 2000: 855).

Z Cars uses older characters retreating from the social order to explore generational conflict that was specific to the fabric of 1960s Britain. One of the distinctive economic trends of the 1960s was the high demand for unskilled youth labour. As the 1960s continued to boast 'full employment', few young people experienced problems finding work. With a 'buoyant job market youngsters were free to move quickly from job to job in search of the highest immediate rewards' (Osgerby 1998: 23). Younger unskilled workers were in great demand because they were cheaper to employ and were happy to accept the relatively high and instantaneous rewards. Therefore employees who had spent their lives specialising in a particular artisan trade were fearful that 'Britain would soon face a serious shortage of skilled workers' (Osgerby 1998: 23). The stable tradition of family dynasties where fathers would pass down their 'skill and craft' to their sons was in decline (Abbott 2003: 125).

Such concerns are exemplified in the episode 'Tuesday afternoon' (4 December 1963), where middle-aged Pawson (Eric Barker) steals a toy car from a shop for his grandson's birthday. Pawson is a sheet-metal worker who has recently been made redundant owing to a takeover of Hutchinson's factory. He is a skilled 'tradesman', as he proudly tells Detective Sergeant Watt (Frank Windsor) when he is arrested. As a result of this takeover, Hutchinson's no longer employs such tradesmen, and there are also no sheet-metal-worker vacancies on Seaport's or Newtown's industrial estates. This shortage of tradesmen's jobs is blamed, in part, on a higher demand for unskilled workers. When Pawson reads job vacancies in the paper all he can find are salesmen positions or unskilled labouring vacancies designed for younger workers. He attempts to achieve a cultural goal (a present for his grandson) but is forced to do so through socially unacceptable means (theft), given the lack of employment opportunities available to people in his position.

This age of full employment and mass affluence, which postwar governments were keen to characterise themselves as the progenitors of, appears to be bypassing the older members of Newtown. Despite the repeated uprating of pensions, the growth of the economy, and rise in consumer spending, the view that poverty was increasing had begun to gain ground in the UK. By 1965 social scientists Brian Abel-Smith and Peter Townsend introduced a new 'relative' definition of poverty into political discourse. People who were unable to participate in the 'conventional and customary' norms of society, including the rise in living standards and new commonplace consumer durables, could now be understood to be living in poverty (Abel-Smith and Townsend 1965: 63). The Government's previous definition of poverty, which had been based on subsistence levels – what Seebohm Rowntree deemed 'physical efficiency' – was now seemingly outdated for having overlooked those who had been living in relative poverty since the end of the Second World

War (Abel-Smith and Townsend 1965: 63). Pawson embodies this 'rediscovery of poverty' gaining prominence in the early-to-mid 1960s as his character also seemingly criticises the postwar settlement for failing to eradicate the 'substantial numbers of the population living below the national assistance level' (Abel-Smith and Townsend 1965: 67).

Claiming the home as a space of male anxiety

The way in which actors handle props in domestic scenes reclaims the home as an extension of the public world of work and enables characters to engage with contemporary developments in anomie theory. In 'Handle with care' (16 January 1962), Jakey Ramsden's (Arthur Lowe) two adult sons, Little Jakey (Michael Brennan) and Ritchie (Anthony Sagar), have stolen some temperamental gelignite explosives to sell to a buyer. The Ramsdens' household is introduced through a close-up of a toy car being crushed by a sledgehammer. The camera patiently observes the sledgehammer slowly flatten the roof of the car with seven blows before the car is dropped into a bucket. The camera then tracks back to reveal Ramsden standing over a kitchen worktop. Having been introduced to the domestic setting through such props and actions, a viewer's expectation is that the events will be taking place in a shed, garage, or warehouse. Therefore the placement of such props within this setting crucially blurs a Hoggartian dichotomy between the private and the public spheres as seen in *Dixon* and *Coronation Street*. These previous programmes entirely omitted 'social or political explanations and contexts' from their storylines in favour of psychological discourse (Rolinson 2011: 185). Soaps in particular would translate public debates into emotional terms by concentrating on characters, and very rarely would 'inanimate objects [be] viewed alone' (Paterson 1980: 65). In comparison, *Z Cars*' social-realist approach uses objects within domestic scenes metonymically to explore criminological debate.

Ramsden agrees with his sons that the scrap metal he is producing is practically worthless. Therefore his actions share an affinity with what Albert K. Cohen defines as 'status frustration'. Building on Merton's anomie theory, Cohen's view was that the norms and values of the middle class are dominant and used to judge the success and status of everybody in society. These norms, according to Cohen, include aspiring to achieve career goals, the rational cultivation of manners, control of physical aggression and violence, and a respect for property. Cohen argues that a young working-class male 'starts out with a handicap' when thrust into a highly competitive social system to achieve such status (Cohen 1955: 110). Therefore Ramsden's smashing of the toy cars in a slow and calculated pressing motion is an act of status frustration, as it exudes a 'bitterness, hostility, and jealousy' (Cohen 1955: 131) towards the middle-class expectation of acquiring material possessions and status through socially acceptable means. All are unavailable to Ramsden, who has stolen the toy cars for the pleasure of defacing them rather than making money from them.

The scene is also pervaded by a general lack of discipline as described by Terence Morris's study of *The Criminal Area* (1957), which built upon Cohen's theory in a British context. Writing about British social class Morris argues that 'the working class child grows up in an atmosphere in which restraint is often conspicuous for its absence', dividing the socialisation of the child among their family and street acquaintants. Because their peers have a much stronger influence from an earlier age, working-class children's 'social maturation is accelerated' and they turn to crime (Morris 1998 [1957]: 172). So, whereas soaps at this time presented the home as a 'place of safety where there is some protection from the harshness of the world outside', *Z Cars* contains signifiers of the public world of work within the private domestic sphere to depict the home as a sort of 'battleground' that a Hoggartian social realism was keen to avoid (Geraghty 1991: 83). Not only are the Ramsdens warring against middle-class values but they also steal, deceive, and fight with one another. When Ramsden finds the gelignite, instead of asking his sons about it, he secretly steals a piece for himself and hides it in a tea caddy. His reluctance to admit he has stolen a piece for himself results in an explosion, transforming the home into a literal battleground of sorts. Portraying the domestic space as an unsentimental and unstable extension of the outside world, and blurring the boundaries between the two, helps *Z Cars* address deviant subculture theory.

A viewer's focus through all of these domestic scenes is informed by working-class men and the suffering they endure from societal change. Compared to *Dixon* and previous social-realist series belonging to the soap-opera or 'glossies' genre, the home is no longer presented as a safe, often feminine, haven from the outside world. The home is a combative setting where men's frustrations manifest in response to challenges from the public world of work. Consistently an audience witnesses either young working-class men retreating from the social order, as a result of being unable to enter the labour market, or older working-class men retreating, having little material reward for their conformity to the social order and its labour market. Both the old and the young are resentful of this lack of (legal and illegal) access to such cultural goals, and so attack signifiers of the middle classes. Collectively these various working-class men work through a number of strains of

The 1950s and 1960s 29

anomie theory. This means the ideology at work in *Z Cars* is multifarious. The series could be agreeing with Morris that citizens are subject to the 'inherent economic entrenchment of inequality in our class system' (Morris 1998 [1957]: 165). However, at the same time *Z Cars* does not necessarily subscribe to Morris's view that 'serious delinquency occurs more frequently among the families of unskilled workers than amongst semi-skilled workers, white collar workers or skilled artisans' (Morris 1998 [1957]: 168). Pawson and George are skilled, albeit elderly, tradesmen who feel compelled to commit crime. By concerning itself with the particularly vulnerable types of working-class men who have fallen through the cracks of the postwar welfare state, *Z Cars'* civilian scenes are concerned with sociologists' 'rediscovery of poverty' and prominent deviant-subculture theories of the era. However, it is a series that looks beyond deviant-subculture theory's obsession with 'juvenile delinquency', as then recognised as 'merely one aspect of the behaviour pattern on underprivileged neighbourhoods' (Mays 1954: 147).

The (police)man of the house

So far this chapter has established that within *Z Cars'* Newtown station CID pose the main challenge towards community-oriented policing, as they dismiss humanitarian concerns as trivial matters in relation to the theft of goods. When examining these station scenes in isolation, *Z Cars* would appear to be criticising CID's cavalier attitude in comparison to the uniformed police officers' acceptance of social work. However, this reading is largely undercut by scenes set within civilian spaces, because here the camera's gaze is resolutely focused on working-class men and their reasons for committing crime. The supposed critical view of Newtown's CID is complicated because the principal interest of the series now assimilates with the impersonal CID characters. Domestic scenes also exclude women to assume a 'masculinist discourse' that exclusively deals with the social concerns and personal crises of male characters (Sydney-Smith 2002: 168). This is, however, both partially furthered and questioned by the depiction of PC Bob Steele and his wife Janey (Dorothy White) within their home. In all of the *Z Cars* episodes that escaped being wiped, the private lives of police officers do not feature prominently beyond the pilot episode, 'Four of a kind'. This episode has attracted a large amount of scholarly attention because here it is revealed that Bob has given his wife a black eye. This caused, following the Chief Constable of Lancashire's visit to the BBC, 'the credit thanking the Lancashire County Police for their co-operation' to be 'quietly dropped' (Lewis 1962: 307). This black eye alone represents the ideological shift from the paternal and faultless George Dixon to a hypocritical police force that does not always abide by the laws it serves to uphold.

Initially the camera is responsive to Janey Steele's movements when we are introduced to her and her husband's home. The camera pans with her as she moves around the space, waiting on the visiting PC Lynch, as she explains how her husband bruised her. There is an interest in Janey's suffering as the camera follows her around the space to capture the stressful nature of her domestic work and the impact of domestic abuse. However, when her husband enters the space the camera repositions itself to remain fixed on Bob Steele and Lynch as they squabble at the head of the dining table. Janey now either has to walk into the frame to be seen by the camera, or interrupt their conversation to warrant a quick close-up of her face. The camera is no longer drawn to her. With Bob's entrance she is discussed without being given any space to voice her opinion. Here, the feminine disappears just as it does in the station at the behest of CID.

Whereas Dixon's upright and ensconced demeanour is interchangeable between both Dock Green station and his front room, Bob Steele's character within his home environment behaves differently in relation to his persona at Newtown station. This is the first police series to share an affinity with Edward T. Hall's scientific study of proxemics, which states: 'Men have two or more distinct personalities, one for business and one for the home. The separation of office and home in these instances helps to keep the two often incompatible personalities from conflicting and may even serve to stabilize an idealized version of each which conforms to the projected image of both architecture and setting' (Hall 1966: 99). When Bob Steele arrives at his home Lynch reveals a hotpot stain on the wall that was not previously visible. Lynch brings this aspect of the space into existence by pointing to it and asking 'is this the stain the hotpot made?'. In response to this question Steele moves one of the wooden dining chairs. In a close-up shot a loose rung falls from the back-rest as Steele claims 'look at t'broken chair where a very frightened husband threw himself to avoid being blinded for life'. Steele's touching of the chair rung and Lynch's pointing to the wall draw the camera's gaze to particular aspects of the *mise-en-scène* that reveal the cracks emerging beneath the surface of this seemingly functional household that could not have been unearthed by the cinematographic discourse of *Dixon*. The scene reveals that, like the other residents of Newtown and Seaport, Steele is adjusting to a middle-class culture and values at home and at work. Living in an underprivileged neighbourhood Steele's learnt behaviour from his working-class origins, where 'father's comfort is usually put first and his meal must be ready for him whatever else happens by the time he gets home from work' (Mays 1954: 86), clashes with the middle-class values that govern society: so much so that 'A number of viewers did not care for the way the members of the Newtown police force were portrayed ("as wife-beaters and gluttons"), and hoped that such details as "the undignified eating" were not meant to be true to life' (BBC 1962: 1). The relationship between Bob and Janey Steele has a similar dynamic to the abrasive marriages featured in 'Handle with care' and 'Hi jack!', where Fielding feels compelled to steal to satisfy his wife's materialistic desires, and 'Incident reported' (28 May 1962), where Stan Carron (Patrick Halstead) assaults his family causing property damage and physical injury. However, unlike these marriages Bob achieves reconciliation to the dispute by apologising, embracing his wife, and kissing her in the kitchen. This apology and open display of affection are what sets him apart from the criminals. Janey's submission and acceptance are, however, surprisingly swift as she claims that the bruise will give her some 'respect along this street now'. This black eye means that she will no longer be socially isolated from her working-class community where, it was believed, 'the general ethical level is extremely low and the area abounds in all manner of vice and immorality' (Mays 1954: 122). Like her husband, Janey Steele struggles to assimilate both with the culture and behaviours of her surrounding underprivileged neighbourhood and with the middle-class norms and standards of society that her husband's occupation serves to uphold.

Whilst this scene reveals the clashes occurring between middle-class and working-class cultures it also manages to abide by public expectations of marriage at the time. Mary Grant's problem pages in *Woman's Own*, and other marital advice books published from this era, identified an 'increasing importance attached to sexual intercourse as a method of communication between husband and wife' (Richards and Elliot 1991: 38). The fact that the dispute between the Steeles is reconciled by a kiss reasserts the view that sex was 'a part of marriage where openness, sharing ... and closeness have particular value' (37).

There is a complex dynamic at play here. Whilst Bob Steele's agency in the abuse of his wife cannot be dismissed, at the same time she is the source of the conflict, as the assault Bob has committed was to stop her throwing the hotpot. Bob does apologise to Janey, and the marriage can be considered relatively companionate (a marriage where spouses are treated as equal companions) in comparison to the other marriages of Newtown where no affection is openly displayed. Through the Steeles' embrace Bob is shown to be appreciative, open, and sharing through these affectionate terms. The scene is interested in Janey's suffering in a way that viewers do not have access to in any of the other civilian scenes that concentrate on the types of alienation suffered by working-class men and how this causes them to commit crimes. However, this access to Janey Steele's perspective is brief before the scene abides by a classic patriarchal narrative, whereby the use of heterosexual romance, the kiss, resolves a dispute and offers absolution, if not justification, for violence towards women. Much like criminological discourse at that time the series is preoccupied with concentrating on the types of crimes men commit and their reasons for doing so.

Conclusion

Z Cars proved to be a very popular programme that helped to shake the BBC out of a militantly Reithian treatment of drama in anticipation of Sydney Newman's takeover. Its documentary approach to researching character and environment, its high-octane pace, and its use of six mobile video cameras created a drama that was distinctive in distancing itself from a nostalgic register to capture 'real life as it is lived' (Lacey and MacMurraugh-Kavanagh 1999: 65). The greater number of shot scales available to each scene adds a distinctive visual discourse to proceedings. In comparison to *Dixon* the way characters gesture, handle props, and position themselves in public and private spaces adds a new ideological dimension to the narrative in addition to the spoken dialogue. Scenes that unfold at Newtown station critique CID's conduct whilst revealing that a relatively close relationship still exists between the police and the public that is not as fractious as unit-beat policing was feared to be. The way characters interact with one another and their surrounding *mise-en-scène* in domestic scenes enables the series to engage with a wide variety of criminological thought emanating from Robert Merton's anomie theory, be it visual articulations of Albert K. Cohen's status frustration or Morris's observations of working-class life. These domestic scenes are also informed by socio-economic anxieties, including the buoyancy of unskilled youth labour and the types of men unprotected by the postwar settlement who are likely to retreat from society. Here the boundary between the public and private is blurred in relation to other popular television of the time, as a sentimental view of the home is superseded by a domestic space that is vulnerable to the harshness and disorders of the outside world. This is something PC Bob Steele has to contend with. Witnessing Steele's character in a private capacity recognises that a boundary still exists between the public and the private given that one's conduct can change in correspondence to one's environment. Ultimately, though, it is a series predominantly interested in the social anxieties of working-class men where the domestic space is used as a means of expressing their frustrations with the outside world. Through *Z Cars*, police series of the 1960s abide by the same masculinist discourses informing prominent criminological theory and wider social concerns of the time.

Nevertheless, by Sydney Newman's appointment as BBC Head of Drama in 1963, *Z Cars* had arrived as one of the BBC's flagship programmes. The momentum was now back with the BBC as their audiences returned in great numbers. Newman recognised *Z Cars* as an integral part of the BBC's new strategy for drama, and the series ran until 1978, just outrunning *Dixon*, which ended in 1976. Under Newman the BBC would launch its signature *Wednesday Play* (1964–1970) and *Play for Today* (1970–1984) anthology series. These weekly plays developed a 'progressive social realism tradition' that merged documentary with drama to present the human impact of political issues, from backstreet abortions to deindustrialisation (Cooke 2015a: 104). It is hard to imagine British television drama making this progression without *Z Cars* having first used the domestic setting as a means of accessing wider social and political issues and concerns. The 1960s began with the British police series as a genre through which to repeat reassuringly patriarchal depictions of law and order as approved by the status quo, police force, and government. By the end of the 1960s, the police series had instigated a new form of televisual social realism complete with a social 'extension of dramatic material to areas of life which had been evidently excluded' from mainstream drama (Williams 1990: 232). Equipped with a 'conscious political viewpoint' this televisual social realism initiated by *Z Cars* would question and challenge injustice and inequality from an authentic working-class perspective (Williams 1990: 233): a prestige its spin-off series *Softly, Softly* (BBC, 1966–1969) and *Barlow at Large* (BBC, 1971–1975) never quite emulated.

Notes

1 Recent articles include: Barnes (2016), Copping (2014), More (2017), Sylvester and Thomson (2016).
2 A number of standalone BBC dramas written by Liverpudlian Colin Morris and directed by Gilchrist Calder entitled *Tearaway* (1956), *Who, Me?* (1959), and the four-part *Jacks and Knaves* (1961), had already relocated BBC crime drama in northern England. Their cutting humour was at odds with the stoic London-based George Dixon and filmed series *Fabian of the Yard* (BBC, 1954–1956).
3 These figures are an average of the numbers for the first six episodes.

4 John Mays interviewed fifty police constables in 1953 at an undisclosed divisional headquarters in a working-class area of Liverpool (the type of location where *Z Cars* is also set) just prior to the nationwide launch of unit beat-policing.
5 Cloward and Ohlin's study of 'conflict subculture' builds upon Merton's anomie theory and is widely considered to be a more comprehensive examination of why adolescent males resort to attacking people (assault), property (vandalism), and each other (gang fights) within gangland USA.

The 1970s: an action-fuelled filmic decade? 2

> I felt very strongly that we ought to pioneer a film technique ... there were things we were very good at in comparison with a tape production in the TV studio – they were action and two-handed dialogue on the run.
>
> *The Sweeney* producer Ted Childs
> (quoted in Alvarado and Stewart 1985: 57)

Academic studies of British police series broadcast in the 1970s often grant too much significance to the programmes that utilise 16 mm film cameras on location and the transformative impact they had on the genre. Whilst *The Sweeney* (ITV, 1975–1978) incorporated high-octane action sequences into the iconography of the British police series, such a programme is not wholly representative of what people were watching at the time. This chapter redresses the balance by investigating *Hunter's Walk* (ITV, 1973–1976), a series just as popular as *The Sweeney* shot using video cameras at Associated Television's (ATV) Birmingham studios. A comparative analysis of *Hunter's Walk* in relation to *The Sweeney* will explore in what manner each series was able to engage in debates surrounding class and gender inequality in light of second-wave feminism and the fracturing postwar settlement. The chapter will inspect how each series negotiated a changing public and political attitude towards crime that was increasingly sympathetic to the rational-actor model of thinking.

Production context

The Sweeney and *Hunter's Walk* were commissioned by a television industry that had considerably changed. Exporting drama to the USA had become a highly profitable venture dictating ITV's 'economic imperatives' (Chapman 2002: 228). Through the 1960s both ABC and ATV made use of London-based Elstree and Pinewood film studios to produce action adventure series including *The Avengers* (ITV,

1961–1969), *The Saint* (ITVm 1962–1969), *The Champions* (ITV, 1968–1969), and *Department S* (ITV, 1969–1970). These series are characterised by an emphasis on action, suspense, and international espionage rather than authentically capturing methods of domestic policing experienced in real life. Shot on 35 mm film in technicolour these exhilarating yet playful depictions of swinging-sixties culture proved popular with American audiences.[1]

Given this change in priority Thames Television, formed in 1968 to serve the London area through a merger between ABC and Associated Rediffusion, set up Euston Films in 1971. Thames's subsidiary company was founded by its Controller of Drama Lloyd Shirley, Head of Film Facilities George Taylor, and Director of Programmes Brian Tesler. Their rationale was to produce films for television using 16 mm-film cameras on location with a view to selling successful programme formats abroad. Euston Films grounded their drama in a verisimilitude that was not as fantastical as ABC's and ATV's action adventure series shot on 35 mm film at Pinewood and Elstree studios. Correspondingly the directors hired by Euston were television documentarians, who regularly used 16 mm-film cameras, as opposed to feature-film practitioners. Euston's aim was to incorporate the 'wobbly scope' techniques of documentary filmmaking into their drama (Alvarado and Stewart 1985: 48). By distancing themselves from what they saw as producing episodes on a 'factory basis', where 'directors had very little power and very little say in what was done', producer Chris Burt felt 'television oriented people' provided their drama with 'more realism' (Alvarado and Stewart 1985: 47). Thus the action sequences produced by Euston were grounded in a more tangible sense of reality than had been achieved by ABC's and ATV's escapist fare. This strategy worked, as *The Sweeney* was Euston's first major hit, peaking at 19.1 million viewers.[2] Congruently *The Sweeney* is frequently lauded for harnessing the full potential of film technology to ensure the British police series was 'shaken out of the drama documentary format of slow moving narrative and static camerawork' associated with studio-based productions (Clarke 1992: 237).

Meanwhile, the ITA felt ATV was too preoccupied with producing drama for the American market through its sister organisation ITC (Incorporated Television Company). A licence was granted to ATV to provide programming for the Midlands in 1968, with the prerequisite that their centre of operations be moved from Elstree to Birmingham. In response, Director of Programmes Bill Ward moved to Birmingham with the programming planning and scheduling staff. However, the appointment of Creative Controller Francis Essex at Elstree caused an 'ambiguity and blurring of responsibilities' between both production sites (Potter 1990: 39). Whilst ATV's Birmingham studios produced cost-effective, studio-based dramas shot on videotape, including *Crossroads* (ITV, 1964–1988) and *Hunter's Walk*, ATV's London base continued to create lavish productions for the international market, such as *The Persuaders!* (ITV, 1971–1972).

Despite these circumstances, *Hunter's Walk* is pivotal to the British police series' stylistic and thematic development. The programme attracted up to 16 million viewers. In 1973 and 1974 every episode of series 1 and 2 made the top twenty most-viewed programmes of the week in which they were broadcast, often reaching number 2.[3] Nevertheless, the series has evaded critical recognition from landmark studies of British television drama, including works by Alan Clarke (1992), John Caughie (2000), and Lez Cooke (2015a).

A muted critical response from the press is also particularly notable. The only mention *Hunter's Walk* receives in a national newspaper, outside the television listings pages, is a question posed by *The Times* asking: 'What is the difference between *Hunter's Walk* and *Dixon of Dock Green*?'. Journalist Quentin Crewe's view is that each programme represents 'acts of cowardice' and 'copies of tried formats' (Crewe 1974: 11). Such an opinion piece epitomises the national press's critical consensus. Often what it saw as unremarkable, lowbrow, and cheap drama did not warrant comment or sustained coverage. A corresponding view was adopted by ATV, as each episode was systematically wiped, and only ten episodes, out of a possible thirty-nine, now survive. Consequently this production context, which marginalised *Hunter's Walk* at the expense of ATV's flagship London-based filmed series, has had a far-reaching impact that this chapter will rectify.

Hunter's Walk and *mise-en-scène* interaction

Invented by *Dixon of Dock Green* creator Ted Willis, who had no regular input beyond designing the programme's format, *Hunter's Walk* follows Detective Sergeant Smith (Ewan Hooper) and uniformed associate Sergeant Ken Ridgeway (Davyd Harries) policing the fictional Midlands town of Broadstone. With exterior scenes filmed in Rushden, Northamptonshire, both detective and sergeant operate from a small-scale station equipped with two further police constables and an additional detective constable to protect their rural community. There is a relaxed dynamic between Ridgeway's uniformed division and Smith's CID. The two branches do not conflict with one another and each episode centres on lengthy discussions between Smith and Ridgeway on how to keep their community at peace.

There are a number of reasons for this change in working dynamic between PCs and detectives. Particularly prominent factors include *Hunter's Walk* being the first successful British police series to focus on rural policing. Official police adviser to the programme Stanley Woolfenden notes, 'an officer on a rural beat ... knows all inhabitants on his "patch" by their first names ... if there is any hooliganism, he will probably know the culprits' (quoted in Deane Potter 1976: 15). Thus the working practices of the police are considerably different from the inner-city policing of previous series. Second, Robert Mark was appointed London Metropolitan Police Commissioner in 1972. From the outset Mark made it clear he wanted a greater CID–uniform interchange. On 24 April 1972, seven days after taking his post, Mark announced every detective constable and detective sergeant successful in passing their promotion exams would return to uniform for two years. This interchange between divisions had an impact on constabularies throughout the country and is highly likely to have been inadvertently recognised by the programme's advisers and scriptwriters.

Interestingly, the collaborative working relationship between PCs and detectives depicts fractures in the relationship shared between the police force and the public. In *Z Cars* (BBC, 1962–1978) gesturing and positioning between the public and uniformed police signifies a mutual respect undercut by the repositioning of cameras in response to CID's orders. *Hunter's Walk*, in comparison, shows the uniformed officers and CID working closely through a mutual, yet cynical, distrust of the public. The interior of Broadstone station is first revealed in the debut episode, 'Disturbance' (4 June 1973). For this establishing shot the camera is placed in the large office behind the police desk where the uniformed officers work. The public who enter are separated from this area by a large wall and can only interact with the police through a small cubbyhole. PC Coombes (Charles Rea) sits with his back to the desk, unlike Sergeant Twentyman of *Z Cars*, who attentively stands behind the desk awaiting public enquiries.

The scene commences with Dennis Kenwright (Doug Fisher) standing behind the cubbyhole in the background of the shot. Significantly, Kenwright is not shown entering the space, suggesting he has been waiting a while. Coombes does not acknowledge Kenwright's presence and slowly finishes his paperwork before turning round and walking in a leisurely fashion to the desk. There is no sense of urgency or shared concern, as seen in *Z Cars*, to help the public with their individual problems. When Kenwright tells Coombes 'I want to speak to someone', Coombes turns his head around to meet the other officer's look, knowingly rolling his eyes back and sniffing. Coombes is instantly dismissive as if this query is overly familiar. The placement of this cubbyhole, designated for visitors, in the background of the shot implies that interaction with the public is kept at arm's length. The police appear to be distancing themselves from the public and dealing with them is not necessarily a priority.

As Coombes locates Ridgeway to help with Kenwright's enquiry, an audience sees the first full view of the station area designated for public use. Here a set of swinging doors, which do not extend beyond hip height, are placed in the narrow hallway to prevent the public from entering the rest of the station. The entranceway to the station is uninviting, as people who enter are confined to this small space. Unlike *Z Cars*, where the public freely share the desk space with police, Kenwright is unable to share a camera shot with the police officers comfortably. Instead of receiving reassurance as he waits, Kenwright nervously lights a cigarette and a close-up focuses on his anxiously shaking hands. When Sergeant Ridgeway appears he directs Kenwright through the swinging doors by motioning his hand with a swift slashing gesture as if he is herding cattle. Similarly, when Ridgeway learns Kenwright wants to collect his possessions from his wife, who has decided to live alone, Ridgeway exclaims they do not work as an 'escort' for domestic disputes. He then sends Kenwright home. Standing by the swing doors Ridgeway tilts his head to the side, commanding Kenwright to leave.

Whereas intimate gesturing in *Z Cars* articulates a relatively strong and mutual bond between the public and uniformed officers, the use of gesturing in *Hunter's Walk* now emphasises a strong divide. The police are no longer as subservient to members of the public, and ensure that citizens act on the police's terms. Each gesture Ridgeway uses to allow Kenwright to enter and leave Broadstone station is accompanied by Ridgeway holding on to the swinging doors with his right hand, thus relying on a strong division between the police force and the public. There is an 'abrasive quality' to these interactions, which were believed to be increasingly common between the police and public throughout the country (Ascoli 1979: 76). Prominent criminologists claimed the 'growth of squads with specialising functions and the spread of technological devices to improve the efficiency of crime control' changed the policeman's role from 'peacekeeper' to 'crime fighter', thus weakening 'the remaining links between police and community' (Hall *et al.* 1978: 46). Scenes in Broadstone station articulate this disparity between the police and their community through the set design and the actors' interactions with it. On the surface the narrative and immediate dialogue (illocutionary markers) of police officer characters portray them as being successful peacekeepers. However, PCs' physical gesturing and interaction with the surrounding set design (attitudinal markers) expose the police as hardened crimefighters who are desensitised to, and dismissive of, personal crises.

Correspondingly, this calm working dynamic shared between Ridgeway and Smith is accentuated by how they ensconce themselves within Broadstone station. When Coombes locates Ridgeway to deal with Kenwright's enquiry, he finds Ridgeway in a dark room lying down, listening to the radio, with his eyes shut. Then, later in the episode, Ridgeway is interrupted from sitting back reading a 'Cooks Golden Wing' holiday brochure by a phone call informing him Kenwright is now on the loose with a shotgun. Similarly, in 'Outcast' (18 June 1973), Ridgeway informs a superior over the phone that the station is too understaffed to help out with a picket line in Northampton. Yet, at the end of the scene, Ridgeway reclines to read a tabloid newspaper with the headline 'Dancing bride who slammed the door on loving'. There is an underlying cynicism communicated visually through the actors' interaction with their *mise-en-scène*. In tandem with the narrative trajectory, where Smith and Ridgeway successfully restore the peace, Ridgeway is culpable for this loss of community, as he prioritises his personal interests over public concerns.

Whilst this is a different working practice from the ever attentive uniformed division of *Z Cars*, both series observe characters from a relative distance to criticise aspects of policing. As such, a viewer has a relative degree of autonomy to pass judgement on the police's conduct. With seventeen minutes devoted to station scenes on average, compared to *Z Cars*' eight minutes per episode, an audience now witnesses lengthier discussions between the police and the public.[4] The visual framework of these discussions is exemplified in the episode 'Reasonable suspicion' (9 July 1973). Here a debate ensues between Ridgeway and Neil Yeldon (Brendan Price) with regard to the 1967 Criminal Law Act. Having been arrested without a warrant Yeldon feels that the police's use of this law has undermined his civil liberty. In comparison, Ridgeway understands their actions as necessary to upholding the law. During this discussion each character is given an equal number of close-ups and time to argue his perspective and understanding of the law. Without the series necessarily favouring one argument over the other, the conclusion remains open-ended, leaving the viewer to make up their own mind. One of the most predominant reasons for the camera retaining an observant gaze, and not favouring a particular character's view, can be ascribed to the mechanics of the studio drama production method. According to television producer Irene Shubik, the electronic studio provides a director with six cameras 'operating simultaneously' (Shubik 1975: 150).

Compared to filmed drama, which has to be 'built up with a single camera', scenes can be shot in one whole piece, 'ready edited' without the need for constant lighting changes (Shubik 1975: 151). As a result, studio production provides a 'mixing between a variety of views of the scene but makes it difficult to cut into the middle of it and identify the look of the spectator with the look of the character' (Caughie 2000: 122). Whilst this may have been seen as a limitation of the studio technique it certainly permitted police series to approach multifaceted issues from a range of perspectives with a degree of objectivity.

Introducing film technology

Although *The Sweeney* is frequently lauded for distancing the police series from the naturalistic studio approach, this is not how it was originally conceived. *The Sweeney* was created by Ian Kennedy Martin.[5] His idea was to explore the impact Robert Mark's appointment as Commissioner of the Metropolitan Police was having on detectives working in the Flying Squad. The Flying Squad was a mobile unit established in 1919 and then reorganised by Met Commissioner Sir Nevil Macready to detect and prevent armed robbery and related professional crime.[6] Kennedy Martin, however, felt this purpose was being impeded. His friend from the Flying Squad informed him detectives were being told they 'had to work in a different way' (quoted in Alvarado and Stewart 1985: 120). They were now instructed not to make contacts within the criminal fraternity as, supposedly, their work 'could all be done from a desk in an office on the third floor of Scotland Yard' (Alvarado and Stewart 1985: 120). This change in approach is what intrigued Kennedy Martin.

Based on his friend's experiences Kennedy Martin wrote a television film for Euston Film's *Armchair Cinema* anthology series (ITV, 1974–1975) entitled 'Regan' (4 June 1974). Here the eponymous protagonist, Detective Inspector Jack Regan (John Thaw), investigates the death of his colleague Cowley (Del Baker) alongside Detective Sergeant George Carter (Dennis Waterman). From the outset this television film was planned as a pilot for the subsequent series *The Sweeney*.[7] However, Ian Kennedy Martin's perception of how the series would work was diametrically opposed to that of his producer, Ted Childs. A dispute between them both, before 'Regan' entered production, resulted in the departure of Kennedy Martin from the project altogether. For Kennedy Martin, 'schooled in the traditions of BBC naturalism, all that was needed for the Sweeney to be both entertaining and realistic was to knock the stories into shape with as few frills as possible' (Alvarado and Stewart 1985: 120). Childs, however, envisioned the series abiding by the recent spate of American crime films, including *Dirty Harry* (1971) and *The French Connection* (1971). Childs was 'taken by that sort of realism', and so *The Sweeney* emulated rogue-cop movies directed by Don Siegel, where policemen cut through bureaucratic complexities and broke the law to enact justice (Alvarado and Stewart 1985: 120). Here, 'squeamishly liberal lawyers, unprincipled politicians and the spineless policemen running police departments' were depicted as additional enemies (Alvarado and Stewart 1985: 123). A similar outlook also governs the thematic construction of station-based scenes in *The Sweeney*.

Under producer Ted Childs's desire to replicate the style of 1970s American crime movies, albeit with 16 mm-film cameras, station-based scenes use point-of-view (POV) shots at significant moments. In these POV shots a viewer shares Regan's line of vision. In 'Jackpot' (9 January 1975), the audience shares Regan's gaze as he looks for clues as to where the stolen money disappeared to during an arrest. Similarly, in 'Contact breaker' (20 March 1975), a retirement ceremony unfolds in the station's common room. After observing the party for five seconds the camera tracks back to allow Regan to walk into the frame and dismissively roll his eyes at the camera whilst he exits the room. This tracking backwards reveals that the audience has been watching the scene unfold through Regan's point of view and then encourages viewers to share his contemptuous opinion of the situation. The viewer is not invited to consider any opinion of the retiring officer other than Regan's, who refers to the party as 'the crap being spoken in there'. Rather than observing characters operate in the station from a relative distance, like studio-shot drama, a viewer shares Regan's gaze and is encouraged to share his perspective of events. Therefore depictions of police work are less balanced, hardly open-ended, and do not provide much room for a debate, as Regan is always depicted as correct in his judgements.

Unlike previous British police series, *The Sweeney* depicts the police as answerable to, and regularly scrutinised by, regulatory bodies. In the episode 'Golden boy' (27 February 1975), an organisational methods team from A10, a department set up by Commissioner Mark to tackle police corruption, monitors Regan. The viewer is first introduced to A10 representatives, assessing whether Regan fills out paperwork correctly, through a low-angle shot placed behind Regan whilst sitting at his desk. From this angle A10 officer Bradshaw (Peter Miles) looms over Regan, entrapping him and preventing him from leaving the desk. Regan is stifled by this seemingly pointless procedure and manages to evade the situation. Carter deliberately walks into Bradshaw, causing a number of files to fall to the floor. Regan then uses this opportunity to persuade Bradshaw forcibly that they all need a lunch break at the pub, where

Regan proceeds to spike Bradshaw's drink. Instead of exploring the merits and drawbacks of A10, in the way Kennedy Martin may have initially envisioned, Bradshaw is presented as a bothersome bureaucrat with a whiny voice representing a trivial department Regan must neutralise to return to fighting crime.

Given *The Sweeney*'s cinematographic discourse, which encourages viewers to identify with Regan's perspective of events, Commissioner Mark's changes to the Met are not debated from the multitude of perspectives involved. Instead, such conflicts are simplified into an 'interpersonal tension between Haskins, Regan and Carter' (Drummond 1976: 19). These conflicts are 'exacerbated by class difference and professional jealousy' (Bazalgette 1976: 62). Regan's superiors' style of work 'expresses the middle-class values of academicism, theory, abstract reasoning, conformity to the rules, and personal ambition' (Bazalgette 1976: 61). Such career consciousness conflicts with Regan's loyalty to his team, referred to as an 'example of working-class solidarity' (Bazalgette 1976: 61). Regan's oft-cited 'identification with working-class people' can be seen to tap into the broader anxieties felt by working-class men through the 1970s as smokestack, Fordist, and primary industries that relied on manual labour were being replaced by service industries (Bazalgette 1976: 62). This resulted in a deep sense of 'uncertainty' and 'instability' amongst working-class men in the UK as manufacturing jobs declined by 17 per cent (Beynon 2002: 89). Regan and Carter 'never appear in suits, and both have unkempt hair' (Bazalgette 1976: 64). Their demeanour defies this 'unsupportive, entrepreneurial, and bureaucratic' culture creeping into the Flying Squad's working practices (Dennington and Tulloch 1976: 39) – although, beyond tapping into this general working-class anxiety, station scenes provide little exploration into the mechanics and politics of the Flying Squad.

There were a number of factors involved in *The Sweeney*'s production that ensured viewers forged an empathetic identification with Regan at the expense of a wider sociological/criminological dialogue. As Childs writes in his guidelines to production staff, his personal conviction was that a television studio's 'extensive rehearsal facilities' accompanied by 'several cameras for any given scene enable fairly complicated sequences involving several actors to be staged quite easily' (quoted in Donald 1985: 118). For Childs, using a 16 mm-film camera on location meant that complicated dialogue scenes were comparatively difficult to produce, as each scene has to be constructed one shot at a time. It was his belief that they should 'pioneer a film technique' that centred on action sequences and 'two handed dialogue on the run' (quoted in Alvarado and Stewart 1985: 57).

Furthermore, Childs's vision was c ned by the institutional and geographical limitations imposed on *The Sweeney* by Euston Film's constrictive working practices and production schedule. The 'comparative freedom that film allowed was hampered by the fact the production team were only given ten days' to film an episode (Donald 1985: 118). The production team were instructed by Childs to 'shoot an average of five minutes edited screen time a day', meaning no more than ten locations could be used per episode (quoted in Alvarado and Stewart 1985: 59). Moreover, each location used could be no more than half an hour's driving time, at the speed of the generator, from the crew's base in Hammersmith. The production guidelines state 'the more time we spend loading and unloading vehicles and driving around London, the less time, within the ten days, we have to actually make a film' (Alvarado and Stewart 1985: 59). What arises from these production constraints, and the producer's interpretation of these constraints, is a series 'deprived of the abundant geographical "reality" of the metropolis' that 'at the same time itself pares down the structure of the "real" flying squad' (Drummond 1976: 18). Thus, *The Sweeney* deploys 'a limited set of geographical and actantial signifiers, inflected towards the quasi-heroic biographical drama' (Drummond 1976: 18).

Rather than each narrative dictating how long should be spent in Scotland Yard, every episode uniformly had two days scheduled for shooting station scenes inside Euston's stock sets, located in former school building Colet Court. Therefore ten minutes of each episode had to be set within Scotland Yard's offices. This restrictive production practice had an impact on the writers, who were instructed to write 'uncomplicated story lines that dealt straightforwardly with crime' with dialogue scenes that were 'short and sharp rather than intriguing' (Alvarado and Stewart 1985: 61). Correspondingly there was a stark contrast of writers' experiences of working on *The Sweeney* compared to *Z Cars*. *Sweeney* writer Trevor Preston claimed 'I just used to feel like I was writing with my legs crossed most of the time' (quoted in Donald 1985: 118). In contrast, *Z Cars* writer Allan Prior felt he had 'never had the same feeling of freedom, in language and in subject' (Hopkins and Prior 1963: 13). Rather than honouring the scriptwriter, *The Sweeney* writers dictated its writers' approach through stricter production practices. As confirmed in 2007 by writer Troy Kennedy Martin (brought into the series by his brother), producer Ted Childs, and director Tom Clegg, *The Sweeney* had no script editor in its first season.[8] Without a uniform tone or style imposed on the writers, 'cohesion and continuity for the series was perceived to be more a product of the ongoing characters and the fifty minute format than a consequence of any overall strategy' (Turnbull 2014: 53).

It is often argued in accounts of television history that 'the film camera allows much more of a given society to be shown, rather than simply being indicated metonymically through the four walls of the stage or studio set' (Lacey 2005: 200). However, this advantage is lost in *The Sweeney*'s station-based scenes, as the series is preoccupied with following Regan's experience of events. Many factors contributed to this style of shooting. A combined result of Childs's stylistic envisioning of the series, the timely practice of using a single-film camera, and the strict constraints placed on the writers and production staff means viewers are guided through events from Regan's perspective. Such scenes are unable to tackle the political complexity behind the transformations of the Met taking place under Commissioner Mark, and an audience is prevented from observing events from a relatively autonomous distance. There is much less of a disparity between the illocutionary markers and attitudinal markers of actors. The visual discourse of the series feels wedded to the immediate dialogue. The visuals operate in tandem with the narrative, meaning little room is left to interpret characters' motives spatially.

The women of *Hunter's Walk*

What makes *Hunter's Walk*'s representation of civilian life distinctive from *The Sweeney* is its desire to examine middle-class women's domestic labour. Of the ten episodes that escaped being wiped, five focus on women who commit crime or are victims of crime. In 'Vanishing trick' (2 July 1973), Sally Lawrence's (Zuleika Robson) father is killed in a car crash at the very start of the episode, and so the narrative focuses on how Sally copes looking after her younger brothers and reconciling with her mother. In the episode 'Kids' (22 July 1974), schoolgirl Stephanie Coe (Patricia Smith) steals money from her mother (Shirley Cain). The episode focuses on Mrs Coe's attempts to have her daughter explain her sudden misbehaviour. Compared to *Z Cars* the domestic realm is not politicised through the way in which men use objects, signifying the outside world of work, within the home. Like soaps and sitcoms of the era, *Hunter's Walk* broadens the term 'political' to 'include a general interest in everyday life, especially the female-associated spheres of domesticity and consumerism' (Brunsdon *et al.* 1997b: 5). Therefore *Hunter's Walk* deserves recognition from feminist studies of television, as it challenges television's reproduced ideology of separate spheres where the home is considered 'a space of femininity and leisure and the public world as a place of masculinity and work' (Brunsdon *et al.* 1997b: 19). The housewife role is reconceptualised as a mode of work in its own right. Like programmes analysed by Carole Lopate (1977), Tania Modleski (1979), Richard Dyer et al. (1980), Ellen Seiter (1982), and Patricia Mellencamp (1986), *Hunter's Walk* is a series that acknowledges 'the role of domestic labour' and challenges 'inequalities between the sexes' (Dyer 1980: 5).

In the episode 'Disturbance', with the viewer having already witnessed Dennis Kenwright voicing his perspective on his wife's leaving him in Broadstone station, the episode develops by following the stresses experienced by his wife, Janet (Helen Fraser), in their home. In a pivotal scene Janet invites her husband over to inform him that she has filed for a divorce. In a close-up, Dennis sits on a chair talking about how his hopes have been dashed. As his speech unfolds, Janet leans into the frame to dust the coffee table. The camera tracks back to bring her into focus and fill the frame as she continues to dust furiously. She then undercuts his speech, asking 'What was the alternative?'. Her interaction with the table instigates a camera movement that refocuses the viewer's attention towards her suffering.

Once Janet undercuts her husband's self-pitying dialogue, both visually and verbally, she states 'somebody had to do something', which he dismisses with 'not me, never me'. As Dennis says this, the camera pans to follow Janet as she walks behind the sofa, and then zooms in on a cushion. She picks up the cushion and punches it with the palm of her hand once, in a strong, direct, and sustained pressing motion. Although this action is intended to plump the cushion, it signifies her repressed frustrations against her husband. Punching it once, in the centre, with great force while he speaks, reveals her contempt towards him. Following this action, Janet replies to Dennis in a more forceful tone, exclaiming, 'Listen to us, we talk round and round in circles. What's the point?'. She raises her voice to a loud, shrill tone, alluding to the extent of her stress. She then turns around on the spot and dusts another coffee table, placed behind the sofa, to continue her chores.

Through this scene, Dennis sits on the chair looking ahead. He talks about himself whilst his wife rarely remains still as she constantly cleans and primes the space. The living room is a space of work for her, yet through the episode it has been a space of recreation for her male partner. She is positioned in between the table and the sofa by the end of the scene, suggesting that she is trapped by such routines. In a previous scene, the sofa was a space of relaxation for her new partner Ted Peters (John Ringham), as he and Dennis argued for ownership of the household. The *mise-en-scène* helps reveal the cracks in Janet's relationship with Peters, and her role as a housewife. The punch, and then subsequent constricted movements, reveal how the lounge has always been a space of imprisonment and work for Janet. This visual composition echoes the works of Betty Friedan's *The Feminine Mystique* (2010 [1963]) and Germaine Greer's *The Female Eunuch* (2008 [1970]). As Greer states, 'mother is the dead heart of the family, spending father's earnings on consumer goods to enhance the environment in which he eats, sleeps and watches television' (Greer 2008 [1970]: 251). So far British police series from the 1960s and 1970s have been characterised as a form of programming that allows 'the feminine' to be excluded from what is 'a primarily masculinist discourse' (Sydney-Smith 2002: 168). With regard to the domestic settings of *Hunter's Walk*, this is not quite the case.

'Local knowledge'

The *mise-en-scène* of domestic spaces in *Hunter's Walk* is frequently used to foreground women's experiences as a means of engaging with wider public debate. The second episode, 'Local knowledge' (11 June 1973), is particularly poignant in this regard. Here, the audience's focus is on rape victim Christine Lewis (Frances White). Significantly, her husband Phillip (Ian Thompson) is depicted as somewhat villainous for being neglectful and holding his reputation within Broadstone in higher regard than his wife's suffering. The Lewises' front room is dominated by a large window that covers most of the wall. Whenever the curtains are opened all that is visible are two semi-detached houses. Although located across the road, the houses are in very close proximity to the window and exacerbate Christine's feeling of being caged in. She is imprisoned, as the room has a typewriter – symbolising the work she undertakes for her husband's company's magazine – at one end, and the big window – representing the judgements of neighbours – at the other. Not being able to relax in the space is what causes her to go for a walk in the early hours to clear her head, which results in her crossing paths with her attacker.

For Christine, there is seemingly no escape. The centre of the room is decorated with exotic travel memorabilia. A woven Cordoba emblem is mounted on the wall, next to a wooden hand-crafted drinks cabinet and a porcelain horse. Significantly there are no photos of the couple in Cordoba because Phillip visited it alone. These possessions function as a status symbol to the Lewises' neighbours, signifying Phillip's wealth and well-travelled lifestyle. The front room, with its huge window, is designed as if it is a showroom inviting the neighbours to admire the patterns of consumption on display. Here Christine must live as if she herself is an exhibit, as her husband fleetingly visits from endless work trips. It is upon the news of Christine's attack that her husband returns home and cuts a work visit short. When they first share the front room, Christine sits on the sofa opening her arms for an embrace. Instead of responding to Christine's inviting gesture, Phillip walks to the drinks cabinet and stands by his travel memorabilia, causing each character to be framed by two separate shots. Phillip's movement, interaction, and positioning within the space change the scene's macro meaning from one of initial reconciliation to one of division. Christine is treated as a possession. Following the attack, she even claims people look at her as though she is an 'exhibit', unaware that she has always been treated like one.

Public/private dichotomy

Such depictions of domesticity not only bring to light the repression experienced by middle-class women; they also critique how domestic crimes were seemingly trivialised compared to public-order crimes within British law. The 1976 Domestic Violence and Matrimonial Proceedings Act empowered magistrates' courts to 'make an order excluding the aggressor from the home' (Edwards 1989: 5). Similarly, the 1978 Domestic Proceedings and Magistrates' Courts Act, in response to criticisms of the 1976 Act, gave magistrates the power to 'evict the violent spouse under an exclusion order' (Edwards 1989: 56). However, in reality 'violence committed against wives, cohabitees, girlfriends or lovers in the privacy of the home, unlike violence against strangers or acquaintances committed in private or public' was 'rarely dealt with in criminal courts' (Edwards 1989: 73). Therefore, a public/private dichotomy was evident, as dealing with these offences in civil courts reaffirmed the 'belief' that martial violence was 'different from other violent crime' (Edwards 1989: 54).

In response to this public/private dichotomy, feminist lobbying reclassified rape as a crime against women. Before this emergence of rape-crisis centres and consciousness-raising groups, rape was largely considered to be a personal problem where 'women nearly always blamed themselves', and 'remained silent out of shame and guilt' (Bevacqua 2000: 61). Challenging commonly accepted myths surrounding rape provided the 'conceptual framework for the development of a new belief system' to change widespread perceptions of rape (Bevacqua 2000: 58). Asserting that rape was a crime of violence enabled feminists to remove blame from victims. Feminists redefined rape as 'any form of unwanted sexual contact' (Bevacqua 2000).

Similarly, the common misconception that rape was a rare occurrence committed by 'sexual psychopaths whose desire to rape emanates from a psychiatric disorder' was called into question (Bevacqua 2000: 62). Feminists instead advanced the notion that 'any man can commit the crime, regardless of his status in the community' (Bevacqua 2000: 63).

This public/private dichotomy was also publicly challenged amidst the crimes of Peter Sutcliffe. During the Yorkshire Ripper's twenty-three attacks on women from 1969 to 1980, the West Yorkshire Police advised women to stay indoors at night. In response activist women's groups organised 'reclaim the night' marches in Leeds. The police's persistent failure to capture the ripper led to a questioning of their priorities. Such criticisms were further highlighted by Women's Aid, a refuge movement for women and their children who had left home to escape physical, sexual, or mental abuse. The movement grew from housing 2 victims in 1971 to almost 200 by 1977 (Hanmer 1989: 90). Essentially it was felt the Home Office had 'no interest in this newly rediscovered social problem and neither Women's Aid nor the parliamentary select committee saw the police and criminal justice system generally as part of the state able to offer a helping service to women' (Edwards 1989: 91).

'Local knowledge' is an important episode because it devotes the majority of its running time to the consequential suffering experienced by rape victim Christine over the police's process of pursuing the rapist. Christine suffers from her husband's lack of support and understanding. Phillip is of the view that she is to blame for leaving their house alone in the early hours of the morning. Their private domestic space is presented as a political space because it is here she faces judgement from those closest to her. The consequences of treating rape as a personal problem, where the woman is incorrectly blamed, are revealed. It also dispels the myth that rape is a rare occurrence committed by psychopaths, as the rapist, Shepherd (Graham Ashley), is a tradesman and fully functional member of the community. *Hunter's Walk* addresses these complex debates by drawing attention to the female victims the law overlooks. Recording the drama in the studio using video cameras enables the audience to observe with considerable clarity, given the grainier texture of film cameras, the nuanced and uncomfortable interactions men and women have with one another within the domestic space following a traumatic crime. Consistently the series highlights the disparity that exists between how crime is officially dealt with by an increasingly fortified police force and the personal suffering citizens experience as a result. Had the police taken Dennis Kenwright's enquiry seriously they might have been able to prevent him from committing criminal damage with his shotgun. Similarly, Christine Lewis finds herself in a vacuum with no support available to her following her attack. *Hunter's Walk* challenges British television drama's traditional belief in a gendered public/private binary, as a distinctly feminist consciousness underpins the programme's ideology – as was also occurring in soap operas at the time.

Sweeney criminals

Whilst *Hunter's Walk* helps unearth the consequences that arise from a public/private dichotomy in British law, *The Sweeney* occupies a different ideological agenda. By accessing civilian settings where violent robberies are planned and conducted by hardened criminals, the series perpetuates the popular belief that 'the rate of violent crime was on the increase' and there was a 'spread of criminal "empires"' (Hall *et al.* 1978: 9, 48). A prominent view amongst the public, press, and judiciary was that reverting to traditional ' "get-tough" policies would have the 'required deterring effect on those attracted to violent crime' (Hall *et al.* 1978: 9). Prime Minister Edward Heath's Conservative Party capitalised on this feeling through their successful 1970 general election 'law and order' campaign, which vowed to achieve stability through tougher laws and more stringent penalties for offenders. More resources were put into specialist squads such as the Flying Squad, Serious Crime Squad, and Robbery Squad. It was perceived that 'the scale and professionalism of robbery ... and, above all, the greater use of guns and violence and prevalence of a "stop-at-nothing" mentality' were the government's and police's biggest priority in terms of crime prevention compared to, say, tackling domestic crime (Hall *et al.* 1978: 48). *The Sweeney* validates this political priority, as scenes based in civilian settings depict the 'planning and counter-planning in each camp, the military-style conduct of the police and criminals, manoeuvring for tactical and strategic advantage, and the final set-piece battle' (Hurd 1976: 49). Paramilitary policing is depicted as the solution to maintaining public safety, as *The Sweeney* 'refracted rather than reflected its time' (Tulloch 1990: 70).

This change in attitude gave rise to, and coincided with, a reawakening of the traditional 'rational actor' model of criminology. The dominance of a 'predestined actor' model grounded by anomie theory, which sought to reduce crime through attacking ' "root causes" [of crime] with programs that end poverty, reduce discrimination, and meliorate privation' lost political capital (Wilson 1975: 30). Instead, the belief that 'it is possible to lower the crime rate by increasing the certainty of sanctions' and 'incapacitation works' gained significant ground (Wilson 1975: 131, 133). Now treating a criminal as a threat to society, rather than as a candidate for rehabilitation, was led by James Q. Wilson's totemic writings, which stated that 'wicked people exist. Nothing avails except to set them apart from innocent people' (1975: 248).

For criminologists invested in the 1970s rational-actor model their aim was to chart a correlation between an analysis of policy in relation to specific crime rates in order to assess pragmatically the effectiveness of deterrence: a deterrence doctrine. In relation to this perceived rise in urban street crime, including aggravated assault, muggings, and armed street robberies, Jack Gibbs advocates 'an emphasis on incapacitation over deterrence and rehabilitation' (Gibbs 1975: 64). Influential criminologists Franklin Zimring and Gordon Hawkins, however, believe 'crime prevention rather than deterrence', through stratagems including better street-lighting and citizen alarms, is the 'ultimate object of crime control measures' (Zimring and Hawkins 1973: 351). Yet despite this clear disagreement each theorist centres their argument on an individual's choice rather than on the social constraints and conditions that shape these choices. For Wilson, Gibbs, and Zimring and Hawkins all criminals are rational actors, rather than victims of circumstance. For them, those who contemplate a crime undergo a cost-benefit analysis whereby an individual: '(1) views the act as contrary to law (2) knows the prescribed punishment (3) perceives the punishment as severe, and (4) estimates the actual imposition of the punishment as certain. Therefore if the individual commits the act, then the threat of punishment clearly did not deter him or her' (Gibbs 1975: 12). This emphasis on an individual's choice is repeatedly revisited in *The Sweeney*. The initial appearance that any character has been forced into criminal action through social circumstance is promptly dispelled. In the episode 'Jackpot' (9 January 1975), for example, it transpires that Harry Biggleswade (Ed Devereaux) has committed armed robbery to pay for his son's operation to correct a potentially terminal kidney problem. When Carter declares 'I can't help taking my hat off to him', Regan reminds Carter that 'if he'd have had a gun that day he'd have taken your head off'. Following this statement Regan looks at Biggleswade through a peephole in Biggleswade's cell door and the viewer shares Regan's exact point of view. This POV is followed by a cut to previous footage of Biggleswade committing the robbery at the start of the episode. The footage is now slowed down and the camera zooms in on his face. As Biggleswade's face fills the frame Regan claims 'funnily enough all the women hate him, they all say the same thing; you couldn't wish a worse father on any child'. Instead of observing a conflicted character, the writing has Biggleswade's character dictated by Regan's perceptions rather than leaving the audience to decide whether or not Biggleswade's intentions had some merit. The possibility of curing his son's ill health may well outweigh the risk of being caught within Biggleswade's internal cost-benefit analysis. However, Regan affirms that Biggleswade's logic is skewed, and that stricter punishment and immediate incarceration are what protect the public. This swift punishment also deters others – indicated by how Carter's praise for the assailant is instantly quelled – as was believed by the Home Office and criminologists who sought to develop the deterrence doctrine.

Similarly, in 'Chalk and cheese' (1 September 1975), working-class Tommy Garret (Paul Jones) is led astray and exploited by upper-class Giles Nunn (Shane Briant) and Caroline Selhurst (Lesley-Anne Down) to carry out armed robberies. Although at times Garret appears to be a victim of bullying, he nevertheless chooses to ignore advice from his childhood friend George Carter and his law-abiding father Pop Garret (David Lodge). Tommy continues to commit armed robbery to earn financial rewards and respect from his peers. His repeated refusal to ignore advice from his paternal, law-abiding role models, and his decision to engage in violence, result in the murder of a civilian. Despite Carter's initial claim that 'he'd never use a gun', Garret's killing confirms Regan's view that 'anyone who carries a loaded shooter is going to use it at some point' and that they need to put those 'bastards away'. Pop Garret is repeatedly shown to be a responsible father who disciplined his sons correctly, and it is ultimately 'not your fault', proclaims Carter, as it is Tommy Garret who has actively chosen criminality.

Whereas *Hunter's Walk* presents domestic spaces as political settings that discuss and work through social debates, *The Sweeney*, in comparison, depicts villainy as an 'amorphous' concept rendering villains as 'characterless' stereotypes (Drummond 1976: 24). In *Hunter's Walk* a slight alteration in the positioning of an object within an elaborately designed domestic space has the potential to disrupt the composition of the *mise-en-scène* to reveal a character's complex interiority. *The Sweeney* does not achieve this, largely because objects stressed in the series 'have little more than a functional utility' and are only used when they have narrative significance (Paterson 1976: 13). Thus domestic scenes involving Biggleswade and Tommy Garret use props sparingly so as to maintain continuity, given that a single camera has filmed the scene several times from different angles in a very restrictive production schedule. Therefore an understanding of these criminal characters and their motivations is extrapolated through the spoken testimony of others rather than through an observation of their direct actions. As Childs admits: 'Little interest is shown in the character or motivation of criminals, or the detailed logistics of crime and detection. Processes and principles of law-making, complex issues about legal rights and responsibilities or civil liberties, the procedures of courts and prisons – none of these figure in the series' (quoted in Donald 1985: 131). *The Sweeney* reiterates the central philosophy of the rational-actor school of thought fashioned by Wilson, Gibbs, and Zimring and Hawkins, as an individual is solely responsible for their criminality. In legitimating this view *The Sweeney* denies 'the validity of alternatives' and the role socio-economic circumstances have in influencing decisions: something studio-shot police series have repeatedly entertained through domestic scenes (Hurd 1976: 52).

The Smiths and companionate marriage

Hunter's Walk depicts a police force that is distrusting and cynical of its public when successfully solving crimes within Broadstone station. Simultaneously a viewer is encouraged to empathise with the suffering that women endure domestically as a result of the police's lack of social provision. Detective Sergeant Smith's domestic scenes navigate both views, as *Hunter's Walk* is the first major police series to spend a large proportion of its running time in a detective's home. A private/public dichotomy in British law practice is examined further in 'Local knowledge' through the interactions shared between Smith and his wife, Betty (Ruth Madoc). When the rapist, Shepherd, has been arrested, Smith prolongs leaving his home before he begins the interrogation process at the station. He deliberately uses this tactic to unnerve Shepherd. Before he leaves home, the establishing shot shows that the front room of the Smiths' house is divided into two areas. A kitchenette and a lounge area are separated by a counter top with shelving placed directly above it. Initially both Smith and Betty share the space. The camera is placed in the lounge area so that Smith is positioned in the immediate foreground whilst Betty is standing behind the shelving in the kitchen. As Betty stirs some ingredients in a bowl Smith finishes fixing the iron in the lounge. Once the iron is repaired, Smith puts on his coat to leave for the station to interrogate Shepherd. He puts the mended iron on the counter top that separates the kitchen from the lounge; he puts it here as if to place it back in his wife's territory. It is an implement she uses as a housewife and something he does not interact with beyond its servicing.

This brief scene initially seems to suggest that both characters are happy to conform to the roles expected of them as part of a sexual division of labour. Both operate in separate spheres, as Smith is the breadwinner leaving the house to earn his income whilst his wife stays at home. Betty appears visibly caged by the shelving and is rooted to the kitchen area. Nevertheless, she is ostensibly content as she stirs her cooking mixture. She is placed behind the shelving as if being protected by her husband on the other side. Betty is happily abiding by Smith's earlier advice that she should not leave the house unattended given the recent rape of Christine Lewis. Although 'reclaim the night' marches would not be staged until later in the decade, the scene appears to be visually affirming police advice that urged women to stay at home when sexual assaults were being committed within their community.

However, this initial dynamic does alter. At the end of 'Local knowledge' Smith sits on a chair in the lounge area with his back to the kitchenette, looking ahead into the camera. Betty sits on an adjacent chair in another separate close-up shot. Betty asks Smith questions about the case as she looks over the top of her magazine. On hearing the suspect is likely to get ten years in prison she asks him, 'it's not him though is it, really. His wife, the woman, their families. Once something like this happens. How many men did you interview, five? What about their families?'. Immediately after asking these questions, Betty walks into the kitchen area directly behind Smith. She moves away from him because the conversation has become too tense to bear. Smith, so far, has been speaking through gritted teeth, hastily trying to end the conversation with one-word answers. Betty appears upset that the police do not seem to consider the wider sociological implications of their actions.

Betty's statement highlights how many women did not see the police and criminal justice system working for women in vulnerable situations. Nonetheless, this question does cause Smith momentarily to reassess his methods, claiming in a rather inquisitive tone, 'I'd never even thought about it.' He then swiftly qualifies his point of view with the firmer authoritative statement, 'I've got a job to do. I do it the only way I know how. I'm a copper not a welfare officer.' Once Smith has made his views clear the camera cuts to a close-up of Betty's face as she sighs and tilts her head to one side, looking over her husband from the kitchen area (see Figure 1). This motion of her head tilting to the left side of the frame is then replicated, through a match cut, by the action of Phillip Lewis, husband of rape victim Christine, downing a glass of whisky alone in his front room. Standing in profile to the camera, he tilts his head backwards to the left-hand side of the camera's frame in

The 1970s 55

Figure 1 Betty Smith looks over disapprovingly at her husband from the kitchen area, because he has not considered the social support that victims of crime require.

the same direction as Betty's head tilted previously. As Phillip drinks, the camera then cuts to reveal his wife Christine getting into bed on her own. As this is the last image of the episode, Betty is proved correct. The Lewis family are isolated from one another and are without the necessary support they need, despite the apprehension of the rapist. Smith's self-assured authority, advice, and support, as a member of the British police force, are questioned and challenged through these domestic scenes. Whilst gendered divisions exist within the Smiths' household, Betty is never sidelined to focus on Smith. She has an equal share of the camerawork to voice her opinions where she reminds viewers that families of criminals and victims of crime require more support because suffering does not cease with an arrest.

The private life of a police official is again representative of how the British public viewed marriage at the time of transmission. Mainstream marriage guidance in the 1970s 'began to put far more emphasis on the emotional/spiritual aspects of sexuality as opposed to the purely physical side'. Problem pages and advice books became less interested in the physiological nature of sex and drew more attention to 'warm feelings' (Richards and Elliot 1991: 39). Rather than predominantly providing advice on sexual intercourse they advised that both parties within a marriage should be treated on equally empathetic and responsive terms. There was a desire to talk through problems and have a greater understanding of each other. This is reflected in the Smiths' home, which allows for a difference of opinion between each character. This mutual sense of companionship and ability to maintain an open dialogue is what makes for the Smiths' successful marriage in relation to those of the Lewises, Kenwrights, and other officers. Brenda Ridgeway (Diana Rayworth), for example, decides to divorce her husband, Sergeant Ken Ridgeway, for being unfaithful, following her private discussions at home with Betty Smith. This consistent access to domestic spaces populated by women is where *Hunter's Walk* engages with feminism's emergence into mainstream UK culture – a far cry from *Z Cars*, where PC Bob Steele's opinions are final.

Regan and divorce

In comparison to Smith, Regan is divorced and lives alone, having 'sacrificed his personal family life for the greater good of us all' (Clarke 1992: 246). There is little access to Regan's character beyond his professional identity. Occasionally he uses his flat as a place to date women, reinforcing 'the complete demarcation between what is presented as the masculine world, the world of work ... and the feminine obsession with the domestic' (Clarke 1992: 246). In adhering to this convention of American rogue-cop movies, where a detective's family life lies in ruins given their professional obsessions, *The Sweeney* obtains a male gaze. In 'Cover story' (20 February 1975), Regan falls for crime reporter Sandy Williams (Prunella Gee) and is effectively suspended for getting too close to a potential suspect who may be involved with the Whittle gang. Whilst on leave Regan drowns his sorrows in the pub, outwardly dubbing Williams a 'vulture' (see Figure 2). However, Regan's dialogue is counteracted by a black-and-white close-up of Williams's smiling face looking directly at the camera (see Figure 3). Williams is positioned lying down on a bed as the camera slowly zooms closer towards her face for six seconds. These thoughts, most likely from a previous romantic encounter, undercut Regan's immediate dialogue as his calming memory provides him with solace from the crowded pub. This editing provides a viewer with access to Regan's thoughts and what motivates him outside work. Here, in line with Laura Mulvey's male gaze theory, 'an objectified other' whose 'visual presence works against the development of a story-line' freezes

Figure 2 Regan reminisces about Williams whilst alone in the pub on leave.

'the flow of action in moments of erotic contemplation' (Mulvey 1989 [1975]: 17, 19). *The Sweeney*, in its emulation of 'cinematic storytelling' and Childs's attempts to distance the series from the studio technique, has little engagement with the social ramifications of law-and-order policy, as again events are dictated by Regan's perceptions (Paterson 1976: 8).

Regan's relationships with middle-class women provide glimpses of a debonair character with the capacity to dress in a sophisticated fashion, drink wine moderately, and enjoy classical music. This contrasts sharply with his identity at work, where he swears, drinks Scotch heavily, and dresses scruffily to war against middle-class careerists stifling the working practices of the Flying Squad. Nevertheless, the primary function of Regan's domestic scenes is to provide fleeting love interests for a 'main male protagonist' akin to Hollywood storytelling (Mulvey 1989 [1975]: 21). There is no attempt to intervene creatively in sociological debate in a relatively balanced manner, as seen in studio-shot drama, because the camera adheres to the cinematographic grammar of the male gaze to capture Regan's personal life.

Figure 3 The camera cuts to a shot of their previous romantic encounter from Regan's point of view to show what is occupying his mind.

Conclusion

Traditionally the soap opera is regarded as the television genre that overturned a 'deeply entrenched value structure based on oppositions of masculinity and femininity' (Geraghty 1991: 41). Since Lopate's (1977), Modleski's (1979), and Dyer's (1980) feminist television scholarship, Deborah Jermyn's (2008) and Julia Hallam's (2000, 2005) work on Lynda La Plante, and Lynn Thomas's (1997 [1995]) examination of *Inspector Morse* (ITV, 1987–2000) have examined how feminist pressures have impacted upon depictions of women in traditionally 'male' genres. There is, however, hardly any detailed analysis of women characters in British police series predating *Prime Suspect* (ITV, 1991–2006). Therefore, it is imperative to remember that the police series has been interested in feminist concerns since the 1970s, and it is not solely interested in depictions of men, as traditionally perceived. Through an analysis of *Hunter's Walk* this chapter has demonstrated how the British police series, a genre usually affiliated with a 'masculinist discourse', has a history of challenging the sexual division of labour in a similar manner to the soap opera

(Sydney-Smith 2002: 168). Through its regular depictions of domesticity *Hunter's Walk* engaged in feminist debate by questioning the attitudes of a male-dominated police force and its prioritising of public, over private, crime. Smith's wife is particularly important in this respect, as she provides counter-arguments to her detective husband's worldview.

ITV's *The Sweeney* is often considered to be the defining police series of the 1970s for utilising 16mm film technology that heightens the suspense of the police series whilst adding 'a certain amount of grit' to typical action sequences (Buscombe 1976: 68). The series addresses a resentment felt by working-class men amidst a significant decline in manufacturing industries as the Government began to abandon its commitment to full employment. This isolationism is touched on through Regan's personal warring against middle-class colleagues who increasingly envelop Scotland Yard. Regan's delivery of this working-class vernacular, to convey 'a very particular kind of British class antagonism', was considered too impenetrable for American audiences, and so *The Sweeney* was not sold to US broadcasters, unlike previous ITV action series (Sparks 1992: 134). Given its restrictive production schedule, however, *The Sweeney* does not investigate these class politics in any great detail, as events are affixed to Regan's gaze and his corresponding rational-actor view of criminality.

Meanwhile, *Hunter's Walk*, given its observational studio-based approach, scrutinises the social shortcomings of public policy in its inability to protect female victims of crime, and an outdated postwar settlement allied 'to the idea of a male breadwinner model' where women are treated 'as dependants of men' (Lewis and Hobson 1997: 7). These second-wave feminist concerns remained fundamentally uncontested by other, less successful, studio-shot police series, including *Parkin's Patch* (ITV, 1969–1970) and *New Scotland Yard* (ITV, 1972–1974). Overall, *Hunter's Walk* is a text with landmark significance for investing a traditionally masculine genre with women's 'day to day experiences' as a form of political struggle, as was being discussed by groups of women across Britain (Coote and Campbell 1987: 5).

Notes

1 *The Avengers* in particular received £5 million from its sale to American broadcasters alone.
2 Statistics taken from Gambaccini and Taylor (1993).
3 *Ibid*.
4 Statistics calculated by working out the average times from each series' first six episodes.

5 Brother of *Z Cars* creator, Troy Kennedy Martin.
6 For more information see http://webarchive.nationalarchives.gov.uk/20081107220129/http:/www.met.police.uk/history/flying_squad.htm (accessed 10 June 2019).
7 'Sweeney Todd' is cockney rhyming slang for Flying Squad.
8 This information was revealed in a voice-over commentary recorded over the third episode of series 1, 'Thin ice' (16 January 1975), for Network's 2007 DVD release.

The 1980s: emergent feminist thought and resurgent video cameras

3

Women are constantly playing those roles where all you do is pour cups of tea and say, 'what happened next?' I see David Hargreaves, who plays my husband, doing it and he hates it. I say, 'I've done it for fourteen years, being bored and upset.'

Juliet Bravo lead actress Stephanie Turner
(quoted in Beauman 1980: 74).

By *The Sweeney*'s (ITV, 1975–1978) fourth and final series the novelty of staging elaborate action sequences using 16 mm-film cameras was already feeling formulaic and 'clichéd' (Cooke 2015a: 127). Portrayals of specialist forces fighting professional criminals were axed because of plummeting audience figures. Police action series *Special Branch* (ITV, 1969–1974), *Softly, Softly* (BBC, 1966–1976), and *Target* (BBC, 1977–1978) were largely outmoded by the four-part *Law and Order* serial (BBC, 1978) broadcast by the *Play for Today* anthology series (BBC, 1970–1984). Producer Tony Garnett's desire to avoid another 'squealing tyres show' ensured natural lighting and sounds, captured by an observant film-camera, made the verisimilitude of action series obsolete (Garnett 2008: n.p.). Series of the 1980s that proved consistently popular with audiences focused on depictions of small-scale crimes that ordinary frontline officers and detectives were likely to face regularly.

This chapter, then, explores how *Juliet Bravo* (BBC, 1980–1985), *The Gentle Touch* (ITV, 1980–1984), and *The Bill* (ITV, 1984–2010) use video cameras to negotiate the disconnect thought to exist between the British police force's increasingly militaristic practices and the public's favouring of community policing. This analysis will consider how each series interacts with contemporary rational-actor models developed by criminologists in relation to this socio-political disparity. Moreover, the chapter will determine how each series intervenes in debates surrounding class identity and gender roles in relation to Thatcherism, the political philosophy committed to reasserting Victorian values and displacing the responsibilities of the State on to individuals to decrease Government spending.

Although *Juliet Bravo* attracted 10 million viewers weekly, *The Gentle Touch* received audiences of 13 million, and *The Bill* is the longest-running British police series of all time, a comparative academic analysis of each programme has not been conducted.[1] This is largely because television academics believe each series is 'co-opted by the ideology of sexism' (Gamman 1988: 11). Scholarship on *Juliet Bravo* and *The Gentle Touch* briefly examines each programme as a precursor to analysing a crime drama written by Lynda La Plante. Deborah Jermyn examines how Jane Tennison (Helen Mirren) of *Prime Suspect* (ITV, 1991–2006) overcomes the 'gendered matrix of looking and seeing in operation' as her male colleagues repeatedly ignore her gaze to disempower her (Jermyn 2008: 65). Similarly, Gillian Skirrow criticises *Juliet Bravo*, in relation to La Plante's *Widows* (ITV, 1983), for framing its leading actress as 'an unusual specimen under a microscope' as the camera looks 'at her environment in a descriptive rather than expressive way' (Skirrow 1987: 175).

Such academic arguments believe that *The Gentle Touch* and *Juliet Bravo* are inferior to La Plante's crime dramas because they do not overtly subvert a male gaze to challenge patriarchal authority. However, neither author acknowledges that La Plante's dramas subscribe to a different visual grammar, synonymous with Hollywood films, that engages in a system of looks exchanged between characters. Comparatively, *The Gentle Touch* and *Juliet Bravo* were shot in television studios, ready-edited with five simultaneously recording video cameras. Without the ability to cut into the middle of a variety of views, and 'identify the look of the spectator with the look of the character', such a production method inherently observes actors operating within their environments from a relative distance (Caughie 2000: 122). So, to compare studio-shot drama with filmed drama in this manner can be misleading.

Production context

Juliet Bravo was envisaged by BBC1 Controller Billy Cotton, who felt 'we should make a series about a woman detective' (Kennedy Martin 2008: n.p.). Accordingly *The Sweeney* creator Ian Kennedy Martin modelled *Juliet Bravo*'s format on real-life Inspector Wynn Darwin from Great Harwood. The show was located in the fictional town of Hartley based on areas of Lancashire and West Yorkshire. Correspondingly, exterior scenes were filmed in a selection of towns across both counties,

The 1980s 63

including Bacup and Todmorden. Then interior scenes were recorded on videotape at the BBC's English Regions Drama department, based in Birmingham's Pebble Mill studios, which had a remit to 'reflect regional life' of communities removed from London (Millington and Nelson 1986: 25). Coincidentally, executives at London Weekend Television (LWT) independently identified a distinct lack of television starring 'a lady detective' that explored how her family life 'integrated with her work' (Arnell 2008: n.p.). Veteran television-writer Terence Feely developed *The Gentle Touch* as part of LWT's strategy to be 'committed to series programming' as a means of retaining a large and loyal viewership (Potter 1990: 78). The series would be shot in their flagship South Bank studios and follow the work and life of a female Metropolitan Police detective. In this race to broadcast the first police series starring a woman in the lead role *The Gentle Touch* pipped *Juliet Bravo* to the post by just four months.

Despite being studio productions commissioned under relatively similar circumstances a different stylistic grammar is utilised in station scenes. Of the shots used in the *Gentle Touch*'s station scenes, 72 per cent are close-ups, whereas only 57 per cent of shots used in Hartley station are close-ups.[2] Likewise, 11 per cent of shots used in the station scenes of *Juliet Bravo* are long shots, compared to *The Gentle Touch*, where they are sparingly used. Consequently *The Gentle Touch* attains what film-studies criticism refers to as the 'rhetoric' of melodrama, as Detective Chief Inspector Maggie Forbes's (Jill Gascoigne) feelings are repeatedly foregrounded to guide viewers through each narrative (Gledhill 1987: 13). Frequently events are witnessed independently from Forbes's knowledge, including the murder of her husband, her son's shoplifting, and her colleagues discovering that a ring given to her by her boyfriend is stolen property. Thus station scenes often abide by Steve Neale's narrative logic of melodrama, whereby 'discrepancies between the knowledge and point of view of the spectator and the knowledge and points of view of the characters, such that the spectator often *knows more*' produce pathos (Neale 1986: 7).[3] Close-ups observe Forbes learning what viewers already know, comprehending this knowledge, and then working out the appropriate course of action. Such a persistent use of close-ups leaves little room for Forbes to interact with her surrounding space, and so diminishes the viewer's autonomous interpretation of her actions.

Hartley station

In the opposite case, the regular use of long shots in *Juliet Bravo* permits the design of Hartley station to acknowledge wider social issues impacting on the protagonist's work. A gender divide exists between Inspector Jean Darblay (Stephanie Turner) and her male colleagues Sergeant Joseph Beck (David Ellison) and Sergeant George Parrish (Noel Collins). This divide is accentuated by the long corridor central to the design of Hartley station. At one end of the spacious corridor is a small desk space where the uniformed male officers work. At the other end of the corridor is Darblay's office door. The cramped police desk, under Darblay's watchful presence, keeps the male officers huddled together and confines this form of hegemonic masculinity as they attempt to conceal recreational items from her. In 'A private place' (3 October 1981), Beck confidently stands behind the desk eating a bread roll. But when Beck hears Darblay's footsteps he swiftly slouches over the desk to hide his food. Similarly, in 'Cages' (18 October 1980), Darblay discovers PC Roland Bentley (Mark Drewry) reading a holiday magazine with a bikini-clad woman on the cover. In contrast to *Hunter's Walk*, where officers unashamedly read such publications at work, Bentley appears bashful as Darblay slowly unveils the magazine. Skirrow criticises *Juliet Bravo* for treating Darblay as 'an unusual specimen under a microscope' (1987: 175). However, the male officers are also examined with a similar degree of scrutiny. Their self-assured methods of policing, unchallenged through *Z Cars* and *Hunter's Walk*, are exposed by Darblay as being relatively childish, undisciplined, and ineffective. Her character provides the genre with a new perspective removed from the male officers' working practices to question their entrenched attitudes. This scrutiny of police conduct is now an active aspect of station scenes, compared to previous series where such criticisms were exclusively consigned to the wives of police officials within their homes.

This warring between Darblay and her male colleagues is often instigated by public enquiries. The expansive corridor in between the police desk and Darblay's office door affords members of the public a large space to act out their various predicaments. For example, members of a Marxist-Leninist study group use the corridor to protest against the detention of their leader in the episode 'Cages'. Also, health-food-shop-owner Jo Fairbrother (Juliet Cadzow) refuses to be searched in a stand against the 1981 Criminal Attempts Act in 'You can go home again' (23 October 1982). Whenever Beck is dismissive of what he sees as trivial enquiries Darblay intervenes and directs people to her office, where she listens diligently to a range of personal problems. In the episode 'Aunt Sally' (24 October 1981), Darblay does not charge retired store-detective-turned-shoplifter Gwen Fletcher (Margery Mason) with theft. Instead Darblay summons Fletcher's estranged daughter to her office to reconnect the family and provide Fletcher with a support network. The long corridor epitomises the difference of opinion Darblay and her male co-workers hold about the public. Compared to previous series, where the public are confined to small spaces, it is the police officers who have less manoeuvrability in their constricted work areas. Here the larger area designated for public use provides a 'benevolent image of policing' (Jermyn 2010: 34).

However, at the time of *Juliet Bravo* it was becoming more apparent that the priorities of the police and the public were diverging. Lord Scarman's inquiry into the 1981 Brixton riots divided opinion. Scarman suggested the violence, petrol bombing, looting, arson, and assaults on police arose from a mixture of 'poor housing', 'unemployment', alleged over-intensive policing, and a resulting feeling of 'frustration' (Scarman 1982: 35). Scarman was of the view that 'there should be proper consultation with the local community' from the police, who must 'listen to community views' and 'be prepared to modify their plans in light of them' (Scarman 1982: 145). The police's instant response, however, undermined Scarman. The Association of Chief Police Officers provided a public-order manual complete with a new 'doctrine of tactics, training, and equipment for all forces in England and Wales' (Brain 2010: 70). Scarman unwittingly exposed existing divisions between the police and the public. Whilst the police were keen to establish themselves as a 'crime-fighting organisation', the bulk of calls to the police actually related to 'non-crime work' (Rawlings 2002: 218). The public 'favoured beat policing' because it aided their feeling of security (Rawlings 2002: 219). However, Richard Kinsey's survey of Merseyside police officers revealed 'patrol work is not sought after and would not appear to be a particularly high status job' (Kinsey 1985: 8). The police's prioritising of measures to combat public order meant community relations were largely ignored, as Scarman's suggestions were derided for providing a 'timid approach to policing' (Brain 2010: 217).

Darblay's use of the large station's central corridor to accommodate minor public enquiries depicts a constabulary that, under her leadership, is sympathetic and responsive to its community's needs in line with Scarman's recommendations. In visual terms the corridor acknowledges the vast divide in opinion that could exist between those who advocated a community-orientated approach to policing (Darblay located at the far end of the station corridor) and those who prioritised the imposition of public order (the male police officers located at the other end of the corridor). However, contrary to prominent sociological analysis and popular public opinion, *Juliet Bravo* depicts those in authority as modernisers sympathetic to community needs. Given its Sunday night teatime slot the series would have been hard pressed to accuse national police dictates of prioritising enforcement at the expense of public need and community relations. Nevertheless *Juliet Bravo* acknowledges a rift in priorities existing within the police force and progressively develops the genre, as a female protagonist uncovers established gendered conventions as ineffective working practices. Whilst Kennedy Martin was disappointed at 'what could have been a hard-hitting drama' for being 'broadcast pre-watershed', this does not mean the series was unable to engage with wider socio-political debate and concerns (Kennedy Martin 2008: n.p.).

Paperwork

In light of their scheduling, *The Gentle Touch* and *Juliet Bravo* were limited in the extent to which they could explore the disjuncture considered to exist between the priorities of the public and those of the police force. However, each series' station-based scenes are more adept at examining how key legislative changes were affecting the UK police force's working practices. Filling out forms and mandatory note-taking at interrogations were fast becoming an integral aspect of police work. Following the increased number of deaths in police custody, from eight in 1970 to forty-eight in 1978, a royal commission on criminal procedure in 1979 was undertaken. The commission was committed to 'ensuring the civil rights of the citizens' (Irving 1986: 148). It also aimed to eliminate 'coercive and oppressive tactics' of police officers that could lead to false confessions (Irving and McKenzie 1989: 11). The commission's recommendations would form the backbone of the 1984 Police and Criminal Evidence Act (PACE), which introduced a series of forms to be filled in at every stage of an arrest. Thus, PACE provided 'clear authority for police powers while balancing their exercise with increased supervision and accountability' (Brain 2010: 79). Amidst the ongoing research and public debate surrounding the 1979 commission neither *The Gentle Touch* nor *Juliet Bravo* adopts a neutral ideological position regarding how responsibly to implement the law whilst safeguarding citizens' civil rights.

The Gentle Touch takes a sceptical stance towards the stringent following of increased procedure. In 'Rogue' (16 May 1980), Forbes begins her interrogation of brothel owner Sally (Shirley Cheriton) by sitting at the interview-room table with her law papers, notepad, and pen in front of her. Initially Forbes carefully notes down Sally's responses and assuredly quotes the 1956 Sexual Offences Act, expecting her to feel intimidated into confessing. Instead, Sally scoffs when Forbes reveals that the penalty for being caught running her brothel would only amount to a £250 fine, a sum that she could easily afford if found guilty. Following Sally's laughter the scene cuts to Forbes in her office slamming her pen on her desk and then furiously rearranging the papers from the interrogation. Forbes is frustrated by this mechanical interviewing procedure for inhibiting rather than enhancing her process of charging criminals.

Earlier in the same episode Forbes is able to extract vital information by avoiding this procedure. She is assigned to uncover the identity of the person who has been supplying drug addict Peter's (Michael McVey) house with heroin. Again Forbes sits with a notepad and pen. However, it is only when she leaves her own side of the table, turning her back on the process of noting down the interview, that she retrieves the information needed. Forbes walks to Peter's side of the table and crouches down by his chair to maintain eye contact. She declares 'the doctor's waiting outside all ready as soon as you say the word'. Invading Peter's personal space and denying him access to a doctor for his withdrawal symptoms enables Forbes to retrieve the name she needs. Similarly, in 'Affray' (1 January 1982), students are interrogated following the stabbing of a policewoman. Again Forbes extracts a confession by kneeling down to Mary Venn's (Sarah James) level, but this time holds Venn's hand reassuringly. In each instance it is only when Forbes discards her paperwork and the formalities of interrogation procedure that she makes a breakthrough. Moving in closer instigates a close-up exchange between Forbes and her suspect where she is able to coerce a confession.

In contrast, Darblay's interactions with props demonstrate a resolute belief in this new procedure. In 'Cages', Darblay discusses with Beck in her office how to deal with a grizzly bear found in Hartley. She sits at her desk reading through a pile of law books as she dictates the 1976 Dangerous Wild Animals Act whilst slowly brushing her fingers across the words on the page. Once Darblay has consulted these law books she shuts the top book on the pile and rests her forearms on it, clasping her hands together as if undertaking a relaxed and impromptu prayer. Resting on her law books for support and investing her faith in them means she finds the appropriate course of action. Similarly, in 'Heat' (11 September 1982), Janet Worsley (Elizabeth Proud) is interrogated following her arrest on suspicion of arson. Darblay sits upright writing and arranging the paperwork on her desk. When Worsley begins to talk Darblay clasps her hands together in the same position as before whilst resting them on her paperwork. She leans her head to one side, asking what Worsley likes about fires and why she starts them. Darblay expresses an interest in Worsley and abides by the law as a sufficient way of apprehending criminals. Compared to Forbes, who deliberately bypasses procedure, Darblay ensures her success through the use of law books and paperwork. Thus *The Gentle Touch* and *Juliet Bravo* have not necessarily deserved persistent academic neglect, as both, at the very least, interact with the changes the police force underwent in the early 1980s.

Stylistically, however, in a slight departure from earlier studio-shot police series, both *Juliet Bravo* and *The Gentle Touch* attempt to forge a greater empathetic identification between their audience and the lead protagonist. The large proportion of close-ups used in *The Gentle Touch* often isolate Forbes from her surrounding *mise-en-scène* so that situations are communicated through her facial expressions and emotional perspective. Contrastingly, Hartley's station design, providing members of the public with space to talk through their predicaments, directly emanates from Darblay's benevolent understanding of police work. This connection is confirmed by *Juliet Bravo* set designer David Crozier, who says of his contribution, 'the overriding consideration at all times is what is appropriate for the character and their environment' (Crozier 2013: n.p.). Each station space, however, is less interested in debating a number of differing viewpoints held by an ensemble cast. Both series provide the audience with a lessened sense of autonomy, as a single protagonist's perspective is upheld against the uncooperative male environment. This does not mean that the studio-shot series completely loses its observant nature. A spatial reading of Forbes's and Darblay's use of props (attitudinal markers) in relation to their immediate dialogue (illocutionary markers) enables each series to work visually through the implications of police procedure reform.

Employment in the 1980s

To consider how *The Gentle Touch* and *Juliet Bravo* intervened in public conceptions of class and gender identities, an understanding of how these traditional notions were being reformulated must be mapped. The election of Margaret Thatcher in 1979 marked a radical shift in the UK's economic infrastructure, substantially detaching UK society from the principles underlying its postwar settlement. The financial sector now embraced neoliberalism to grow the economy by 'liberating individual entrepreneurial freedoms and skills within an institutional framework characterised by strong private property rights, free markets, and free trade' (Harvey 2005: 2). It was no longer the Government's responsibility 'to provide for full employment', and so total industrial output fell by 15 per cent from 1979 to 1981 (Keynes 1949: 372). Manufacturing industries such as shipbuilding, steelworks and coalmining were no longer State-funded and eventually disappeared (Hill 1985:293). This had an impact on trade union membership and the class identities the unions provided. Those who thrived in this new economic environment were known as 'yuppies' (young, upwardly mobile city workers) driven by a 'ruthless cut-throat determination' to be successful (Beynon 2002: 105). David Bradbury's empirical survey *'Social Class' in Planning Consumer Markets* by the Henley Centre for Forecasting discovered British people 'no longer viewed class as a source of pride', as it was now considered to be one of the 'least important social priorities' in relation to health, physical appearance, and lifestyle (Mort 1996: 104). Masculine identity was being increasingly expressed through patterns of consumption.

Juliet Bravo and working-class masculinity

Viewers of *Juliet Bravo* witness former mill town Hartley transform into a service-based economy dependent on the tertiary sector, and so a series of conflicts ensue between yuppies, adopting a ruthless determination to amass wealth, and industrial men, symbolising 'mass conformity and old patriarchal structures' (Beynon 2002: 105). In 'A private place', elderly, working-class couple Annie and Billy Stamp (Gwen Nelson and Arthur Hewlett) try to stop property developer Charlie Pendle (David Daker) from tearing down their terrace house for a development of flats. Priding himself on his appearance, Pendle wears expensive jewellery and perfects his physique in his own private gym. In 'Home-grown or imported?' (15 November 1980), Greenwood (Allan Surtees) protests against the opening of Peter Palin's (Ivor Danvers) country club, as it complicates access to his own farmland. Also, in 'Trouble at t'mill' (27 September 1980), rich property owner Ted Galway (Alan Lake) is repeatedly reported to the police by elderly lollipop man Israel Smethurst (John Barrett) for allegedly breaking the speed limit. In each episode the entrepreneurial yuppie is presented as a dubious figure in relation to the principled tradesmen. Sergeant Beck (David Ellison) persuades Pendle to delay the new build by threatening to inform Pendle's wife of his romantic affairs. Palin has previously been implicated in illegal money-laundering through his London-based businesses. It also transpires that Galway is harbouring stolen goods for his former employer.

Significantly, *Juliet Bravo*'s set designs help articulate this socioeconomic divide. When Darblay visits Smethurst's council flat she commends the tidiness of his home before sitting beside him as they drink tea. She identifies a photo of his deceased wife above the fireplace. Smethurst's home is then juxtaposed with Galway's mansion. As Darblay asks Galway questions in his front room, he leans against his fireplace glistening his gold bracelet, ring, and watch in Darblay's direction as if to impress yet intimidate her with his wealth and status. Standing in a separate camera shot from Galway, Darblay is not welcomed or permitted to share his perspective. Compared to the memories of a loved one that are central to Smethurst's living space, Galway instead prioritises his appearance, signified by the mirror that hangs above his fireplace centrepiece. Juxtaposing Smethurst's and Galway's homes suggests that upholding one's appearance as a chief priority can be vacuous, inhumane, and detrimental to the social bond. Once Galway is arrested for harbouring stolen clothes in one of his properties, his drive to achieve wealth, possessions, and status is exposed as synonymous with his criminality and lack of regard for Hartley's community wellbeing.

The Gentle Touch and gendered spheres

Thatcher's transformation of the UK's economic infrastructure was accompanied by a contrived political effort to reassert the traditional nuclear family, as family values were highlighted as a matter of public concern. Thatcher stated, 'at this time of rapid social change and accompanying stresses marriage has never been more important in preserving a stable and responsible society' (quoted in Evans 1993: 240). Therefore 'the Victorian model of the two-parent family in which the husband and father went out to work in order to support the wife and mother at home served as the ideal to which all should aspire' (Kingsley Kent 1999: 350). Given this idealisation of the stay-at-home mother and sexual division of labour, little political sympathy was given to feminists' concerns with equal rights. *The Gentle Touch* complicates the politicisation of these moral concerns through a predominant focus on upper-middle-class women: here a particular type of woman who, despite her spacious and material surroundings, is inherently isolated. In 'Shock' (2 May 1980), a woman is found dead in a hotel room, yet no member of her family is particularly anxious when she disappears. Her uninterested husband, company director Brian Rylands (Peter Austin), and son are seemingly unaware of their comparative neglect, which has resulted in this unfortunate circumstance. Her name is not revealed, highlighting the remorselessness of the men who mistreat her.

The social results of reasserting a sexual division of labour are communicated through upper-class characters. In 'Rogue' (16 May 1980), Forbes believes Jessica Sanderson (Moira Redmond) can assist her enquiries. At midday, in her high-rise apartment, Sanderson defiantly refuses to help, claiming she is busy 'enjoying life'. She drinks champagne claiming 'I'm a very selfish woman.' When Forbes questions whether she is truly happy Sanderson retracts her initial statement, claiming that she has the best happiness 'on offer'. Similarly, in 'Something blue' (5 September 1980), Forbes questions Juanita Shervington's (Lynda Marchal) parenting skills, given that both Forbes's son and Shervington's have had access to Shervington's pornographic videos. When Forbes refuses a glass of vodka because it is a 'little early in the day', Shervington pours one for herself. Initially Shervington stands confidently by the drinks cabinet as if boasting her wealth, but Forbes soon criticises her irresponsible parenting, which reduces Shervington to tears. Having previously confiscated the videotape from the Shervingtons without any legal reason for doing so, Forbes has returned to the house under strict instruction from her superiors to hand the tape back to its rightful owner. However, having had her parenting skills criticised, Shervington refuses to take the tape back, admitting that she only used pornographic materials for her husband's benefit.

It has been well documented that *The Gentle Touch*'s implausible dialogue allegedly inspired young television actress Lynda Marchal to become a scriptwriter, subsequently penning *Widows* and then *Prime Suspect* under the pseudonym Lynda La Plante. However, this should not automatically discredit *The Gentle Touch*, as it can still be considered a feminist text. Sanderson's and Shervington's expansive front rooms, initially framed by a long shot, are reduced to mid-shots following Forbes's intrusion. This reframing to a tighter shot-scale changes the scene's macro meaning from one of contentment and power to one of the confinement women could experience in being consigned to the domestic realm. The political effort to establish a dichotomy between the domestic sphere and public sphere is exposed as something that pressurises rich and intelligent women into alcoholism. Rather than simply being victims these women are complex characters who on the surface appear to thrive in this environment. It is Forbes's ability to probe into their private lives that uncovers the deep psychosocial ramifications endured and coping mechanisms employed by women who live in the upper echelons of a neoliberal economy. Essentially, through civilian scenes, *The Gentle Touch* draws attention to a different set of expectations and problems that women are subject to in the domestic space amidst this reasserted sexual division of labour.

Juliet Bravo and domesticity

The Home Office's preoccupation with controlling public dissent in light of the Brixton riots meant crimes committed in the home 'against wives and female partners' could become 'further marginalised and subordinated to the overriding concern with public as opposed to private order' (Edwards 1989: 23). *Juliet Bravo* was commissioned as a family-friendly police drama in response to accusations that the BBC was commissioning too many excessively violent crime dramas. Nevertheless, the programme's 'gentler world of crime' refocuses the concerns of the British police series on women whose domestic experiences were being neglected by law-and-order rhetoric and policy (Clarke 1992: 248).

In 'Rage' (25 October 1980), Kim Buckley (Judy Liebert) experiences a breakdown after her husband, Jeremy, leaves for work and their baby cannot stop crying. First Buckley seems enraged with her role as a housewife, throwing pots and pans in the kitchen to the floor. Then she seems resentful of her husband's work and ability to leave the home, tearing apart his work books. Following this she holds a framed photo of her wedding day and a photo of herself as a teacher. At first she lovingly caresses the frames before suddenly smashing them, perhaps frustrated with the professional identity she has sacrificed to be a stay-at-home mother. Then she throws books against a cabinet, causing a small, hinged door to open and reveal four bottles of whisky, which had previously been hidden from view, before she subsequently smashes them all. This rage, underscored by possible alcoholism, Inspector Jean Darblay tells Jeremy Buckley (Christian Rodska), has been 'a way of making herself heard'. Darblay informs Jeremy that the Buckleys must listen to each other to maintain their family. Like previous studio-shot series, the visual composition of Buckley's breakdown is textually rich and open to a multitude of interpretations, as she regularly alters the scene's macro meaning through her interactions with the *mise-en-scène*: a practice rarely seen in filmed series of the time, as it could lead to continuity errors.

The domestic is a political space where the implications of political attempts to reassert the Victorian model of the two-parent family are revealed. In 'Misunderstandings' (27 November 1982), written by Valerie Georgeson, Lin Mitchell (Amanda Murray) is raped by her neighbour. Darblay recognises the public/private dichotomy of British law, explaining to Mitchell that whilst 'the force puts life and limb before property ... the law doesn't always take the same view'. Having offered Mitchell her support in pressing charges, despite the unlikelihood of a conviction, at the conclusion of the episode Darblay relays her concerns to Detective Chief Inspector Logan (Tony Caunter). Logan dismisses Darblay's unease by exclaiming 'the public get the police force they want', and that, as police staff, 'we are servants, not masters'. Darblay then ends the episode by stating 'well in that case we really ought to sympathise wouldn't you say, *Sir*'.⁴ By deliberately pausing before sternly stressing the word 'Sir', Darblay emphasises that in relation to the men (or 'sirs') in positions of authority, women such as Mitchell, Buckley, and Darblay, having not conformed to the heteronormative mother role expected of them, are subject to a separate set of judgements. Logan convinces himself that Mitchell is to blame for her own attack by asserting that she let her assailant into the house 'of her own free will', is a 'divorcee', a 'good looker', and has a 'reputation for being mean with money', compared to the accused, who is a 'nice enough lad' who 'lives with his mother' with 'no previous record'. In line with second-wave feminism, *Juliet Bravo*'s domestic scenes metonymically challenge institutionalised gender inequalities that were being downplayed by postfeminism.

Rational-choice theory

Whilst *Juliet Bravo* and *The Gentle Touch* can be read as critiques of Thatcher's socio-economic, largely postfeminist agenda, both texts still comply with rational-actor criminology, which dominated UK political and academic discourse. With levels of crime rising year on year until 1993, rational-actor theorists began questioning the limitations of the deterrence doctrine that had proven popular through the 1970s. Rational-actor theorists now partially compromised with the predestined-actor approach, recognising that 'environmental circumstances of the individual play a far greater part than previously recognised in delinquent conduct' (Clarke 1987: 120). A newly developed 'rational-choice theory' believed offenders choose criminality because such actions appear 'rational in the circumstances in which they find themselves and in terms of their knowledge base and cognitive thought processes' (Clarke 1987: 120). The preponderant authors of rational-choice theory argued through the 1980s that controlling aspects of 'the characteristics of offenses which render them differentially attractive to particular individuals or subgroups' (choice-structuring properties) could pragmatically eradicate specific crime rates following an 'accurate identification of the subgroups of offenders' (Cornish and Clarke 1987: 935, 943).

Both *The Gentle Touch* and *Juliet Bravo* present a series of character types who actively decide to engage in criminality having been influenced by their surrounding environment. Crucially, both dramas can be aligned with rational-choice theory over traditional forms of the predestined-actor model. First, these characters either display considerable agency in deciding to partake in criminal behaviour, rather than appearing to be victims of circumstance. Second, small-scale pragmatic solutions are also offered to deter similar crimes. In *The Gentle Touch*, for example, characters such as Shervington; Sanderson; and Susan Scott (Beth Harris), who in 'Help' (25 April 1980) is unaware her daughter is prostituting herself, live indulgent, selfish lifestyles. The solution to their problem, as instructed by Forbes, is to come to terms with, and take accountability for, the bad decisions they have made instead of just blaming 'the system'. It is accepted that a more individualistic neoliberal society, and the corresponding re-emergence of a sexual division of labour, have encouraged rich, successful businessmen to subjugate their wives. The pragmatic solution, however, is for individuals to rediscover their humanity and to maintain caring and responsive relationships among family members to prevent tragic circumstances.

In *Juliet Bravo*, the mind-set, rationale, and cognitive thought processes of yuppie characters are explored by Darblay in relation to working-class tradesmen. She then negotiates a solution to the crimes that arise from this clash of subcultures. Usually, the permissive and reckless lifestyles of the entrepreneurial characters irk the working class tradesmen, who vandalise, assault, or steal in protest. Whilst the series is critical of this materialistic culture, it does not necessarily call for complete economic reform, as neither type of character is completely free of blame. As actress Stephanie Turner felt, 'baddies and goodies have gone. We have people with difficulties ... there's a strong emphasis on unemployment and the way poverty causes crime' (quoted in Beauman 1982: 9). In 'Home-grown or imported?', for example, whilst country-club owner Palin may have broken the law in a previous life, it is farmer Greenwood's son who has thieved goods from Palin. Similarly, in 'Amenities' (18 September 1982), Rennick (George Little) has his office-block development repeatedly vandalised by, it transpires, an aggrieved plumber whom Rennick did not pay. Whilst Baker the plumber has committed the crime in question Darblay disapproves of both men's actions. Therefore the series does not necessarily champion complete economic reform but rather reminds individuals to consider the wellbeing of others and to respect the law regardless of circumstance. Then, in episodes such as 'Rage' and 'Misunderstandings', there is accompanying recognition that certain persistent socio-legal gender inequalities need to be addressed.

Ultimately, in line with rational-choice theory, each series identifies a reoccurring subgroup of offenders, determines why the characteristics of offences are differentially attractive to these subgroups, and then finds pragmatic solutions, having recognised that crime arises from a mixture of individual choices and environmental factors. Whilst to a large degree civilian scenes expose the detrimental effects that Thatcher's economic and social policies were having on a range of people, from working-class men to upper-middle-class housewives, both series look to pragmatic developments in the rational-actor tradition of criminology for solutions.

Marriage

Despite a marked political effort to revert to Victorian values, divorce rates in the 1980s were higher than ever before. By 1988 more than a third of marriages involved a previously divorced partner, and stepfamilies were commonplace. Advice manuals and print columns portrayed marriage as a 'compromise between stability-maintaining and identity-upholding' (Askham 1984: 183). This meant a successful marriage was widely considered to be a balancing act in which both parties were able to 'develop and maintain' their own individual 'unique, personal identity' whilst concurrently being able to 'preserve a sense of stability' as a married unit (Askham 1984: 7, 184). Whereas an optimistic view of companionate marriage was encouraged in the 1960s and 1970s, prominent sociological writings of the 1980s drew 'a sharp distinction between the aspiration and the lived reality' (Finch and Morgan 1991: 63). As a result of these changing attitudes men were now increasingly expected to partake in domestic work, as authors of childcare manuals put an 'unprecedented emphasis on the father's role in bringing up babies' (Abbott 2003: 157). Likewise, for married women, 'paid work had become the norm', even if many young women still saw paid employment as a 'prelude to a spell as a full time wife and mother' (Abbott 2003: 153). Therefore, in comparison to previous 'male series' *Juliet Bravo* and *The Gentle Touch* devote more screen time to the 'domestic situations' of their 'leading characters' (Clarke 1992: 248).

Juliet Bravo and marriage

Juliet Bravo is pervaded by a seemingly anti-neoliberal sentiment that tries to preserve the values of community against increasing combative police practices and an increasingly entrepreneurial political sphere convinced that 'there is no such thing as society' (Margaret Thatcher, quoted in Keay 1987: 30). This ideology is complicated, however, as audiences are regularly subjected to scenes that focus on the difficulties of the Darblays' marriage.

The ground floor of the Darblays' home has an open-plan design that contains an equally sized lounge and kitchen. There is no strict divide separating each room. This contrasts with Hartley station, where the male uniformed officers are clearly separated from Jean Darblay by a small, demarcated desk area. A key feature of the Darblays' living space is a circular table placed inside the lounge. Here both characters can discuss matters and share their meals together. It is at this table that reconciliations following disputes occur. In 'The one who got away' (1 November 1980), Tom Darblay (David Hargreaves) uses the table to write an apology. The Darblays also equally share all chores within the household, regularly standing over the sink as they wash and dry their cutlery together whilst discussing their days at work. The dimensions of the downstairs rooms seemingly promote a companionate marriage where both partners are treated as equals and the man undertakes an equal share of housework.

As the series develops, however, the Darblays' interaction with props undercuts the egalitarian design of their home. Jean is unable to separate her private self from her work. In *Dixon of Dock Green*, *Z Cars*, and *Hunter's Walk* a crucial aspect of measuring a police protagonist's successful conduct is the way in which they carry themselves at home in relation to the values they uphold at work. Comparatively, Jean is expected to leave her public persona at work, and her inability to do so causes marital disputes. In 'Coming back' (11 October 1980), the couple have an explosive argument in the kitchen. Annoyed by his wife for interfering with his cooking and accusatorily remarking on his levels of alcohol consumption, Tom accidentally tips spaghetti from a saucepan into the sink and scalds himself. Both characters stand in profile within the same shot as this occurs, whilst Jean angrily slams down placemats and cutlery onto their circular dining table. She lashes out against the equality and discussion the table signifies. Without a sense of structure, order, or division to this space's structure, as experienced in Hartley station, Jean finds it difficult to maintain appropriate boundaries, often treating her husband like a junior officer. These interactions turn the egalitarian open-plan space into an abrasive one because she is judged by different standards from previous policemen protagonists. Jean Darblay is expected to leave her professional life at work to assume the role of the doting housewife.

Both Jean and Tom represent the emergence of new gendered identities that were challenging enduring assumptions about what a man and woman should be and do. Tom is representative of the 'new man' figure emerging in mainstream culture who was portrayed as a caring husband and father in childcare manuals and Mothercare adverts of the time. Simultaneously, Jean is a career woman who, as in soap operas, provides 'a model in which women act rather than react; a model in which it is necessary for a woman to be self-assertive rather than continually absorbing the pain and punishment on behalf of other members of the family' (Geraghty 1991: 139). However, the arguments that arise from these two characters trying to come to terms with the new roles expected of them do not necessarily mean that the purpose of the series is to scrutinise Jean's authority with 'sadistic curiosity' (Skirrow 1987: 174). Tom's jealousy of his wife's success is exposed as he gradually develops into a short-tempered, petty, and unsupportive husband. At the end of the episode 'Expectations' (8 November 1980), Tom admits that he resents Jean's success because 'everyone regards you as more successful'. Jean dismisses this as 'ridiculous', stating 'you're just trying to find a reason because your job hasn't worked as smoothly as expected'. Her self-assertiveness as a career woman and breadwinner of the household exposes Tom's intolerance of her and of being resigned to the 'domestic background' (Phillips 1980: 74).

The design of the Darblays' home is meant to be a relaxing alternative to Hartley station, and a progressive space that has broken down the sexual division of labour seen in the domestic lives of police officers in *Z Cars* and *Hunter's Walk*. However, their home is subject to regular conflict. The Darblays are never able to find a balance between their collective identity as a married couple and their own individuality as advised in marriage-guidance manuals of the time. This is different from *Z Cars*, where a dispute between the Steeles is resolved by a kiss, and *Hunter's Walk*, where the Smiths work through minor disagreements. The Darblays' marital problems are repeatedly revisited, because they are so difficult to resolve – contrary to the marital advice Jean dispenses in the station – leading Tom to move out Tom moves out in the third series. Like marriage guidance of the time, the series also draws a 'sharp distinction between the aspiration and the lived reality' (Finch and Morgan 1991: 63).

The Gentle Touch and childcare

Alternatively, in *The Gentle Touch* the orderly design of Forbes's home works as a sobering counterpoint to the expansive, disorderly homes of the upper-middle-class characters living indulgent, hedonist, and permissive lives. On the ground floor of the Forbes' living space are a kitchenette area and lounge divided from one another by a breakfast bar. Maggie Forbes and her son Steve (Nigel Rathbone) regularly eat their meals at this breakfast bar whilst discussing family matters. In 'Help', Maggie confronts her son about his underage drinking and instructs him that he will not drink until 'old enough', with which he instantly complies. In 'Something Blue', Maggie addresses the issue of pornographic materials found in Steve's bedroom. In 'Paint it black' (18 December 1981), when Maggie asks Steve why he does not feel tempted by the drug abuse at his school, he claims that those who resort to such excesses live without 'meaning', 'structure', or 'terms of reference' in their lives. The interior design of their house is a visual manifestation of this 'structure', as it helps foster a mutual respect between both characters and an understanding of what behaviour is expected of them within the home. Rather than conversations and disputes going round in circles, here matters are resolved by each episode's conclusion, given the talks that have occurred at this breakfast bar.

This is different from the domestic scenes in *Juliet Bravo*, where the position that the Darblays both reach at the end of an episode is often one of discontent and continued distance. Maggie Forbes's ability to keep her household ordered and assign specific arguments to certain sections of the house is similar to the etiquette experienced at her place of work, although here close-ups share an affinity with the soap opera, rather than with the rhetoric of classic melodrama, as the agreements reached between Maggie and Steve ensure the household 'becomes less of a battleground and more of a place of safety where there is some protection from the harshness of the world outside' (Geraghty 1991: 83). Rather than drawing a 'sharp distinction between the aspiration and the lived reality' of family life, Maggie Forbes's home is a sanctuary from sexist work pressures and the socio-political expectation that she find a male partner to provide a cohesive family unit (Finch and Morgan 1991: 63).

A consequence of this ordered home life is that both Maggie and Steve largely conform to their traditional gender roles. Maggie is the only character in the series consistently to use the kitchen space for long periods of time: usually sitting on the kitchen side of the breakfast bar at mealtimes. However, rather than being caged away in the kitchen from the rest of the space, like Betty Smith in *Hunter's Walk* or Janey Steele in *Z Cars*, Maggie Forbes often uses the kitchen space as a place to stand and survey the rest of the ground floor with her commanding presence. Although her use of the space could be considered to advocate a Victorian sexual division of labour, the skills Maggie has amassed through her public detective persona are intrinsically linked to her successful parenting. Whilst the Thatcher administration was attempting to encourage women to become housewives – for example, through the abolition of the maternity benefit in 1982 – Maggie Forbes meets the challenges of the workplace and of the home, including colleague Detective Inspector Bob Croft's (Brian Gwaspari) repeated attempts to undermine her, believing that her sex is of detriment to her professional capabilities. Whereas Jean Darblay's inability to separate her private self from her public persona maintains a deep rupture between her and her husband, Maggie Forbes's constant combination of both identities suggests a healthy family life can be achieved, against the odds, by a single parent.

Overall, in borrowing characteristics from the soap opera the private lives of Jean Darblay and Maggie Forbes challenge pressures placed on professional women at the time in different ways. The pressure experienced by Darblay to balance a successful career with being a doting partner is revealed to be an unfair expectation, solely expected of women. Meanwhile, the authority Forbes maintains in her home was castigated by television critic Mary Kenny for 'not [being] the least bit women's libbish' and instead occupying a 'feminine fantasy' (Kenny 1981: 18–19). Nevertheless, Forbes's home life asserts that single mothers can effectively balance their maternal responsibilities with career success in the face of increasing pressures to revert to a Victorian ideology of gendered spheres.

The Bill

To create a police series that was distinctive in relation to the success of *The Gentle Touch* and *Juliet Bravo*, writer Geoff McQueen decided his programme would 'keep out of the police officers' homes' because '[if] you go into the police officers' private life, it's the kiss of death to police series' (quoted in Kingsley 1994: 25). A year after receiving his first screenwriting credit for *The Gentle Touch* episode 'Be lucky uncle' (29 October 1982), McQueen had his standalone script about the inner workings of a police station commissioned for Thames's anthology series *Storyboard* (ITV, 1983–1989). Previously rejected by the BBC, 'Woodentop' (16 August 1983), was directed by Peter Cregeen who, inspired by Roger Graef's documentary series *Police* (BBC, 1982), used one handheld video camera to follow PC Jim Carver's (Mark Wingett) first day on the job. Receiving such a positive response meant a twelve-part series was swiftly commissioned, so long as its title reverted to McQueen's original idea: *The Bill*.

The Bill's first executive producer, Michael Chapman (1984–1997), was responsible for shaping the series as a 'police procedural with strong documentary overtones' (Rogers 2009: n.p.). A documentary style was produced by three rules. First, a single lightweight MR Ikegami camera recorded scenes directly on to half-inch tape. Taking video cameras out of Teddington Studios (where 'Woodentop' was recorded) meant the 'crisper image and greater depth of field' of video cameras captured real east London localities (Smart 2015: 69). Events now appeared to occur in a more immediate time and space compared to previous police series, which had uniformly relied on the inferior focusing capabilities and grainier image texture of film cameras to capture exterior locations. This immediacy was intensified by the second stylistic decision to record scenes through long, unbroken takes. Rather than using traditional shot-reverse-shot cutting, the single video camera pans to each character after they have started speaking, as if being shot by a documentarian trying to capture events as they unfold. Consequently, a single protagonist's view does not dictate the narrative, as each episode focuses on more than two members of its large ensemble cast. Lastly, natural lighting was preferred, and was suited to videotape, given that it was 'more adaptable to changing states of natural light than film' (Smart 2015: 69). Whilst *The Bill* was treated as the 'benchmark by industry and audience in judging British television police series' for its twenty-six-year run, little academic analysis exists of its first series: a series that, given these considerations regarding its visual composition, established *The Bill* as a drama invested in the 'minutiae of day-to-day policing' (Rogers 2009: n.p.).

Sun Hill station

Before moving to its permanent Merton Studios base at Morden in 1990, Sun Hill Police Station's first set was a disused warehouse in Wapping. Here *The Bill* was knowingly commissioned against a backdrop of 'inexorably rising crime levels' and 'earth-shaking urban riots' (Brain 2010: 86). When the first episode was broadcast, PACE had passed in Parliament 'in a cloud of controversy' (Lynch 1991: 17). The police soon came to be nicknamed 'Maggie's army', following Home Office Circular 114, which confirmed their 'protected species' status within the public sector. This view was further solidified a year later, after the police's successful containment of demonstrations throughout the 1984 miners' strike (Kingsley 1994: 28). *The Bill* is, however, uninterested in the relationship between the police force and public. Instead, the rivalry between Sun Hill's detectives and its uniformed division is the principal source of station-based drama. The upstairs of Sun Hill station is exclusively occupied by CID's offices. The detectives are nicknamed 'superstars' by the uniformed division on account of their inflated egos and view that the PC role is figuratively and literally beneath them. In comparison, the uniformed division (or 'woodentops', as the detectives call them) work in a more regimented way. Stationed on the ground floor the PCs rarely remain still as they type reports, file paperwork, and are issued orders. Officers are castigated by station sergeant Bob Cryer (Eric Richard) for leaving their desks without permission, making grammatical errors in their reports, and for standing around without appearing busy. Producer Pat Sandys was keen to replicate these intense working conditions for the actors, stating 'When a new regular joins, he or she is given the character's professional background – then that actor is left to find his own space. Some actors were comfortable with this approach. Others were not, and their characters quickly disappeared' (quoted in Kingsley 1994: 45). This was a different approach from *Z Cars*, where actors would discuss 'the complete social background of every character' (Laing 1991: 128). An interest in police officer characters' backgrounds, psychology, and motivations was replaced by a focus on how professionals cope within the cut-throat world of Sun Hill, a working environment intensified by its distinct militaristic working practices and strict compliance with PACE policy.

The stylistic grammar underpinning Sun Hill station scenes is unique, as narrative progression is regularly halted by the process of filling in paperwork. Dialogue exchanges cease when Cryer retrieves signatures from witnesses, suspects, and staff at key stages of investigations. As if suspending the narrative, the video camera focuses on paperwork being signed off in an isolated close-up, in silence, before events resume. This paperwork system records 'every step of the process from initial arrest, or stop in the street, to the final release at a police station', as PACE intended (Cowley 2011: 213). In the episode 'A friend in need' (23 October 1984), Detective Inspector Roy Galloway (John Salter) locates Cryer in the downstairs area of the station when looking for his help. Cryer, however, is busy processing another case, causing Galloway to wait. Releasing the previously drunk-and-disorderly Lampton (Christopher Guinee), Cryer meticulously itemises each of Lampton's possessions one at a time in the foreground of the shot. Simultaneously the camera pans, with Galloway impatiently pacing across the room in the background attempting to find an opportune moment to pull Cryer away. Once all the items have been issued, Cryer instructs Lampton to 'sign here', and the camera frames the sheet of paper in a close-up for Lampton to sign. Once it is signed, Cryer chooses to acknowledge the presence of Galloway, who then issues Cryer with an order regarding a recent spate of bomb scares. Similarly, at the episode's conclusion Carver is keen to thank Galloway for providing a testimony that helped him avoid dismissal following Lampton's accusation that Carver stole his wallet. This time, however, Carver has to wait for Galloway to sign the appropriate paperwork so that the prank callers responsible for the bomb scares can be detained. Galloway instructs Carver to wait 'just a minute' as he signs the form and underlines his signature in a seven-second close-up before the camera pans back up to resume the dialogue among Cryer, Galloway, and Carver. This procedure that documents every stage of the investigation is central to the regimented working practices of the police force. With parallel investigations unfolding, the narrative switches its focus from one case to another once the investigation at hand reaches a significant development, which is signed off.

The Bill advocates a more stringent following of procedure than *Juliet Bravo*. In comparison to *The Gentle Touch*'s Forbes, Darblay is driven by a resolute faith in the system whilst her humanitarian nature aids her crime-fighting ability. Repeatedly intervening in the personal social circumstances of victims and perpetrators is what produces breakthroughs. However, the human-interest element of the genre does not feature in Sun Hill station. Whenever anybody expresses an interest in a civilian's personal circumstances they are ridiculed for being a 'social worker'. PC Carver is disciplined on his first day by Sergeant Jack Wilding (Peter Dean) for 'playing the social-minded copper', having clipped a pair of thieving youths round the ear instead of arresting them. In 'A friend in need' Carver faces dismissal for escorting the drunken Lampton home whilst off duty. A seething Cryer informs Carver 'you are a policeman first and *not* a bloody social worker'. Although Carver 'felt sorry' for Lambton, Cryer informs him 'he's not our problem ... do it by the book, that way it's safe'. Accordingly, personal opinions cloud the professional judgements of Sun Hill officers. In 'Death of a cracksman' (15 January 1985), Cryer refuses to be on the alert for prison escapee Alfie Mullins (Paddy Joyce) because he disagrees with the prison's claim that Mullins 'dangerous'. However, once Mullins is murdered by a criminal gang Galloway reminds Cryer 'if you had done your duty he would still be around'. Therefore all procedure must be followed to the letter and not questioned, as it operates in the public's best interest.

Ultimately, the hustle-and-bustle of *The Bill*'s station scenes, captured through its unique stylistic approach, evokes the fresh array of pressures constabularies were facing, including directives issued by central government, the obligation to comply with new accountabilities implemented by PACE, public pressure to solve particular crimes, and the rivalry that arises between PCs and detectives when unburdening the station's larger workloads. Surprisingly, amongst this assortment of stresses, Sun Hill station is impervious to gender inequality. In 'It's not such a bad job after all' (13 November 1984), WPC June Ackland (Trudie Goodwin) professes to be annoyed with being exclusively assigned 'disgusting' jobs such as helping 'snotty nosed kids' or 'searching women for drugs'. Unable to convince Galloway that Amanda Jenkins's (Cindy Day) death was not a clear-cut suicide, Ackland informs Cryer she will resign. Cryer responds, as the camera zooms into a close-up of Ackland's face, by instructing her to take leave and stop mentioning 'this resigning nonsense'. As the shot zooms out to its original position Ackland complies, asserting that she will 'see the case through', to which Cryer favourably replies, 'that's my girl'. Essentially, this short, sharp shock spurs Ackland into succeeding. At the episode's conclusion, once it is proven that a pornographic film producer took advantage of Jenkins, Ackland drinks gin in Galloway's office. At first the camera focuses on Ackland's despondent expression, her head bowed, as the detectives talk around her. When Galloway asks Ackland whether the process was worthwhile, she sits up straight and her face breaks into a smile as she states 'it's not such a bad job after all'. This smile initiates a succession of close-ups of her male colleagues as they laugh and drink.

Dispelling Ackland's accusations of inequality as being a symptom of what Cryer identifies as her own personal 'exaggerations' complies with postfeminist thought. Postfeminism argued that gender equality had been achieved. Major reductions to the budget of the Equal Opportunities Commission and the core funding provided to women's groups by the Greater London Council recast issues such as the gender pay gap or sexual discrimination as private problems. With growing numbers of women achieving high-profile jobs, Thatcher decreed 'the battle for women's rights has been largely won' (quoted in Wilson 1987: 205). Correspondingly, texts classified as postfeminist focus on a woman's personal inadequacies that prevent her from assimilating into mainstream society as a 'problematic she', rather than exposing societal obstacles that deter women from succeeding as an 'unproblematic we' (McRobbie 2007: 29). *The Bill* complies with postfeminism as Ackland is snapped out of her moping by Cryer to learn she is not discriminated against and only has to prove her ability.

Overall the station scenes of *The Gentle Touch* and *Juliet Bravo* direct the focus of their audience on to one principal protagonist and their isolation within their workplace. *The Bill*'s return to an ensemble cast partially recasts the station as a space open to debate from a number of differing viewpoints. However, the handheld video camera highlights particular aspects of interest, such as paperwork being completed, and so provides the viewer with less opportunity autonomously to read an actor's attitudinal makers in relation to their illocutionary markers from a relative distance. This focusing on the macho rivalry experienced between detectives and PCs means gender discrimination is barely acknowledged, despite actress Trudie Goodwin's research that uncovered scores of WPCs who were 'desperate to be treated the same as the men', given 'rampant sexism in the force' (Goodwin 2007: n.p.). Ultimately *The Bill* conforms to an image of the police that the government and police force itself were keen to uphold, partially as a result of the programme's continued approbation from the Metropolitan Police.

Clayview council estate

From the beginning, *The Bill*'s creator, Geoff McQueen, made it clear that:

> Nothing should be shown without one of our police men or women being there. So you'd never see two villains talking, planning a job. You'd never see a man beating his wife in their house or see an accident or a fight happen on the streets unless one of the police characters was passing by or knocking at the door or trying to make an arrest. (Quoted in Kingsley 1994: 25)

Following McQueen's complete departure from *The Bill* in 1988, executive producer Michael Chapman safeguarded this commitment until 1997, agreeing the 'particular character' of the series lay in 'every scene always having a police presence in it' (Kingsley 1994: 6). However, this clear stylistic objective adds a large degree of happenstance to the narrative of each episode. Officers on foot patrol regularly stumble across crimes being committed or civilians in need of help. In 'Funny ol' business – cops & robbers' (16 October 1984), Carver and PC Francis 'Taffy' Edwards (Colin Blumenau) are informed by the communications desk that suspicious figures are tampering with cars near to their location, resulting in an immediate arrest. Similarly, in the same episode a woman who realises she has been burgled is able to report the crime to PC Dave Litten (Gary Olsen) walking past her house. In 'Death of a cracksman', Taffy returns a lost boy to his mother before seeing wanted robbers acting suspiciously across the road. This strict but efficient procedure, as witnessed in the station, directly ensures the uniformed officers are in the right place at the right time to protect the public. Including the police in every scene propagates the 'popular image of the police as the prime agents in the discovery of crime', when 'no more than one out of every seven crimes was discovered (directly or indirectly) by the police' (Bottomley and Coleman 1981: 43).

The way in which police officers occupy civilian locations enables *The Bill* partially to explore the relationship between welfare reform and crime, which was the topic of much political debate, particularly given the regular depiction of 'bleak council estates', including the Bronte,

Abelard, Clayview, and Jasmine Allen (Brunsdon 2001: 43). Economists argued that economic performance since the Second World War had been undermined by the Government's strong commitment to the welfare state, as a central tenet of the postwar consensus, which took 'a disproportionate share of resources' and crowded out 'economic investment in more productive areas' (Fraser 2009: 289). For the first time since 1945, the 1980 budget announced a reduction in social security benefits that would reduce the income of poorer families. The 1982 Social Security and Housing Benefit Act, which tied benefit increases to prices over wages and taxed benefits, ensured that within Thatcher's first two years the total value of State support for an unemployed couple with two children fell by 48 per cent (Abbott and Wallace 1992: 122). The 1980 Housing Act also reduced social housing stock, and subsidies were withdrawn from councils that had previously kept the level of council-house rents down to affordable levels. By 1985, 4 million families were at, or below, the poverty line: a two-fold increase since 1979 (Abbott and Wallace 1992: 85).

Concurrently, the Broadwater Farm riot in Tottenham on 6 October 1985 had, according to the independent inquiry team chaired by Lord Gifford, QC, arisen from a lack of 'education and economic development', 'high unemployment', the 'social isolation' experienced by the unemployed residents, and 'an appalling state of distrust and hostility ... between the police and the people who lived in ... Broadwater Farm' (Gifford 1986: 34, 222, 225, 190). The police struggled to maintain control of the 500 rioters over the course of a day as they were attacked with petrol bombs, bricks, and concrete blocks, and PC Keith Blakelock was stabbed to death. The estate was pertinent because it had been identified by Met Commissioner Kenneth Newman as one of the four 'symbolic locations' where members of the community were beginning to take control of their own social problems and might 'seek to impose their authority over police' (Brain 2010: 110). Given that Chief Superintendent Crouch had ignored warnings that a riot was being pre-planned, rumours circulated that 'no go areas' had been adopted as unofficial policy by the Met. Lord Gifford's linking of the riots to poor social conditions contrasted with the Social Science Research Council, which concluded in 1983 that evidence was not sufficient to establish a link between violent crime and unemployment. Admitting as much would have been tantamount to undermining Thatcher's social and economic philosophy, one reason why Gifford's inquiry was independently funded by the council without support from central government.

Parallels can be drawn between perceptions of Broadwater Farm and the fictional Clayview estate, as it is also depicted as a 'no go' area populated by people who police themselves. The episode 'Clutching at straws' (13 October 1984) opens with teenager Billy March (Adam Armstrong) being beaten for not paying gangster Terry Collins (Jonathan Stratt) a fee for accessing the flats and having relations with Betty Hilmore (Debbie Killingback), or, as Collins sees it, 'giving it to one of our girls'. Later, PC Litten and PC Carver are told by the caretaker, who found March, that Collins is always beating people up without consequence. Billy refuses to disclose the identity of his attacker to the police, instead giving the information to his older brother, Paul (Bruce Payne), with the knowledge his stronger brother will punish Collins. When the police approach Paul for information he explains 'we take care of our own troubles'. To change these ingrained social attitudes Carver takes it upon himself to open a new youth club for the estate's teenagers, despite their low self-esteem and collective belief that 'something's bound to go wrong'. When Carver returns to Clayview, off duty, to initiate youth-club planning he overhears Paul March beating up Collins. Carver intervenes, arresting March to prevent rough justice being enacted. As Carver emerges from the fight with March in handcuffs, the teenagers look at Carver with dejected expressions. A succession of close-up shots of their faces looking at Carver in silence is followed by a teenager's utterance, 'told ya he's still a copper'. Essentially the youth club cannot be re-established because the separate rules the community operate by directly clash with the law. Furthermore, in 'The drugs raid' (20 November 1984), Galloway informs the Clayview Tenants' Association that the drug epidemic is claiming lives because it is 'your kids doing the pushing'. This view is reaffirmed when it is revealed that responsible community leader, police informant, and parent Tombo Robertson (Norman Beaton) has been hiding a heroin addiction all along. Clayview scenes are at odds with the Scarman Report's recommendation that police be responsible for 'the provision of opportunities for operational officers to get to know the community they are policing' because the deep divide depicted between law-abiding society and alleged 'no go' areas is pragmatically unbridgeable (Scarman 1982: 145).

It is not the police's job, as *The Bill* sees it, to intervene in the social circumstances of their communities or individuals. Carver is repeatedly castigated for taking an interest in Clayview because running a youth club is not 'what the tax payer pays you for'. Similarly, younger officers are advised 'never get involved in domestics' and to 'avoid domestics like the plague'. At the end of 'Clutching at straws', after it transpires that the previous manager of the dormant youth club, Simon Doleman (Anthony Ingram), has been abusing children, Doleman is found to have committed suicide in his bed to avoid arrest. Galloway confidently states to Cryer 'well we can close the book on this one Bob', to which Cryer replies 'you sure?', as the camera cuts to a close up of Doleman's frail mother (June Brown) suffering from dementia. Throughout the course of the episode Doleman threatens his mother with physical abuse once the police have left as retribution for the beatings she inflicted on him as a boy. The episode finishes on an unsettling disquiet, suggesting the social complexity of cases like this will never be truly rectified given that these closed communities are governed by unlawful behaviours that are misguidedly passed down through generations. Rather than attempting to draw specific links between social deprivation and rising crime rates, which could counter Thatcher's agenda, *The Bill* draws attention to the types of crimes poorer communities are likely to endure, how the police deal with them, and their apparently inherent cyclical nature. Domestic crime is portrayed as the responsibility of individuals. Therefore *The Bill* does not argue for a socially benevolent police force to involve itself in the individual social problems of its community as recommended by Scarman, Gifford, *Juliet Bravo*, and *The Gentle Touch*.

Routine activity approach

In terms of criminology *The Bill* is more invested in the 'routine activity' theory that also grew from the paradigmatic orthodoxy of the rational-actor model. Rather than determining the characteristics of offenders, as was the practice of rational-choice theory, Cohen and Felson developed an approach that concentrates on the circumstances in which an offender 'intentionally takes or damages the person or property of another' (Glaser 1971: 4). Their belief is that three categories of variables increase the likelihood that persons will be victims of predatory crime within a locality. The first variable is the presence of motivated offenders (usually young males); the second is the availability of suitable targets in terms of persona or property; third is the absence of capable guardians against crime. Cohen and Felson hypothesise that criminal acts require the convergence of 'likely offenders, suitable targets and the absence of capable guardians against crime', and 'the dispersion of activities away from households ... increases the opportunity for crime and thus generates higher crime rates' (Cohen and Felson 1979: 588). Therefore 'the timing of work, schooling and leisure may be of central importance for explaining crime rates' (Cohen and Felson 1979: 591).

In 'Clutching at straws', Paul March informs PC Cryer that he was unaware his younger brother had been beaten because he 'works nights' and 'only just found out'. Paul's brother was a victim of crime because he was a suitable target in a concentrated area of potential offenders at a time his guardian against crime was absent. Given Carver's failed attempt to restart the youth club, *The Bill* concurs with Cohen and Felson's conclusion that 'the opportunity for predatory crime appears to be enmeshed in the opportunity structure for legitimate activities to such an extent that it might be very difficult to root out substantial amounts of crime without modifying much of our way of life' (Cohen and Felson 1979: 605). Domestic abuse will remain endemic to Clayview, and the best police can do is pragmatically stop predatory crimes when called upon as 'capable guardians against crime'.

Conclusion

Through the 1980s the police series was a genre that utilised video-camera technology and included women police officers as central characters to explore the political currency of daily life in a similar manner to melodrama and the soap opera. *The Gentle Touch* and *Juliet Bravo* use the video camera's clearer image-texture to scrutinise the police's working methods from a woman's perspective within the station, rather than keeping these criticisms reserved to domestic spaces. In light of PACE, *The Gentle Touch* takes a sceptical stance towards increased paperwork procedure, whilst *Juliet Bravo* believes in the merits of these working practices, which were introduced to protect civilian's rights. Despite these differences in opinion both programmes maintain that a benevolent interest in individual citizens and their social problems is integral to police work. In contrast, *The Bill*'s use of handheld video cameras portrays a station that is much more of a stressful, high-pressure environment, given PACE's implementation. Focusing on an intense rivalry experienced between CID and PCs means the human-interest element of police work is sidelined, leaving *The Bill* impervious to gender inequality in aligning with postfeminist thought.

In terms of civilian settings, studio productions *Juliet Bravo* and *The Gentle Touch* present the domestic as a political space where the psychosocial effects of Thatcherite attempts to reassert the Victorian model of the two-parent family are revealed. Each series, akin to rational-choice theory, identifies a reoccurring subgroup of offenders; determines why the characteristics of offences are differentially attractive to these subgroups; and then finds pragmatic solutions, having recognised that crime arises from a mixture of individual choices and environmental factors. Yuppie characters and working-class tradesmen commit certain crimes given their perspective on society, which emanates from their socio-economic position. However, neither series necessarily attains a complete anti-neoliberal agenda, but rather reminds individuals to consider the wellbeing of others, to respect the law regardless of circumstance, and to be accountable for their decisions. Accompanying this view of crime, though, is recognition that an increasing gender-inequality epidemic needs addressing. Gamman has stated both that series are 'co-opted by sexism' because Jean Darblay and Maggie Forbes have few professional 'equivalents'. However, collectively, civilian characters through the course of both series stand in as equivalent characters who also attain a feminist stance against gender inequality as experienced in the public and domestic realms. Both leading police characters are subject to the same pressures at home to conform to heteronormative family units overseen by a male breadwinner. Their reluctance to conform to the subjugated housewife figure continues the objective of the women's movement in relation to postfeminist denial.

In contrast, *The Bill*, in its repeated visits to the Clayview council estate, identifies the types of crimes poorer communities were likely to endure given the UK's largest spate of welfare reform. In line with routine-activity theory, the predatory crimes committed are portrayed as inevitable, and so it is not the job of the police force to involve itself in the individual social problems of its community as recommended by Scarman, Gifford, *Juliet Bravo*, and *The Gentle Touch*. The police are guardians against crime who exist to deter criminals. Without access to the personal lives of Sun Hill's officers and detectives, the disparity that was thought to exist between the police and the public regarding the police's prioritising of public enforcement over the public's preference for a community oriented force is upheld and justified. By the decade's end, studio-shot police series using videotape had depoliticised the domestic realm.

Notes

1 Figures obtained from Gambaccini and Taylor (1993).
2 These statistics have been calculated by analysing the first six episodes of both series.
3 Italics used by Neale.
4 Italics have been used to emphasise my point.

The 1990s: transitioning from film to digital 4

> We should be tough on crime and tough on the underlying causes of crime.
>
> Shadow Home Secretary Tony Blair (Blair 1993: n.p.)

This chapter examines the tremendously popular, critically revered, and somewhat controversial *Prime Suspect* (ITV, 1991–2006), *A Touch of Frost* (ITV, 1992–2010), and *Cracker* (ITV, 1993–2006). Each programme utilises the visual iconography of the horror film as a response to increased censoring of the police series. In July 1988, the time of *The Bill* (ITV, 1984–2010) was brought forward to 8 p.m. to target *Coronation Street* (ITV, 1960–) viewers. According to script editor Zanna Beswick, this meant 'violence, blood and gore ... are never included in the writing' (quoted in Kingsley, 1994: 41). As a direct result of this rescheduling, actor John Salthouse left the series, proclaiming, 'you can't make a contemporary series about the police without including some violence' (Kingsley, 1994: 29). Thus, the following chapter analyses how *Prime Suspect*, *Frost*, and *Cracker* use film cameras to portray violence and capture a rising dissatisfaction with the criminal justice system's continued adoption of rational-actor policy. First, the chapter considers how each series challenges the essential nature of the police station. It examines how images of abject violence question business management practices borrowed from the private sector to measure police performance. Then, it explores how each series uses horror-film conventions to depict perceived threats to society, including the underclass of *Prime Suspect*, middle-class femininity in *Frost*, and *Cracker*'s working-class 'masculinity in crisis'. Next, the sombreness pervading the private lives of detectives is explored to deduce how each series' presentation of civilian life engages with notable socio-political concerns that the early 1990s were a period of moral decline. Lastly, an examination of *The Cops* (BBC, 1998–2001) determines how digital, handheld cameras combine docudrama's emotional realism with the 'horizontality' of contemporary social realism to embody the precariousness of Anthony Giddens's 'new individualism' whilst critiquing New Labour's adoption of 'left realism' criminology.

Production context

The 1990s are often deemed the UK television industry's 'most significant decade for change' (Cooke 2015a: 173). Following the 1986 Peacock Report's recommendations, the 1990 Broadcasting Act ensured 25 per cent of BBC and ITV programming was produced by independent production companies, and ITV franchises were awarded through competitive tendering. As Carlton Television outbid Thames Television for the lucrative London weekday contract, it was able to gamble on a new detective series with a feature-length format. Based on the novels of Colin Dexter, *Inspector Morse* (ITV, 1987–2000) became one of the most popular television series of the late 1980s. Regularly attracting 15 million viewers, *Morse* won six BAFTAs and was sold to 200 countries. Given the launch of Channel 4 (1982) and satellite television (1989), Morse became the benchmark for retaining large audiences whilst receiving consistent critical acclaim within an increasingly deregulated marketplace. Despite being set in contemporary Oxford, the Blackbird Leys estate is omitted in favour of helicopter shots of village greens and church spires. This Oxford is anchored by the aesthetic tradition of heritage dramas providing 'a visual present of a fantasy past' (Brunsdon 2000: 119). *Morse* does not address 'queries about the roles and power of the police' as expected from a police series (Sparks 1992: 100). Instead, the drama is invested in the dynamic between its 'single investigator and his sidekick' as an 'English country-house' whodunnit (Brunsdon 2000: 202). In retaliation, Christopher Menaul directed *Prime Suspect* as an 'antidote' to the 'glossy' style of *Morse*, *Poirot* (ITV, 1989–2013), and *The Adventures of Sherlock Holmes* (ITV, 1984–1994) (quoted in Paterson 1991: 136). This 'sombre realism' subsequently informed the style of post-Morse police series *Frost* and *Cracker*. Here, as in horror films, the grainy texture of the film camera image accentuates dark, unsettling settings; intensifies the tense POV gazes exchanged between murderers and victims; and adds a grisliness to scenes of graphic violence. Combined, this iconography criticises criminal investigation procedure and uncovers the extent of the postwar settlement's break-up (Jermyn 2010: 70).

Police and crime

To stifle criticisms that the rate of violent crimes was being perpetuated without any sign of slowing down, the 1994 Police and Magistrates

Court Act and the 1996 Police Act provided chief constables with financial devolution and new management freedoms to allocate budgets to staff, vehicles, and equipment. Similarly, Prime Minister John Major's 1991 Citizen's Charter was an initiative designed to improve public-sector standards by assessing the quality of services through published targets. Following these competitive working practices, common to the private sector, Home Secretary Michael Howard set national policing objectives. The Police Authority and chief constables incorporated these objectives into an annual local plan complete with set targets to measure police efficiency. Therefore the Authority's role changed from maintaining an 'adequate' police force, as detailed in the 1964 Police Act, to maintaining an 'efficient' and 'effective' service measured against seventeen quality standards and forty-five key performance indicators (KPIs) set by the Inspectorate and Audit Commission (Rawlings 2002: 220). Given increased pressure on chief constables to produce timely results, the murder investigations of *Prime Suspect*, *Frost*, and *Cracker*, which attract mob outcry and media outrage, result in 'hasty police judgements' or even the arrest of innocent suspects to meet essential objectives and satisfactorily conclude enquiries (Piper 2015: 73).

Prime Suspect

La Plante's Detective Chief Inspector Jane Tennison (Helen Mirren) overcoming the Metropolitan Police Force's institutional misogyny was an extraordinary critical and commercial success. Winning three BAFTAs and two Emmy awards, *Prime Suspect* was instantly lauded for lingering on peripheral aspects of the genre – for example mortuary slabs, crime photos, and 'grisly evidence' – in cold, hard focus (Paterson 1991: 124). Basing her protagonist on Merseyside's Assistant Chief Constable Alison Halford, who pursued a tribunal upon failing to secure promotion nine times from 1987 to 1990, La Plante shadowed homicide detective Jackie Malton in incident rooms and crime labs to understand how women coped in male-dominated environments. La Plante wrote the first three *Prime Suspect*s before severing ties with Granada, as Mirren insisted that more screen time be dedicated to Tennison's private life.

Southampton Row

Tennison challenges the patriarchal authority that oversees the Metropolitan Police's target-led working practices by mimicking the 'monstrous feminine' figure of horror films. Barbara Creed identifies monstrous feminine characters as a staple of horror because the genre consistently works through Julia Kristeva's abject theory. The abject is a sight that reminds one of one's materiality. Discovering 'the border' of one's 'condition as a living being' provokes trauma in the form of 'a gagging sensation' and 'spasms', causing the 'forehead and hands to perspire' (Kristeva 1982: 3). Creed agrees that in order for society to function horror films must inevitably deposit the abject 'on the other side of an imaginary border which separates the self from that which threatens the self' (Creed 2003: 9). Like horror films, *Prime Suspect* also explores 'the boundaries between the human and the non-human' (Creed 2003: 14).

Before Tennison takes leadership of the murder investigation in the first *Prime Suspect* (7 and 8 April 1991) a clear boundary exists between the abject and the station.[1] When Detective Chief Inspector John Shefford (John Forgeham) is in charge, he and Detective Sergeant Bill Otley (Tom Bell) visit the morgue. As the mortician directs the viewer's gaze towards graphic close-ups of cut wrists, a slashed chest, and bruised arms Otley and Shefford look at the mortician and exchange uneasy glances to avoid acknowledging the injuries as chilling reminders of their mortality. Once Shefford has the information he requires, he refuses to see the victim's vaginal bruising and repositions himself alongside Otley at the other side of the room to maintain a comfortable distance between himself and the corpse. To Shefford, confronting the abject is not conducive to charging a suspect within thirty-five hours of a discovered body: an unbeaten record he wants to beat. This attitude contrasts sharply with Tennison, who, unconcerned with plaudits, comprehensively scrutinises the victim's injuries in her own time to discover the victim has been misidentified.

Compared to the discomfort experienced in the morgue the male detectives are ensconced in the station's incident room. Officers are relaxed when exchanging beers, jokes, and high fives because this makeshift social club is removed from the abject contained within the morgue. Tennison soon redraws this boundary between the living and the dead by enlarging pictures of the mutilated corpses and pinning them to the incident room's central noticeboard. When conducting briefings an opposition is drawn between the solitary Tennison standing in front of these corpse photographs and the 'brooding sea of men' grouped together at the other side of the room, refusing to meet her gaze (Jermyn 2010: 64). Tennison confronts the men by channelling a maternal form of the monstrous feminine character prominent in horror film. According to Creed, images of bodily waste, including the secretion of blood, vomit, and faeces, threaten the unified subject, who can control such pollution as instructed by the paternal social order. Images of secretions 'hark back to an archaic period when the child's relation to its mother was such that it did not experience embarrassment and shame at the emergence of its bodily wastes' (Creed 2003: 356). The men avoid Tennison's gaze not just as a means of 'disempowering her' but because they are disgusted by the mutilations that Tennison is 'symbolically aligned' with, which hark back to the vulnerability of their childhood (Jermyn 2008: 64–65).

By the final briefing, however, there is a marked change, as the men acknowledge the abject as an essential component of their investigation. Images of George Marlow's (John Bowe) victims are projected across the wall as one detective at a time provides a profile of each victim and identifies commonalities between injuries. The male detectives in attendance are no longer brooding and instead note down information with undue attention. An image or video of the victim when they were alive is juxtaposed against their mutilated corpse through the projector as the boundary between the living and the dead is now a focal element of detective work. Whilst some feel Tennison 'makes no change to the structure or the ethos of the institutions with which she engages', examining Tennison's use, as a monstrous feminine figure, of the station confirms her revolutionising of the Met's working practices (Hallam 2005: 84).

A Touch of Frost

Over an eighteen-year run and forty-two feature-length episodes, *A Touch of Frost* won four BAFTAs and peaked at 18.2 million viewers. Based on R. D. Wingfield's novels, *Frost* is remembered as a family-friendly drama that cemented actor David Jason's status as a national treasure. However, the first and second series, predominantly scribed by *Hunter's Walk* writer Richard Harris, were muted, serious affairs. Honouring the public's appetite for 'gritty realism during the recessionary gloom', *Frost* provided an 'opposition to the golden deep-focus cinematography and heritage locations of *Inspector Morse*' (Piper 2015: 45).

Denton station

Like Tennison, Detective Inspector Jack Frost (David Jason) is doubtful of a target-led culture, and so instructs his subordinate (who changes in every episode) to complete crime report returns retroactively to mislead Central Control about his KPIs. Frost is given such a short timeframe and lack of resources to charge suspects his post-mortems are decidedly brief. No injuries are shown, as the camera provides a shot-reverse-shot sequence of Frost's face in close-up and the mortician's face in close-up to explain the cause of death. Analogously, team briefings are no longer of fundamental importance. Where Tennison's briefings piece together forensic evidence, Frost's briefings are last-ditch attempts to brainstorm ideas. In 'Widows and orphans' (16 January 1994), Frost attaches small A4 photos of victims' facial injuries to the noticeboard behind him. Following this action the camera pans with Frost as he walks amongst the officers, never to recapture the photos again. In 'Stranger in the house' (30 January 1994), Detective Chief Inspector Allen (Neil Phillips) stands behind Frost holding up two photos revealing victims' injuries. Whilst the photographs are clearly visible to the officers, the camera is positioned behind Allen so that the viewer cannot see them. The abject is referenced by the working practices of Denton station but its significance is drastically reduced, as a comfortable boundary is largely re-established between the human and non-human.

Such direction comes, in part, from Frost's direct superior, Superintendent Norman Mullet (Bruce Alexander). Mullet does not just 'represent the police norms from which Jack must dissent' (Piper 2015: 53); he is demonstrative of a public-relations-management culture, completely removed from the abject, that dictates the police force's priorities. Rooted to his office, Mullet threatens Frost with disciplinary action through fear of falling behind with national crime figures, overspending, or attracting negative press attention. During every conversation with Frost, Mullet takes off his glasses and holds them atop his paperwork and calculator, signifying how he wants Frost aligned to his vision of police work, which is informed by the metrics of police efficiency. In 'Stranger in the house', Mullet informs Frost that the Chief Constable is willing to dispense major resources to identify and arrest a serial rapist before it becomes a national scandal. This contrasts with Mullet's instructions, in 'Care and protection' (6 December 1992), to avoid using a helicopter or overtime to find a missing girl, as they are already 'pushing the bloody budget'. Similarly, in 'Not with kindness' (13 December 1992), Mullet informs Frost that their 'number one priority' is to achieve a 'quick result' without extra manpower. Additional resources are only granted to crimes that attract negative press attention. Therefore chief constables' budgetary freedoms are exposed as a means of preserving the police's public image. This top-down obsession with public relations results in a lack of sustained engagement with the abject, as the detective's role has been refashioned to prioritise the achievement of various KPIs.

Cracker

Cracker emerged from ITV's directive to replace *Morse* during its temporary retirement. In response to a circular from Granada Head of Drama Sally Head, producer Gub Neal constructed an outline for a police series that centred on a criminal psychologist.[2] Jimmy McGovern, who had cut his teeth writing episodes of the soap opera *Brookside* (Channel 4, 1982–2003), was hired, and wrote six screenplays. Despite fuelling debates around the 'perceived excess of violence and sex on television' *Cracker* quickly built a regular audience of 14 million viewers and won fourteen BAFTAs (Duguid 2009: 26). As in *Prime Suspect*, there is a 'determination to confront death … in all its brutality and finality', as each feature-length episode strives to understand its murderer (Duguid 2009: 80).

Anson Road station

Psychology lecturer Dr Edward 'Fitz' Fitzgerald (Robbie Coltrane) scrutinises the inner workings of the 'no-nonsense, common sense-oriented' Greater Manchester Police, where 'real justice and the demands of the criminal justice system' are 'perversely incompatible' (Duguid 2009: 51, 60). In 'One day a lemming will fly' (1 and 8 November 1993), knowing an innocent suspect has been detained, Detective Chief Inspector David Bilborough (Christopher Ecclestone) refuses Fitz's request to overturn the charges. Bilborough fears being lynched by his boss, a 'distraught family', and 'a vengeful, frightened public' gathered outside the station 'urged on by a baying media' (Duguid 2009: 60). Compared to Mullet, Bilborough upholds his decision to protect his staff as much as his own skin. Sustaining the charges secures the safety of his detectives, who are increasingly vulnerable to an incandescent public awaiting the swifter efficiency promised to them by the Citizen's Charter. Bilborough's duty of care to his staff is repeatedly evidenced by the way he uses his office as a space to counsel detectives on their private problems. Unlike Mullet, the focus of Bilborough's attention is on whoever sits at the other side his desk. Bilborough's desk is never obstructed by calculators or paperwork, and his computer forever lies dormant in the corner of his office. He is less invested in public-relations directives, and as a figure of relative authority he instead prioritises the psychological wellbeing of his team as conducive to achieving results.

Therefore, in further contrast to Mullet, Bilborough's office is not a cosy alcove decorated with wooden furnishings and comfortable seating to host informal discussions with politicians and journalists over cups of tea. Instead, Bilborough's office is attached to the detectives' incident room by a thin glass partition. This partition has a two-fold function, permitting Bilborough to be actively involved in the day-to-day work of his detectives whilst simultaneously shielding them from the abject. Photos of injuries, dead bodies, and murder weapons are pinned to Bilborough's office wall in a corner that cannot be seen clearly from the incident room. Akin to a horror film, *Cracker* uses the divide between Bilborough's office and the incident room to explore the 'border which separates the self from that which threatens the self' (Creed 2003: 9). In 'One day a lemming will fly', amidst the investigation of a murdered schoolboy, Bilborough summons Detective Sergeant Jane Penhaligon (Geraldine Somerville) into his office to discipline her for publicly suggesting his private live is 'interfering' with his work. After Penhaligon apologises, Bilborough tries pinning a photograph of the dead schoolboy's shoe to the wall alongside images of the body and murder weapon. Fatigued, Bilborough fails to exert enough pressure to the affix the photo to the wall and it falls to the floor. He then confesses to Penhaligon that his pregnant wife is a week overdue and he is not sleeping. This act of dropping the photograph reveals the extent to which concealing the trauma of the abject from his staff exacerbates Bilborough's personal problems and compromises his professional capabilities.

Criminologists have accused *Cracker* of 'creating a misleading impression of what offender profiling can achieve' (Ainsworth 2013: 6). Despite this dramatic licence, however, being unanswerable to police protocol means Fitz has the freedom to criticise detectives openly, admit to feeling the same animalistic urges as his suspects, and understand suspects' childhood trauma. This tactic cajoles criminals into confessing. Therefore, Fitz's perspective unearths how the logic of quantifying detectives' achievements through a series of metrics and national targets is detrimental to achieving true justice. Fitz's skillset unburdens Bilborough from suffering the abject alone, and this has the perceived benefit of preserving the senior incident team's mental wellbeing to achieve timely results. Instead, Fitz uses his expertise to have detectives prioritise true justice and expose the 'classic policing error', as he sees it, of concentrating efforts into securing convenient results.

Overall the pressures of producing timely results to correspond with national targets are revealed as being incompatible with justice. In each series a protagonist with an outside perspective is required to reorder the workings of the station to achieve, or at least recognise, true justice. In *Prime Suspect* Tennison's adoption of the monstrous feminine figure forces her male colleagues to confront the abject and the suffering endured by victims to displace the competitive, individualistic culture of beating records to achieve a successful arrest. *Frost*'s public-image-conscious management requires an elderly protagonist with a belief in his intuition to navigate through trivial modern protocols to solve cases and, at the very least, acknowledge the abject. Lastly, Fitz's psychological expertise means that, as an outsider, he is better equipped to undertake interrogations. He is not answerable to the metrics of police performance and so can deal with, and help unburden Bilborough of, the psychological ramifications of regularly scrutinising the abject alone to preserve the wellbeing and efficiency of the senior incident detective team.

Domestic horror

With the abject established as a focal aspect of the police station, this chapter will now determine how accompanying horror-film cinematography manifests in domestic spaces. It is well documented that *Prime Suspect*, *Frost*, and *Cracker* are saturated with the 'social dissatisfaction of their era ... punctuated by references to a sharp economic recession, homelessness, social exclusion, the welfare state and the broader disintegration of civic and community values' (Piper 2015: 66). This thematic outlook is framed by a visual appetite for the 'spectacularization of the body and site of crime', as was occurring in horror films such as *The Silence of the Lambs* (1991), and literary crime fiction by Patricia Cornwell, James Patterson, and Minette Walters (Brunsdon 2000: 216). The rest of this chapter, then, unpicks the relationship between each series' horror-film style and its social ideology in relation to the aforementioned station scenes.

1990s social decline

In 1990, financial deregulation and reckless lending produced high inflation. With higher interest rates introduced to defend the pound's plummeting value, investment reduced and lesser profits triggered another recession. Mortgage rates rose 15.5 per cent, 1991 saw 48,000 businesses declare bankruptcy, and in 1992 unemployment rose to 3.5 million as GDP diminished by 2.5 per cent (Pugh 2017: 458). On 16 September 1992 ('Black Wednesday') the Government withdrew the pound from the European exchange rate mechanism, having failed to keep it above its agreed lower limit. Thus, the pound was further devalued by 15 per cent, with the Bank of England having spent £60 billion to save it (Pugh 2017: 458). Furthermore, the decade was tainted by a number of high-profile crimes that horrified the general public. Two-year-old James Bulger was abducted, tortured, and killed by ten-year-olds Jon Venables and Robert Thompson in February 1992. Rachel Nickell was stabbed forty-nine times in front of her two-year-old son on Wimbledon Common five months later. Then the 1996 Dunblane school massacre resulted in sixteen dead primary school children. Journalists, sociologists, and politicians proclaimed there was increased social decline. Shadow Home Secretary Tony Blair identified the Bulger murder as one of many 'ugly manifestations of a society that is becoming unworthy of that name' (Blair 2010: 57). Political scientist Charles Murray used the term 'underclass' to label those he felt were 'contaminating the life of entire neighbourhoods' through their 'illegitimacy' (lone parenthood), 'violent crime', and 'idleness' (exiting the labour force) (Murray 1996 [1989]: 26). As unemployment and social collapse became etched into the UK's social fabric, a 'new iconography of ... casual, indiscriminate violence' (Lacey 2007: 140) entered the police series.

Prime underclass

To capture this apparent social deterioration, the *mise-en-scène* of *Prime Suspect* is 'as dark as the crimes under investigation' (Piper 2015: 68). Mundane spaces are transformed into 'sinister sites of mutilation', consisting of 'a lock-up garage bearing the evidence of sexual assault and torture, a charred council flat with an unidentified cadaver', and 'a homeless boy dying of AIDS in a makeshift shanty town' (Piper 2015: 68). According to film theorist Robin Wood, killers who conduct such acts threaten bourgeois culture and so are punished by a horror film's conclusion. Like slasher films, then, *Prime Suspect*'s civilian settings perpetuate 'myths of working-class squalor and sexuality' to justify the repression of the proletariat, which 'has escaped its colonization by bourgeois ideology' (Wood 2001 [1979]: 27). In the first *Prime Suspect* Jermyn believes the 'cosy colour palette' of serial killer Marlow's home integrates him into 'the fabric of a common social world' (Jermyn 2010: 77). In keeping with horror-film logic, however, repeated behaviour displayed by Marlow, and his fiancée Moira Henson (Zoë Wanamaker), signifies their affinity with Murray's underclass that threatens bourgeois ideology. Initially Henson is undeterred by her fiancé's courting prostitutes, and evidences her promiscuity by flashing her breasts to the officers conducting surveillance of their home. Resolution comes when Henson retracts her alibi following Tennison's threat to prosecute Henson for her benefit fraud whilst unveiling photographs of Marlow's victims' injuries. Henson withdraws her alibi because she is cleansed of her underclass perspective. Her gagging in abjection towards the corpse photographs demonstrates she is now repulsed by the grave consequences of idleness, illegitimacy, and crime.

In *Prime Suspect 2* (15 and 16 December 1992), rapist and killer James Reynolds (Matt Bardock) also belongs to Murray's 'underclass' subdivision of the proletariat. He is derided in a restaurant for being 'of that sort' on account of his loud cockney accent, unkemptness, and lack of table manners. Furthermore, his criminality is protected by his family, who also voluntarily subscribe to Murray's 'illegitimacy' and 'idleness'. Eileen Reynolds (June Watson) is deliberately ignorant of her son's makeshift photography studio where he takes photographs of himself raping and murdering women. Eileen knows that the photography business is likely to be illicit, given that he possesses large amounts of cash and yet lives in a caravan, but she willingly turns a blind eye. It also transpires that James's uncle David Harvey (Tom Watson) helped him bury his first victim: a young, middle-class woman viewing the property Harvey resided in with a view to becoming a tenant. Lastly, in *Prime Suspect 3* (19 and 20 December 1993) a 'clear distinction is drawn between the ratty alleys where the rent boys and vagrants hang out, and the glitzy bars where drag queens sing for a crowd of incognito politicians' (Chappell 2012: n.p.). This underworld of homeless child prostitutes is overseen by pimp James Jackson (David Thewlis), who despite being a handyman by trade patrols the streets at night like an 'animal who should be caged'.

Prime Suspect abides by the style and thematic composition of contemporary slasher films, as working-class murders arise in the dead of night to kill middle-class women before being avenged by the bourgeois criminal justice system. Concurrently *Prime Suspect* agrees with political scientists such as Murray who believe a distinction should be made between 'low income as such and the behavioural poverty that results from conduct which is both antisocial and self-harming' (Green 1996: 20). Marlow, Reynolds, and Jackson are all young men who have grown up without a father within impoverished neighbourhoods. They look to figures like Harvey, whose casual attitude towards work and paying rent sees him evicted from the house where Reynolds killed his first victim. This supports Murray's view that 'plentiful examples of good fathers' have significantly diminished in poorer neighbourhoods, leading to an autonomous underclass whose questionable attitudes towards work, crime, and the family threaten the bourgeois way of life (Murray 1996 [1989]: 32).

Bourgeois *Frost*

Prime Suspect depicts a highly polarised society where uncouth characters belonging to an underclass threaten the safety of the law-abiding middle classes. However, *Frost* is concerned with crimes that emerge from recessionary pressures experienced by suburban middle England. Consistently respected community members turn out to be murderers, be it a teacher in 'Not with kindness', a business owner in 'Nothing to hide' (23 January 1994), or a bus driver in 'Widows and orphans'. These brutal assaults occurring in quiet suburbs are portrayed as a symptom of the traditional family unit's decline. By 1995, 70 per cent of children under ten experienced their parents' divorce. The number of lone-parent families trebled to the highest rate in Europe. Two-thirds of single mothers did not receive their income support, and six in ten employed lone mothers worked part-time (McRae 1999: 1–33). Rather than using the horror film's visual style to re-establish the bourgeois colonisation of the proletariat, here crime now emerges from post-traditional, middle-class families who struggle to balance recessionary economic pressures with the untenable social ideals they are expected to uphold.

In 'Care and protection', a mismatch between social expectation and economic reality results in the disappearance of schoolgirl Tracy Uphill (Rebecca Ricketts). Linda Uphill (Claire Hackett) is late picking up her daughter from her social club because her gentleman caller Brian Farnham (Sion Tudor Owen) 'was late'. Uphill is a single mother who is only given part-time hours at the supermarket and so works as a prostitute to supplement her income. However, there is more to Uphill's lateness than she admits. In the opening scene, having slept with Farnham, Uphill informs him he cannot stay because she needs to pick up her daughter. Once Farnham has left, Uphill then remakes the bed, takes off her clothes, and walks out of her bedroom to shower and change. Despite running late she finds the time to cleanse herself and her bedroom to hide evidence of her work. Wood believes that the horror film's obsession with cleanliness is 'closely associated with ... bourgeois sexual repression' to distance the bourgeoisie from 'the myths of working-class ... sexuality' (Wood 2001 [1979]: 28). Frost reveals that such a way of life, intrinsic to *Prime Suspect*'s underclass, is now endemic to Denton's middle class. Frost tells Detective Constable Clive Barnard (Matt Bardock) that lots of 'respectable middle-class ladies ... like her' need to 'sell' what's 'available'.

Maintaining bourgeois cleanliness is a recurring theme, not necessarily as an 'outward symptom' of bourgeois sexual repression, as in the contemporary horror film, but as a means of concealing evidence of sexual promiscuity from other middle-class characters (Wood 2001 [1979]: 28). When cleanliness is exposed for concealing evidence of promiscuity or the denigration of marriage, a crime is committed. In 'Not with kindness', teacher Michael Bell (John Vine) kills his fifteen-year-old pupil Paula Bartlett because, following their sexual encounter, Bartlett lay naked on his recently deceased wife's bed, put his wife's lipstick all over her face and laughed in a way he felt was 'grotesque'. Furthermore, the reason Bartlett let herself into the house was because she couldn't bear the thought of her mother in bed with her stepfather. In 'Stranger in the house', seventeen-year-old Alison Cook goes missing after unexpectedly walking in on her mother Pauline (Amelda Brown) cheating on her father with another man. Also, in 'Widows and orphans', evidence of Ronald Gould's (Christopher Fulford) capacity for killing is revealed when Frost forces him to admit his mother was a 'dirty little tart with only one thing on her mind', having abandoned him at three months old.

Occasional scenes that depict civilian life independently from Frost's perspective are fundamental to the series' visual tone and ideology. In 'Care and protection', Uphill's home, where she prostitutes herself, is coloured by pastel greys to provide a cold, uninviting space rather than the wholesome warmth and comfort expected of a family home. It is also peculiarly dark inside the house, despite its being daylight outside. Similarly, at the beginning of 'Nothing to hide', Ray Butler (Gerard Horan) walks through the dark interiors of his house, again despite the light outside, to discover his home has been ransacked by his brother-in-law. As Ray picks up the phone to ring the police, his wife Anne (Felicity Montagu) rushes downstairs and forcibly puts the receiver down, vowing to sort the matter herself. Both sequences borrow key tropes from British gothic television drama. The scenes are darkly lit with a *mise-en-scène* dominated by 'drab and dismal colours, shadows and closed-in spaces' (Wheatley 2006: 3). Both scenes are accompanied by unnerving yet ethereal flute music scored by Barbara Thompson and John Hiseman. This form of music, as used in gothic television to connote a supernatural presence, eerily foreshadows the death that will occur. Like previous British gothic series, notably *Hammer House of Horror* (Hammer, 1980), this visual and aural composition indicates the family is 'a simultaneously threatened and threatening institution' (Wheatley 2006: 82). Unlike gothic series, however, this style does not offer a textual space in which anxieties surrounding the subjugated nature of the woman in the home may be 'worked through' (Wheatley 2006: 121). Instead, ideologically those domestic scenes that occur independently of Frost's perspective are closer to contemporary American horror. If Linda had left her home promptly she could have picked up Tracy on time and prevented her disappearance. Similarly, had Anne Butler not prevented her husband from ringing the police her brother would have been detained and protected from his murderer. Therefore, in *Frost* the sexual 'autonomy' of women, as discussed by Wood, is what threatens the stability of the traditional family as much as the recession (Wood 2001 [1979]: 27).

Cracker in crisis

So far civilian scenes have subscribed to Wood's horror-film theory. In *Prime Suspect* the middle-class public must be protected from an abject underclass. Meanwhile, *Frost* uses gothic imagery to portray middle-class women's sexual freedom as an eerie danger to the traditional bourgeois family. *Cracker* intervenes in this binary by highlighting the challenges that McGovern felt working-class men, either stereotyped by *Prime suspect* or overlooked by *Frost*, were experiencing. At this time a 'crisis of masculinity' referred to the state of siege men felt they were experiencing from feminist criticism and the radical reorientation of UK industry. The economy's new reliance on service industries over manufacturing overthrew 'labour roles that had sustained male identity in the industrial age' (Duguid 2009: 53). *Cracker*'s depictions of civilian life are situated within this distinct social milieu, as stigmatised working-class men misguidedly target their frustrations at middle-class institutions they feel have abandoned their interests. Rape and murder scenes have been likened to *Psycho* (1960), *Carrie* (1976), *Halloween* (1978), and *Friday the 13th* (1980) by Duguid (2009) and Piper (2015) – although how *Cracker* adopts slasher-film cinematography to explore working-class masculinity has been overlooked. This is especially startling given that, just as in these films, *Cracker*'s murder scenes balance between the first-person assaultive gaze, where murderous men perform acts of violence, and the reactive gaze, which is gendered as feminine by focusing on the 'wide, staring eyes' of a female victim 'expressing stark terror ... to an ultimate threat' (Telotte 1980: 151).

Repeatedly in 'To be a somebody' (10, 17, and 24 October 1994), the camera navigates the axis between assaultive and reactive gazes. Following the death of his father, welder Albie Kinsella (Robert Carlyle) murders a psychology lecturer, detective, and *Sun* journalist to avenge the Hillsborough disaster he believes aggravated his father's cancer. With his father dead Kinsella struggles to cope with the sudden realisation that the orthodoxies of the left, which have sustained his identity as a trade unionist Labour Party voter, have disappeared. This realisation comes when the proprietor of his local corner shop, Shahid Ali (Badi Uzzaman), will not allow Kinsella to owe the extra 4p he needs to pay for a copy of the *Guardian* and a pack of teabags. When Kinsella visits the shop, the camera providing the establishing shot is placed alongside Ali at the counter as Kinsella walks unassumingly towards his till. Assuming Ali's perspective of the space puts Kinsella in a position where he is too embarrassed to meet Ali's commanding gaze. On Kinsella's return, however, these roles are reversed. Kinsella's POV is now used as the establishing shot as he surveys the shop. Kinsella then marches towards the till with the camera shaking in his wake, signalling the 'force ready to be unleashed' (Clover 1992: 189). Then the scene cuts between Kinsella's assaultive gaze, framed by a slightly low angle, and Ali's reactive look, framed by a high-angle shot from over Kinsella's shoulder. Now Kinsella retains a degree of confidence over middle-class surroundings. From this moment Kinsella's adoption of the horror film's assaultive gaze provides him with the platform required to be 'an articulate spokesman for working class anger and alienation' (Piper 2015: 85). Kinsella assumes an assaultive POV to stalk *Sun* reporter Clare Moody (Beth Goddard) at her newspaper offices and to frame the wide-eyed reactive gaze of Professor Nolan (Glyn Grain) in a university photocopying room. Both characters have publicly stereotyped Kinsella as an unskilled and unemployed football hooligan. Therefore, obtaining an assaultive POV provides Kinsella with a platform cathartically to confront middle-class prejudice. In these murder scenes he forcibly demonstrates he is a loving son and educated welder who enjoys the music of Mozart and Rossini, despite mainstream sociopolitical thinking that 'assumes the right to treat' white working-class men 'like scum'.

The same cinematographic grammar is adopted in 'Men should weep' (21 and 28 November, 5 December 1994), as Floyd Malcolm's (Graham Aggrey) experiences of racial discrimination as a mixed-race taxi driver fuel his warped reasoning for raping his boss's wife and murdering his welfare officer's wife. Repeatedly, the audience shares Malcolm's assaultive POV when giving his victims taxi rides. As in slasher films, Malcolm is doomed to fail, as 'the vision of the subjective camera calls attention to what it cannot see' (Clover 1992: 187). Within these moments only the rear-view mirror, covering approximately one-third of the shot, is in focus. The correspondingly blurred two-thirds of the image represent the 'recesses' of Malcolm's vision that call attention to his 'vulnerability' and inevitable failure (Clover 1992: 187). To some extent the ideology of the contemporary American horror film is upheld, as it is certain Kinsella and Malcolm will be punished for severely criminalising the people Kinsella terms 'bourgeois lefties'. However, the concluding scene of 'To be a somebody' sees *Sun* journalist Moody killed when she opens Kinsella's letter bomb. Therefore, *Cracker* also challenges the horror-film formula it embodies. *Cracker* suggests that a satisfying conclusion occurs not just when the bourgeoisie have colonised the proletariat, but also when the bourgeoisie face judgement for their discriminatory treatment of the proletariat. This argument is articulated through Kinsella's and Malcolm's assaultive gazes. These POVs provide characters with a platform to articulate how they have been unfairly ostracised and present a reasoning as to why they seek agency over middle-class people and settings.

Ultimately, the station scenes of *Prime Suspect*, *Frost*, and *Cracker* use the abject to ask serious questions of a detective culture increasingly obsessed with achieving targets and KPIs over the suffering endured by victims and successfully punishing the guilty parties responsible. However, this view is somewhat complicated by *Prime Suspect*'s depiction of a feral underclass and *Frost*'s sexually transgressive middle-class women. Both representations are caricatures that, as in slasher films, serve to refract, rather than reflect, existing moral panics: in this case a supposedly expanding underclass and a decline in the moral standards traditionally symbolised by marriage. In response, *Cracker*, whilst it 'never shirks from condemning the crime', uses slasher-film cinematography to suggest that to 'understand the criminal' better can help redress supposedly perpetuating rates of violent crime and wider social decline (Piper 2015: 75). Therefore, the extent of each programme's refractions of social concerns, particular to the 1990s, will now be determined by an analysis of each protagonist's private life.

Tennison's abject home

Prime Suspect initially demarcates Tennison's home from the sombreness of Southampton Row station and other civilian locations. The first time an audience witnesses Tennison in a private capacity is whilst Shefford leads the investigation. Following a typical day of menial courtroom work Tennison returns home to her partner, Peter Rawlins (Tom Wilkinson), keen to make a good impression on Rawlins's son Joey (Jeremy Warder) and ex-wife Marianne (Francesca Ryan). There is an academic consensus that the scene is rendered feminine, given that the 'golden pine cupboards and soft yellow lights' produce 'softer tones that distinguish this domestic space from the office and incident room' (Hallam 2005: 81; Jermyn 2010: 41). Tennison's 'elegant pencil skirt with a flattering cream silk blouse and simple gold jewellery' make an outfit 'quite removed from the sombre attire of police uniform' (Jermyn 2010: 41). Combined, the *mise-en-scène* humanises Tennison as a gentler character than witnessed in the station, who displays maternal instincts. Marianne admits 'she's not at all what I expected'.

When Tennison takes leadership of the case, however, she becomes a monstrous feminine figure in the eyes of her partner. Having been granted leadership Tennison spends her first evening in charge at her dining table taking notes. Lit by a solitary lamp, she is surrounded by darkness as she looks through forensic photos of mutilated body parts that signify the materiality of the human condition. The detectives' bashful reluctance to meet her gaze in the following scene, where she conducts her first briefing, is predetermined by Rawlins, who watches her in the background of the shot, unnerved by her obsession with photos of mutilations that prevent her coming to bed. From this moment onwards domestic happenings continue to scare Rawlins. Tennison's actions provoke wide-eyed reactive gazes from Rawlins, who is visibly scared of his partner and the threat she poses towards the unified self. When they watch her night-time television appeal in their darkened bedroom, Tennison decides to arrest Marlow immediately, as she wants the 'shit scared out of him'. Rawlins exclaims 'Jesus Christ' in direct response, as if expressing 'disgust' towards her desire to produce 'bodily wastes' from another human subject who Rawlins is not yet convinced is guilty (Creed 2003: 356). In another instance Rawlins flinches in terror when Tennison swipes a copy of the *News of the World* from his grip in a fit of rage, following his jocular reading of an article that claims she is an 'obsessive woman'.

Tennison's and Rawlin's relationship ends when she fails to attend an evening meal with some potential clients who could save Rawlins's fledgling business. He confronts her in her darkly lit hallway, accusing her of caring 'more about your lads, your rapists, and your tarts'. To Rawlins, Tennison is a monstrous feminine threat for prioritising her alignment with signifiers of the abject and representatives of the proletariat over opportunities to grow his business or procreate. Whilst redrawing the boundary between the living and the dead produces a more efficient police force, Tennison's personal life is doomed because bourgeois domesticity and the abject are revealed as fundamentally incompatible. The ideology of the station scenes is partially undercut because the viewer is encouraged to share Rawlins's terrified reactive gazes, which frame Tennison's obsessive behaviour as monstrous and threatening to bourgeois patriarchal capitalism.

Existential *Frost*

In comparison to Tennison's home, which counteracts the feminist ideology of *Prime Suspect*'s station scenes, Frost's private life adds an existentialist dimension to the programme's critique of bourgeois culture. Existentialism re-emerged in the 1990s, as philosopher and sociologist Anthony Giddens believed self-identity had become a more reflexive project that a person continuously works and reflects on. Thus, one's notion of the self becomes more susceptible to fragility as 'the existential question of self-identity is bound up with the fragile nature of the biography which the individual "supplies" about herself' (Giddens 1991: 54). *Frost* is a series that shares an affinity with traditional existentialist writings keen to disassociate themselves from postwar Europe's bourgeoisie. Because individuals are not provided with any 'values or commands that could legitimize our behaviour', traditional existentialists feel that from the moment the individual is 'cast into the world, he is responsible for everything he does' (Sartre 2007 [1945]: 29). In line with this view, Denton's middle-class community, amidst social decline, looks to bourgeois expectations of the traditional family unit for guidance. At first Frost's home could seemingly be 'just another drab, suburban house with dated décor, cast in a palette of browns, dull greens and beige' (Piper 2015: 46). However, Frost actively demarcates himself from Denton's middle class. Like Jean-Paul Sartre's Roquentin, Frost is nauseated by bourgeois materialism, and its obsessive cleanliness in particular.[3] In 'Widows and orphans', Frost's neighbours Mr and Mrs Bright (Ian Dunn and Louise Yates) make persistent demands of Frost's private life. Mr Bright corners him on his way to work, requesting he fix his unkempt garden as 'it really isn't very nice'. Later, when Frost returns home in the dead of night, he pulls into his driveway to see the Brights standing at their front window with the lights on, decorating, and enthusiastically waving at him. Frost exhales in irritation, unable to exist in liberty from bourgeois judgements. Similarly, when Frost's wife dies he reveals 'she suddenly became more house-proud' when they discovered they could not have children, leading him to 'dread going home to see that look of disappointment in her face'. As existentialism prophesies, all these domestic scenes reveal that 'the effect of any form of materialism is to treat all men – including oneself – as objects' (Sartre 2007 [1945]: 41).

Frost's private life furthers the patriarchal logic of civilian scenes that depict female sexuality as a threat to the capitalist family. All the women in Frost's life represent a capitalist family unit, as vacuous as the systems of authority that existentialists felt were incapable of providing citizens with a responsible moral compass. Both Frost's wife and his sister-in-law conform to types of women that the prominent existentialist – and Sartre's wife – Simone de Beauvoir identifies as being complicit in their own subjugation. Frost's wife is what de Beauvoir calls a 'woman in love' because she sacrifices her identity for her privileged husband. Frost reveals the pressure he endured to 'make something of myself' that awakened suicidal thoughts. He explains he only won the George Cross medal because he was willing the assailant he disarmed to 'shoot me'. Like de Beauvoir's 'woman in love', Frost's wife is 'disappointed and vexed' that 'he does not live up to the images she has put in his place' (de Beauvoir 1993 [1953]: 665). Furthermore, Frost's sister-in-law, Marion (Annabel Leventon), stands in as de Beauvoir's 'narcissist', using her appearance as her sole source of value at the expense of freedom. Following her sister's death, Marion stays with Frost to look after him, but he finds his private life imposed on. Whenever he walks to his front door he can hear her aggressively ordering her husband over the phone to buy particular clothes. When in his front room, Marion moves ornaments, turns off lights Frost has already put on, and books him in for a vitamin B injection with his doctor. Visually, Marion's bright-pink blouse, large gold earrings, dyed blonde hair, red lipstick, pink blusher, and shining white teeth appear garish in sharp contrast to Frost's drab decor. The audience is encouraged to find her decisions to 'bestow as much care on the furniture and ornaments that enframe her as on her costume' as disagreeable as de Beauvoir found women displaying these narcissist tendencies to be (de Beauvoir 1993 [1953]: 646); thus the viewers are led to find Marion as insufferable as Frost does.

Overall, Frost's domestic life provides an existentialist critique of bourgeois domesticity, as he is trying to establish 'the human kingdom as a pattern of values in distinction from the material world' (Sartre 2007 [1945]: 41). According to *Frost*'s ideology, in accordance with contemporary horror film, de Beauvoir's archetypes must be overcome by a male protagonist, rather than functioning to teach women how to challenge their subjugation as de Beauvoir intended. Instead, Frost's wife and sister-in-law are merely an extension of the material world that hinders Frost's efficiency in pursuing justice. Richard Harris's previously scripted *Hunter's Walk* drew attention to how women were being othered by domestic work, as was being argued by Friedan and Germaine Greer. Now, when Frost discusses his wife's death in the pub, the camera zooms into his face further to cut out his wife's female carer from view. The audience is completely focused on Frost's perspective of women and how he feels that bourgeois domesticity and cleanliness are to blame for social decline and are psychologically damaging towards his ability to uphold law and order successfully.

Kafka

Whilst Frost maintains a Sartre-esque existential view of the world, Fitz is amidst the throes of an existential crisis, wearied by 'modernity's drive to make sanitised middling versions of us all' (Piper 2015: 79). Like the murderers, enduring a masculinity in crisis, Fitz finds comforting agency in his chaotic drinking habits and gambling addiction. Like a protagonist in a Kafka novel, Fitz is trapped between memories of a bygone world that he once belonged to, and a present world that he must 'attempt to come to terms with, within the 'social organism' of which he must 'find a place' (Winkler 1962: 42). As a former working-class Glaswegian, Fitz has socially ascended into 'middle class professionalism' (Creeber 2002: 170). Therefore Fitz is fixed amidst 'the public evaluation of masculinity' that leading sociologists felt had 'undergone a profound shift' (MacInnes 1998: 47). Fitz has been brought up in an environment where 'independence, detachment, courage, strength, rationality, will, backbone, and virility' were deemed to be 'manly virtues' (MacInnes 1998: 47). Now he is expected to perceive these traits as destructive 'vices' and must develop an ability to 'be flexible, to communicate, to empathise, to be soft, supportive or life affirming' (MacInnes 1998: 47). This quandary is first expressed when Fitz enters his house. As he rushes to find money for an awaiting taxi, the film camera frantically spins around Fitz whilst he navigates through the 'chaos of the domestic maze', unable fully to 'negotiate the unfamiliarity of his home' (Creeber 2002: 177). The camera momentarily stabilises when Fitz clings on to a whisky bottle, enabling him to regain his footing on the journey to his study, where he can drink in peace in the company of a large poster of actor Humphrey Bogart. In his study the camera steadies because Fitz is grounded by the hard-boiled model of masculinity, synonymous with Bogart, that is 'tough, stoic, honest, and loyal to his own values, fighting for a lone battle against urban chaos' (Munt 1994: 3). This contrasts sharply with Fitz's demeanour in the lounge, where he has to ask his son Mark (Kieran O'Brien) for money three times before his panicked request is understood. In relation to these alienating communal areas, Fitz finds solace in his study or bathroom, where he can drink or, as we see in the first episode, tearfully mourn his murdered student behind locked doors.

However, as the series develops, its domestic scenes increasingly present Fitz's stoicism as destructive to the mental and physical health of himself and his family. Where the bathroom once provided comforting solace, in 'To be a somebody', Fitz willingly locks himself in there to drink whisky when experiencing what appears to be the onset of a heart attack (later diagnosed as a panic attack). Unlike Frost, Fitz acclimatises to the domestic arena. However, this is only because his wife, Judith (Barbara Flynn), is able to recalibrate his Bogart-inspired wordview, underpinning his Kafka-esque crisis, closer towards her own perspective. The disputes they have in the kitchen 'associated with genres such as the female melodrama or soap opera' reformulate Fitz's perspective (Creeber 2002: 176). Not only was their arguing in the kitchen a trigger for Fitz's panic attack; in the same episode Judith uses the same room forcibly to instruct Fitz to stop gambling. Similarly, in 'One day a lemming will fly', when preparing a meal Judith presents Fitz with a bank statement to explain the financial predicament his gambling is causing their family. The poster of Kafka is prominently displayed next to her head when she states, 'you like a crisis, it gives you an excuse to drink and gamble', exposing Fitz's existentialism as a deliberate act of self-indulgence.

Once Fitz acknowledges Judith's point of view he can face 'the limitations and boundaries of his hard boiled persona' and embrace 'family intimacy and emotional responsibility' (Creeber 2002: 176). Following their argument in 'One day a lemming will fly', the episode concludes with Fitz walking out into the garden on a bright summer's day. As he enters the garden the camera zooms out into a bird's-eye view to observe the whole family comfortably sharing the space. Then, in 'Men should weep', once it transpires that Judith is five months pregnant she lies on the couch in the centre of the living room whilst Fitz kneels by her side in a brightly lit space, aurally saturated by birdsong from outside, and with a large, bay-window view of their idyllic garden. Bathed in sunlight they profess their love for one another. At last Fitz appears comfortable in the space he felt disoriented by in the first episode. Thus a solution is found to the perceived masculinity in crisis, as the 'problems caused by the confusion of sexual genesis and sexual difference' have been appropriately balanced (MacInnes 1998: 59).

Examining the private life of each protagonist reveals how, in accordance with the conservatism of horror-film ideology, each series longs to reinstate a division between the 'home as a space of femininity and leisure and the public world as a place of masculinity' to offset 1990s social decline (Brunsdon *et al.* 1997a: 19). Despite *Prime Suspect*'s radical feminist critique of the misogynist Metropolitan police force, Tennison's home life grows increasingly darker and isolated as she becomes obsessed with the abject underclass in a professional capacity that turns her into a monstrous feminine figure. Frost's longing for a return to a public/private dichotomy is driven by an existential distaste for bourgeois cleanliness that needs to be contained for having obsessed middle England with the inhumane, vacuous pursuit of materialism. However, *Cracker* suggests that domesticity, as the realm of femininity and leisure, can provide a moral compass and comforting sanctuary for those who are amidst the throes of a masculinity in crisis and are increasingly tempted by criminality. Despite each protagonist's successfully rebellious working practices, then, the detective figure is in their most vulnerable state yet when at home, suggesting that some suggests that some sort of wider social intervention is required, beyond rational-actor law-and-order policy, to reverse wider societal, moral decline.

The Cops

With feature-length ITV police series dominating television ratings, the BBC fought back in 1998 with *The Cops*. This series assesses New Labour's attempts to reverse rising levels of crime, which reformulated a rational-actor approach to law and order. Following the work of uniformed police in the fictional town of Stanton (in reality Bolton), *The Cops* ran for three series and won a BAFTA for best drama series in 1998 and 1999. Producer Tony Garnett's World Productions had already gained prominence for J. C. Wilsher's controversial *Between the Lines* (BBC, 1992–1994) and its depiction of the Criminal Investigations Bureau's work on police corruption.[4] Alternatively, *The Cops* was revolutionary because it was the first police series recorded on digital betacam instead of film. The lightweight and cheap, yet high quality, digital video format meant eight minutes of an episode could be shot in one day over a greater number of locations. Operating with a 'low budget' for a 'minority channel' (i.e. BBC Two) provided Garnett's team with a degree of creative freedom (quoted in Cooke 2015a: 191). Therefore, the conventional two-camera set-up, which obeys the rules of continuity editing, was banned in favour of capturing events with a single camera on one axis. Camera operators were usually unaware of what would happen, and so had to pull focus quickly to capture events. By following the action rather than shaping it a heightened 'reality' was created whereby 'what was being enacted was an unrepeatable event' witnessed together by the camera and audience (Garnett 1998: n.p.).

Unwittingly this verisimilitude is similar to the mode of realism employed by docusoaps, which dominated weekday evenings with 8–12 million viewers. Programmes including *Airline* (ITV, 1998–2006), *Airport* (BBC, 1996–2008), *Clampers* (BBC, 1998), and *Driving School*

(ITV, 1997) also used digital cameras to scale down production and enhance a viewer's sense of 'unmediated connectedness' (Biressi and Nunn 2005: 38). Docusoaps were different from straightforward documentaries because they captured the day-to-day lives of service-industry workers through a distinctive 'emotional realism' (Biressi and Nunn 2005: 71). People's stories are 'interleaved in soap opera style' as personality clashes, prolonged arguments, and relationships govern each episode (Biressi and Nunn 2005: 63). In sharing this digital technology *The Cops* is partially invested in this emotional realism, as the camera focuses on the facial expressions of characters reacting to events so that the viewer can make sense of what occurs through the way in which characters emotionally process them.

Stanton station

As a result of this emotional realism, the division between a person's professional and personal identities is significantly blurred. In the very first scene, Mel Draper (Katy Cavanagh), in a nightclub toilet having just snorted a line of cocaine, discovers she is running late for work. As Draper catches a taxi and runs into her workplace it is revealed that she is a police constable as she hurriedly enters the station locker room. Here, through one long unbroken take, each officer changes into their uniform and cleanses their appearance of their private identity. Whilst the camera fleetingly captures Draper brushing her hair and PC Danny Rylands (Jack Mardsen) straightening his tie, camera movement is motivated by characters' reactions to certain lines of dialogue. The camera pans from face to face as characters ask questions of one another's night before: for example how long they were out drinking, and members of staff they would like to sleep with. A camera move is prompted once a character directs a comment towards somebody else, and so the camera moves to capture the respondent's reaction. Whilst, in terms of narrative significance, the purpose of the scene is to establish the start of the constabulary's working day, the camera remains invested in the personal views of officers and how they are informed by their private lives. The camera's movements counteract the characters' readying for work because they emphasise that the subjections of each officer will dictate their conduct throughout their shift. The uniform and surrounding station space are largely arbitrary, because for the first time in the genre police officials are civilians first and foremost who happen to work as police officers.

As in docusoaps, each officer is led by their 'assumptions, habits and attitudes' as prejudices, petty rivalries and personal taste determine how work is carried out (Lacey 2007: 148). However, the severe humanitarian consequences of their prejudices are made clear. PC Natalie Metcalf's (Clare McGlinn) prolonged harassment of Brian Skillet (Steve Ramsden), as revenge for breaking her arm when she previously worked as a housing officer, results in his death. Similarly, PC Roy Bramwell (John Henshaw) plants drugs on Vincent Graves (Paul Oldham) to ensure he receive a six-month prison sentence. Bramwell acts because he holds Graves responsible for the death of his close friend Sergeant Poole, who died from a heart attack when chasing Bramwell. In 1998 the Human Rights Bill had passed through Parliament to bring British law into line with the European Convention on Human Rights. Its promise that 'no one shall be subjected to torture or to inhuman or degrading treatment or punishment' has not affected the working practices of Stanton officers (HMSO 1998: 16).

The Cops partly blames the hierarchical structure of the police force for such inhumane policing. Chief Inspector Newland (Mark Chatterton), with a photograph of Tony Blair framed above his desk, represents 'the new order of accountability' and 'locus of power' (Lacey 2007: 148). The New Labour Government further progressed public-sector reform by ensuring the Inspectorate monitored efficient police delivery through a series of thematic inspection reports in 1997. Constabularies were required to provide 'unequivocal evidence of progress towards compliance' (Brain 2010: 270). Whereas previously the Chief Constable had enjoyed moderate financial freedoms in achieving local targets, now all had to comply with national guidelines, fuelling criticism of the continuing empowerment of a 'policy-making elite' (Wall 1998: 316). Correspondingly, the gulf between the upper echelons of management and PCs is 'unmistakable' (Lacey 2007: 148). In marked contrast to the 'local argot' of his officers, Newland prefers management-speak, talking of a 'client responsive ... proactive approach' (Lacey 2007: 148). When Newland reveals he will not pass on Sergeant Edward Giffen's (Rob Dixon) complaint to the Chief Constable regarding Bramwell's concerning conduct, Newland is busy readying his office for a conference. Newland interrupts Giffen's reservations to criticise canteen staff for providing food that pales in comparison to the quality of food provided at a previous London event. Compared to Tennison's and Bilborough's devotion to teamwork, or Mullet's obsession with his team's public image, Newland prioritises impressing his London-based superiors. This depiction of authority is weary of modern law-and-order policy's tendency to be increasingly 'technicist and state-centred' in offering 'top-down expert solutions for social problems and disorders' (Garland and Sparks 2000b: 10).

Left realism and New Labour

In advance of *The Cops*' broadcast there had been a large shift in criminological consciousness within the academy. 'Left realism', created by Jock Young, John Lea, and Roger Matthews, criticised left-leaning criminology for ignoring vulnerable, working-class victims of crime. Attention was now drawn to those living in high crime areas whose experiences of 'mugging, burglary and interpersonal violence … have a real and destructive impact on the poor' (Lea and Young 1993: vii). Correspondingly, Lea and Young's 'square of crime' theory argues that crime materialises from a combination of the behaviours enacted by, and structural preconditions underlying, front-line agents representing the State, the victim, society, and the criminal offender. Controlling crime involves 'intervention at each part of the square of crime' (Young 1992: 41). This view influenced the New Labour Government and its 1998 Crime and Disorder Act. A balance was now sought between tackling offending behaviour and intervening in the socio-economic conditions that made such behaviour a rational option for many. Aspects of the 1998 Act abided by rational-actor thinking, such as reversing the rule of *doli incapax* to ensure fourteen-year-olds were personally culpable for their actions. Simultaneously, the 1998 Act also subscribed to aspects of the predestined-actor model, as youth offending teams were deployed to divert young people from offending to re-engaging in education. However, this Government policy was criticised by the left realism school for constructing a binary of inclusion/exclusion where 'the excluded exist in an area which is spatially segregated and socially and morally distinctive' (Young 2003: 390). It was felt that a model for making criminal justice 'democratically accountable' had been turned into a 'device for the authoritarian regulation of the poor and marginalised' (Lea 2010: 148).

Skeetsmore

The Cops engages with left realism as crimes occur exclusively within the Skeetsmore council estate, where vulnerable residents are exposed to regular drug addiction, domestic abuse, theft, and violence. Garnett's inflexible rule for writers was that the narrative follow the actions of PCs to 'create a sense for the viewer that she or he had accompanied the police on their journey through a society, experiencing the violence, poverty and social disintegration as they did' (Lacey 2007: 147). After a dead body is found, PC Draper pieces together evidence to learn the deceased died from his daughter's neglect. Theresa Riley (Caroline Pegg) was stealing her dead father's prescribed diazepam and pension to feed her heroin addiction, resentful of having cared for her abusive, housebound father since she was fourteen. In another instance, PC Rylands dismisses Dave Wilcox's (Malcolm Pitt) pleas to retrieve his six-year-old from his mentally ill ex-wife Pauline (Lisa Millett), who has failed to return her daughter home after her allocated hours. Rylands repeatedly dismisses what appear to be trivial concerns to discover alongside the viewer that Pauline has killed her daughter through a drug overdose. Therefore, by depicting the types of abuse vulnerable members of the working class could be unduly and repeatedly victim to, *The Cops* recalibrates dominant societal conceptions of an 'underclass'. Whereas Murray's writings were popular for characterising illegitimacy, crime, and joblessness as a matter of personal negligence, here an audience is encouraged to confront 'the results of grinding poverty through the generations' (Garnett 1998: n.p.). Killings committed by members of a marginalised underclass arise not from evil premeditation, as depicted in *Prime Suspect*, but from a complex interrelation of abuse, poverty, and mental illness.

Whilst, as in docusoaps, all events are framed through the emotional perception of white-collar protagonists, *The Cops* returns this perspective to the 'terrain of social realism' (Lacey 2007: 144). *The Cops* channels British television's stark, unnostalgic tradition of televisual social realism, which had, in part, been instigated by *Z Cars* (BBC, 1962–1978) to inform the *Wednesday Play* (BBC, 1964–1970) and *Play for Today* (BBC, 1970–1984). *The Cops* also socially extends 'dramatic material to areas of life which had been evidently excluded' by entering 'parts of our society that we are not shown on television' (Williams 2013: 214; Garnett 1998: n.p.). Also, as Skeetsmore is clearly a 'class-based community in crisis', *The Cops* also reflects British social-realist cinema of the 1990s that revealed how deindustrialisation and mass unemployment 'altered the social character of the British working class' (Lacey 2007: 145; Hill 2000: 179). However, this is not the feel-good social realism of *Brassed Off* (1996) or *The Full Monty* (1997) that revolves around 'a recovery of pride and self-dignity in the face of economic adversity and social decay' (Hill 2000: 179). Nor is this the progressive social realism of *The Wednesday Play* or *Play for Today* underlined by a character's 'politicised perspective on events' to instigate change (Williams 2013: 183). Instead, Garnett's series channels a similar pessimism to that which dictates Ken Loach's Channel 4 Films, from *Riff-Raff* (1991) to *The Navigators* (2001), as individual acts of frustration constitute 'the main form of resistance to the status quo' (Hill 2000: 179). Underage sex workers and shoplifters Chris (Andrew Whyment), Sarah Midgely (Vinette

Robinson), and Ryan Tunce (Alan Halsall) reoffend because the 1998 Crime and Disorder Act has not delivered the resources required to deter those predisposed to crime. Instead, a PC's role is to segregate the poor and marginalised Skeetsmore residents from the adjoining middle-class Stanton community: i.e. to 'put a lid on the rubbish', as Giffen instructs his officers.

Lives of officers

Interestingly, *The Cops*' thematic concerns, which can be linked with the broader developments of 1990s social-realist cinema, are communicated through a key visual device that would be refined through forthcoming social-realist films. In using handheld digital cameras, *The Cops* treads a fine line between utilising the 'emotional realism' of docusoaps whilst concurrently foreshadowing the 'horizontality' of contemporary British social realism. Much like the films of Lynne Ramsay, Shane Meadows, Andrea Arnold, and Duane Hopkins, *The Cops*' camera relies on its horizontal axis to provide a combination of 'motion and a restricted view' (Dave 2017: 130). Here 'an uneasy sensation of being deprived access to off-screen space and a feeling of vulnerability' are 'naturally intensified in a narrative context of crime in which we are primed to expect danger' (Dave 2017: 130). For example, when Draper cautiously enters Riley's flat to find his dead body, the camera tentatively follows her from behind. Then, upon her seeing the body, the camera pans horizontally with Draper as she backs out into the corridor to vomit in abject repulsion. Similarly, when PCs Colin Jellicoe (Steve Garti) and Dean Wishaw (Danny Seward) are trapped in their police van by surrounding rioters, the camera remains rooted to the inside of the van, anxiously panning from side to side to capture rioters as they menacingly approach, jeer, and knock on the van's bonnet. The handheld camera's hesitancy actualises the apprehensiveness of police officers and compounds their vulnerability in forbidding situations.

Therefore, *The Cops* can be considered a progenitor of contemporary social-realist films that have perfected 'horizontality' as a 'political aesthetic'. As identified by Paul Dave in his analysis of contemporary British social realism, a fear of falling into instantaneous poverty overhangs every character and informs the camera's hesitancy. Draper is a former resident of Skeetsmore, aware she could have suffered a similar fate to Skeetsmore residents. She even identifies her former schoolmate Nico (Paul Simpson) in hospital, having been beaten up by his drug-dealer employers. Furthermore, PC Jaz Shundara (Parvez Qadir) feels compelled to stay employed as a police officer despite the racial discrimination he endures at work and the shunning he receives from his surrounding community because his father asserts it is a 'secure salary'.

The hesitancy underpinning this horizontality often arises from characters struggling to come to terms with what Giddens termed a 'new individualism'. In previous generations the exercise of a person's individual choice was largely determined by the professional life-course of their parents. According to Giddens, however, life in the 1990s had 'become an open project, creating new demands and anxieties' for people who were now tasked with pursuing a life that suited their particular needs and ambitions (Giddens 1992: 8). With people aged under forty increasingly living alone to develop their career before committing to heterosexual cohabitation, the number of single-person households between 1979 and 1997 increased from 370,000 to over 1 million (Pugh 2017: 466). In reaction to this socio-cultural shift, *The Cops* is concerned with how the anxieties of PC protagonists manifest privately. When PC Mike Thompson (Steve Jackson) returns home, having admitted to himself he has fallen out of love with his fiancée, his partner Colleen (Suzanne Hall) is leaving for work. The camera remains focused on Thompson's despondent face as he slumps against the wall and Colleen instructs him to change his shoes and attend his final suit-fitting for their wedding. Throughout the sequence the camera remains fixed on Thompson's face as he vacantly stares ahead, seemingly depressed and unable to interact.

Repeatedly docusoaps provide revelatory scenes where emotionally articulate white-collar workers relish their conflicts with others to achieve social mobility. Such programming believes a citizen's 'most pressing obligation to society is to empower her or himself privately' (Hay and Ouellette 2008: 3). As in a docusoap, then, a viewer processes Mike's returning home after a day's work through his emotional interpretation of the event. However, unlike a docusoap, the scene does not use this emotional realism to endorse the social mobility that new individualism afforded certain people. Instead, *The Cops* reveals the psychological consequences of new individualism as we see Thompson unable come to terms with the wrong life-choice he has made. Correspondingly, viewers witness officers failing to exercise control over their private affairs. PC Rylands is unable to accept that his younger, student girlfriend Jenny (Sarah Byng) wants to end their relationship. In line with Giddens she find a 'new balance' between her 'individual and collective responsibilities' as she wants to prioritise her new friends, sport, and studies over Rylands because she 'can't fit it all in' (Giddens 1991: 37). In contrast, Rylands is unable to appreciate the 'consequences of what we do and the lifestyle habits we adopt'; he is so frustrated with her decision that the argument escalates and he physically assaults Jenny and her friend within their student accommodation (Giddens 1991: 37). The emotional distress is furthered by the camera's wobbly horizontal movements as it is struggles to capture and follow the highly charged assault in its entirety. Ultimately, then, *The Cops'* visual interest in the emotional realism of its police-officer protagonists is anchored by an unnerving social-realist horizontality tied to the anxieties of young professionals struggling to cope with the pressures of new individualism.

Conclusion

The 1990s were interesting sociologically, politically, and philosophically. The increasingly global and competitive nature of economic and political life presented a 'puzzling diversity of options and possibilities' under which one had to construct one's own identity (Giddens 1991: 3). Now a person's ontological security was increasingly susceptible to existential introspection and anxiety. As such, popular 1990s British police series have been recognised for working through the 'anxieties and exclusions of contemporary citizenship' (Brunsdon 2000: 197). The use of film-camera technology in *Prime Suspect*, *Frost*, and *Cracker* utilises horror-film iconography over a number of feature-length episodes to reassess 'the boundaries between the human and the non-human' (Creed 2003: 14). In each instance an outsider is required to circumnavigate the increasingly competitive target-led culture of the station to achieve true justice, be it a woman challenging patriarchal sexism, an unorthodox detective who refuses to abide by the Chief Constable's obsession with public relations, or a psychologist who is better equipped to deal with and unpick the minds of psychologically disturbed murderers.

In terms of civilian life a visual appetite for violent crime is used to access fears of social collapse. *Prime Suspect* uses slasher-film iconography to depict a highly polarised society where a feral underclass threatens the safety of law-abiding middle classes. Whilst *Frost's* style is grounded in the gothic television tradition of horror, ideologically it suggests that the sexual transgressions of middle-class women are what aggravate recessionary gloom. Meanwhile, *Cracker* intercepts this binary by using the assaultive gaze of the slasher film to understand why certain working-class men in crisis seek agency over middle-class people. However, in capturing the homes of police-officer characters, *Prime Suspect's* subversion of police-drama ideology is largely undone when the audience is encouraged to share the terrified reactions of Tennison's partner as her obsessive and monstrous behaviour threaten bourgeois patriarchal capitalism. The existential Frost distances himself from Denton's middle-class pursuit of vacuous materialism. Fitz, however, in trying to overcome his Kafka-esque masculinity in crisis, embraces 'family intimacy and emotional responsibility' (Creeber 2002: 176).

The police series began in the 1990s as a genre utilising horror-film iconography to prey on societal fears. Then, by the decade's end, it returned to its social-realist roots, albeit with a more pessimistic flavour mediated by digital betacam and docudrama's emotional realism. The use of digital cameras in BBC Two's *The Cops*, for the first time in the genre's history, saturates all settings with a distinct anxiousness. Divisions between the public station and private civilian homes are largely arbitrary, as police-officer characters are civilians first and foremost who happen to work for the police. In keeping with Loach's pessimist social realism of the time, the extent of the suffering endured by the underclass Skeetsmore community is uncovered. The way in which the lightweight digital cameras frame the young police-officer characters partially utilises docusoap's emotional realism and acts partly as an early progenitor of social-realist 'horizontality'. This political aesthetic unearths the inherent precariousness underlying new individualism to expose how the role and responsibilities of the police can be inhumanely exercised over others below themselves in the social chain.

Notes

1 *Prime Suspect* established the distinctive format of broadcasting a three-hour-long, feature-length episode over two instalments, a practice subsequently adopted by *Cracker*.
2 Neal had been harbouring this idea since working as a producer on *Prime Suspect 2*.
3 See Sartre (2000 [1938]).
4 J. C. Wilsher had been a long-term writer on *The Bill*.

The 2000s: looking to the past 5

> Just your regular run of the mill time travelling cop show.
> Life on Mars co-creator Matthew Graham (Graham 2008: n.p.)

A macabre visual style associated with the horror film, combined with the sensibility of modern social realism, made 1990s police series decidedly worrisome in working through the anxieties surrounding contemporary citizenship. Following the turn of the millennium, however, digital cameras, digital editing techniques and special effects refreshed the police series with a flamboyant visual style to navigate the postmodern condition. *Waking the Dead* (BBC, 2000–2011), *New Tricks* (BBC, 2003–2015), and *Life on Mars* (BBC, 2006–2007) all make sense of the 2000s by excavating memories of the past. *Waking the Dead* and *New Tricks* depict the work of specialist teams assembled to fix unsolved cold cases. Comparatively, Detective Chief Inspector Sam Tyler's (John Simm) time travel in *Life on Mars* permits him to solve past crimes in the 1970s directly. To make sense of an era increasingly saturated by information technology, each series channels the iconography of the science-fiction genre with a self-consciously playful tone. This chapter examines how these series provide differing views as to how technological innovations can be balanced effectively with traditional methods of detection to combat crime and maintain a stable society. Then the chapter considers how each series explores the impact the internet and associated surveillance technologies had on civilian life, given increased postmodern awareness that a person's identity can be fragmentary, temporary, and contingent over time.

The digital age

The 2000s heralded a digital age of broadcasting. BBC Four and BBC3 were launched on 2 March 2002 and 9 February 2003 respectively to increase the BBC's drama provision. To compete with this changing digital landscape, on 2 February 2004 ITV merged its two largest franchises, Granada and Carlton, into a £5.8 billion broadcasting giant, ITV plc. This ITV conglomerate would oversee the running of ITV2, launch ITV3 on 1 November 2004, and then introduce ITV4 a year later on 1 November 2005. Original drama produced for ITV2, BBC Three, and Channel 4's *E4* (launched 18 January 2001) was aimed at the eighteen to thirty-five demographic and so made full use of digital-camera capabilities to create a 'visual style distinguished by rapid cutting, unusual camera angles, zooms, slow motion and a colourful mise-en- scène' (Cooke 2015a: 238). These new technological norms became commonplace within mainstream drama. Meanwhile, the new television regulator, Office of Communications (Ofcom) was legislated by the 2003 Communications Act to promote greater competition among content providers. Therefore, certain dramas often employed 'a faster narrative tempo and a quirky, non-naturalistic style' to maintain visibility within an overcrowded television schedule (Cooke 2013: 126). This stylistic shift had a seismic effect on the police series as the sixth and penultimate *Prime Suspect: The Last Witness* (9 and 10 November 2003) cultivated a 'glossier look' and a 'hi tech finish' to foreground a sense of 'spectacle' (Jermyn 2013: 107–108). Compared to the first *Prime Suspect* (7 and 8 April 1991), which rejected the glossiness of *Inspector Morse* (ITV, 1987–2000), the programme's style had been subsumed by a significant change to British television drama's verisimilitude.

Policing a new century

In addition to this change in televisual realism the police series also developed an increasing fascination with how modern science and intelligence-gathering were redefining the nature of British policing. The Home Office stipulated that to reverse the fall in detection and conviction rates, 'advances in technology must be matched by the police service being able to exploit them to the full' through the newly designed National Intelligence Model (NIM) (Home Office 2001: 19). Accordingly, intelligence collection was now undertaken by each constabulary's Intelligence Bureau. Intelligence officers and analysts would collate and evaluate masses of data and produce strategic assessments every three months to determine their control-strategy priorities. In 2004 an evaluation of NIM across Lancashire, Surrey, and the West Midlands found that consultative meetings were dominated by 'concerns about performance', with a resistance to NIM based on 'ignorance' and 'dislike of its academic structure and language' (John and Maguire 2004: 5). Uniformed officers often felt the local intelligence unit was 'detracting from the real policing of the streets', and intelligence units complained because only up to three of their constables were operational at any one time, meaning they did not have 'enough of a proactive capability to use the intelligence' received (James 2013: 165).

The National Intelligence Model was also accompanied by the Home Office's DNA expansion programme. In April 2000 the England and Wales police forces were provided funding to take DNA samples from all known offenders and extract more DNA material from crime scenes. Subsequently there was a four-fold increase in DNA detections, with 3 per cent of the total police workforce employed in forensic-science posts by the 2004–2005 financial year (Green 2007). However, a Home Office report noted that whilst the timeliness of DNA submissions was quickening there were 'significant delays in most of the forces in commencing an investigation following receipt of the identification' (Blakey 2002: viii). It also criticised the 'multiple false identities appearing on the National DNA Database', and so instructed chief officers to 'ensure that sampling policies are both clearly understood and implemented' (Blakey 2002: vii, x).

Waking the Dead

A fascination with forensics had been gaining momentum in the late 1990s following the transmission of *Silent Witness* (BBC, 1996–) and *Trial and Retribution* (ITV, 1997–2009). This interest culminated with *Waking the Dead*, which peaked at 9.2 million viewers and won an International Emmy in 2004. As one of the BBC's most successful programmes of the decade, *Waking the Dead* helped BBC One become 'the country's most watched channel for the first time since ITV surpassed it in 1956' (Piper 2015: 11). The series depicts the investigations of Detective Superintendent Peter Boyd's (Trevor Eve) Cold Case Unit. Boyd announces in the first episode that the unit's remit is to utilise 'new weapons' in the form of 'forensic expertise' and 'new psychological profiling' that can 'dig into the past' to ensure 'there is no longer such a thing as an unsolved crime'. Boyd's staff consists of psychologist Dr Grace Foley (Sue Johnston), Detective Sergeant Spencer Jordan (Wil Johnson), Detective Sergeant Amelia 'Mel' Silver (Claire Goose), and forensic pathologist Frankie Wharton (Holly Aird).

The role of technology

Following sceptical depictions of police stations in the 1990s, *Waking the Dead* reaffirms the essential nature of the station, given the technology affixed throughout the Cold Case Unit's offices. Often the camera is focally interested in the large, flat-screen televisions; laptop computers; closed-circuit television (CCTV) cameras; mobile phones; and bluetooth headsets that populate the space. The programme's enthusiasm towards the increased intelligence capabilities associated with these appliances is underscored by the technical wizardry employed by the camera itself. Rarely stationary, the camera effortlessly pans and tracks in long and smooth graceful motions to create the impression of a dynamic space operating at a faster tempo than previous detective units have managed. Often this slick, roaming camera revolves around key pieces of technology in isolated close-ups to provide them with an inherent mysticism. In the 'Pilot' (4 and 5 September 2000), when kidnapper-at-large James Marshall (Finbar Lynch) telephones Boyd, the scene commences with the camera focusing on Boyd's answer machine in his empty office in a close-up. The distressed sounds of the crying schoolgirl-hostage Jodie Whitemoor (Amelia Warner) emanating from the answer machine prompt the team to enter Boyd's office, where the camera awaits. As Whitemoor reveals Marshall's demands the camera revolves around the machine in a 360-degree motion, solely focusing on it before cutting to reveal the reactions of the detectives in a panning motion. Similarly, in the episodes 'The blind beggar' (25 and 26 June 2001) and 'Every breath you take' (9 and 10 July 2001), when uncovered CCTV footage is being analysed by the detectives, the camera focuses on the images being displayed on a flat TV screen. In these regular occurrences the technology is prioritised over observing the detectives' attitudinal markers (gesturing) in relation to their illocutionary markers (dialogue). The camera revels in the technology's ability to enhance the capabilities of the intelligence operatives.

This 'flashy aesthetic style' was also intrinsic to the US series *CSI: Crime Scene Investigation* (Channel 5, 2000–2015), which debuted on US television four months after *Waking the Dead*. Boyd's Cold Case Unit is equally imbued with an air of 'spectacle' as spaces are dramatically illuminated by reflective surfaces, glass partitions, bright overhead lights, and stainless-steel fixtures (Jermyn 2013: 108). The *mise-en-scène* of the detectives' offices shares a close affinity with the literary science-fiction genre, which also provides an 'imaginative framework' that is relatively 'alternative to the author's empirical environment' (Suvin 1988: 37). A focal point of this imaginative framework is a small laboratory with four glass walls obtaining a central position within the Cold Case Unit that can be seen from any point in the space. This frequently enables pathologist Wharton to interrupt briefings, private meetings, intelligence-gathering, and interrogations with her forensic discoveries, immediately to alter and dictate the unit's line of enquiry. Located to the side of the laboratory behind a door are two purpose-built interview suites. Both suites can be overlooked simultaneously via an 'obs room' containing a pair of two-way mirrors. Often, interviews of suspects and witnesses are carried out simultaneously. Then, through the use of wireless bluetooth earpieces, detectives can inform those conducting an interrogation of new information obtained from the adjoining interview room, forensic discoveries in the lab next door, or breakthroughs in intelligence-gathering. The climactic, ten-minute ending to 'Every breath you take' is particularly demonstrative of how each member of the team can concentrate on their own area of expertise whilst sharing their findings with one another. The team know that either Detective Inspector Steven Maitland (Thomas Lockyer), his wife Fiona Maitland (Tessa Peake Jones), or daughter Anna Maitland (Paloma Baeza) murdered Sergeant Debbie Britten (Joanne Farrell). Anna is revealed as the murderer, following Silver's and Jordan's mobile-phone database searches and satellite scans, Wharton's concurrent discovery of glass fragments in Steven's coat pockets, Boyd's interrogation of Steven, and Foley's simultaneous psychological assessment of Anna. Each operative shares their discoveries in real time via their wireless headsets to pool their knowledge collectively and conclude Anna is the murderer.

This representation of detective work exceeds what was achievable in the real world, given the speed of forensic discoveries and the way various experts are able to work cohesively with little conflict over competing priorities or concerns about performance. In partial alignment with postmodernism, then, *Waking the Dead*'s depiction of the station maintains a degree of Jean Baudrillard's 'hyperreal'. Alongside other dominant representations of police stations and forensic labs, police series of the 2000s were beginning to bolster perceptions of what forensic detection could achieve by 'substituting the signs of the real for the real' (Baudrillard 1994: 2).[1]

Forensic humanism

Despite *Waking the Dead*'s close stylistic proximity to postmodern concerns, Martin Willis feels the high-tech *mise-en-scène* leads 'not to an appreciation of the wonders of forensic science but to the human narratives and actions that created that evidence' (Willis 2016: 45). This 'forensic humanism' comes directly from Boyd's leadership. Boyd has a photograph of his missing son placed on his desk to occupy his gaze and obstruct his view of the unit's central lab, as a reminder of his humanistic reasoning for forensically investigating cold cases. In 'Burn out' (18 and 19 June 2001), Boyd gives into Marina Coleman's (Angela Griffin) pleas that his team investigate the suspicious circumstances surrounding her father's death after looking at the photo. His missing son reminds him of his own first-hand experience of the trauma that Coleman is going through, and this coaxes him into accepting the case. Repeatedly Boyd affirms that his job is to pursue the 'truth ... at any cost' and that 'we don't do this to satisfy ... performance targets'. In 'A simple sacrifice' (2 and 3 July 2001), Deputy Assistant Commissioner Ralph Christie (Simon Kunz) instructs Boyd to prove the guilt of convicted child killer Annie Keel (Harriet Walter), in light of her appeal to the European Court of Human Rights, because being 'tough on crime is a vote winner' and 'innocence costs money'. Instead, Boyd uses his resources to uncover the truth and prove Keel's innocence, causing Christie great embarrassment. Boyd's commitment to the truth is a far cry from the cynicism underpinning 1990s detectives in equivalent positions of power, who prioritise results through fear of being chastised by the press, their superiors, and the public. Therefore Boyd's forensic humanism overrides the station's close aesthetic proximity to postmodernism. Instead, underpinning the station's somewhat fantastical *mise- en- scène* and marvelling camerawork is an ideological commitment to achieving a definitive, accurate, and uncontested understanding of the past: a position that is antithetical to postmodern thought, as postmodernism sought to complicate perceptions of history by highlighting the 'incredulity toward metanarratives' (Lyotard 1984: xxiv).

Essentially, Boyd's Cold Case Unit functions as a model of technological utopianism that utilises technology to achieve 'the maximum fulfilment of individual human potential' (Booker and Thomas 2009: 65). Rather than being a postmodern, hyperreal space that dismisses a utopia as an unachievable 'lost object', the Cold Case Unit offices are invested in the ideals of the Enlightenment, resembling utopian sci-fi novels published around the turn of the twentieth century (Baudrillard 1994: 123). In a similar manner to Edward Bellamy's *Looking Backward* (2000 [1888]), William Morris's *News from Nowhere* (1993 [1890]), and H. G. Wells's *A Modern Utopia* (2006 [1905]), there is repeated 'faith in the ability of reason and rationality' to 'build a better world' through a dependence on technological efficiency (Booker and Thomas 2009: 76). In line with Marxist understandings of technological utopianism, by alleviating his staff from Christie's job-target pressures, Boyd prevents his detectives from being alienated by their labour through an 'embracing and celebration of the possibilities of technology' (Levitas 1990: 131). Therefore, the Cold Case Unit's ideological relationship to technology serves as a guiding framework for forensic detection. In comparison to the widespread resistance that intelligence policing was receiving, on account of individuals' concerns with their own performance, the 'flashy' camerawork and *mise-en-scène* of *Waking the Dead* are grounded by Boyd's leadership. The working environment overseen by Boyd removes detectives and analysts from these hierarchical pressures so that staff can focus all their energies on enhancing their individual specialisms and capabilities. Central to this working practice is a communications system where all knowledge and discoveries can be pooled together simultaneously and effectively. These communication technologies are what enable a range of specialists to work cohesively, continuously to guarantee civil society's safety and security.

New Tricks

A positive audience response to a *New Tricks* pilot resulted in a full series being commissioned, which, with eleven subsequent series, managed consistently to maintain its BBC One primetime 9 p.m. slot. Averaging 7–8 million viewers meant *New Tricks* was the most watched television drama after *Coronation Street* (ITV, 1960–) and *EastEnders* (BBC, 1985–). This success, in part, came from maintaining its baby-boomer target audience. Those born between 1930 and 1960 were now dominating the broadcasting market, as younger viewers were turning to alternative viewing platforms in greater numbers. The programme depicts the work of the Unsolved Crimes and Open Case Squad (UCOS), overseen by Detective Superintendent Sandra Pullman (Amanda Redman) and staffed by retired senior Metropolitan Police and widower detective Jack Halford (James Bolam); ageing playboy Gerry Standing (Dennis Waterman); and Brian Lane (Alun Armstrong), haunted by a death he oversaw in custody. The squad are provided cases from the 1970s to the early 1990s where new evidence challenges the original conclusion. UCOS's services are required because an understanding of the working practices followed during the original investigations is needed to uncover the truth.

Smart policing

New Tricks defies the digital aesthetic that dominated primetime television drama in the 2000s, as embraced by *Waking the Dead*. Instead of employing a fast editing tempo and mobile camerawork, *New Tricks* utilises what has been dubbed a 'traditional, functional TV aesthetic' with a camera that barely moves, a slower editing pace, and a *mise-en-scène* that exists to 'serve the text and not to bring attention to itself'

(Wickham 2010: 72). The UCOS office does not contain an air of spectacle, as the team occupy a damp, dark, and quotidian office in the basement of the Metropolitan Police building. Rather than the latest in communication technologies being affixed to the space, any technology featured, whilst essential, retains an understated and less domineering presence that does not invite the camera's fixated gaze. Each detective has a computer on their desk that is placed to one side and is usually displaying a screensaver. The four detectives each have a desk to themselves, and each one is placed just in front of one of the office's four walls. Sat behind their desks the detectives can maintain eye contact with one another without being obstructed by technologies. Instead of there being a lab centrally attached to the office, the large, unused central floor space ensures that detectives can engage in conversation with one another whilst at their desks to exchange ideas and memories when processing the physical cold-case files.

Whilst *New Tricks* values the developments made in forensic science, the series is not visually fascinated by technology, nor is it narratively anchored by forensic discoveries. Science complicates UCOS's enquiries, causing the detectives to pool their knowledge, intuition, and memories in person to overcome the puzzling stalemate often created by forensic evidence. In the pilot, 'The Chinese job' (27 March 2003), UCOS are assigned to prove gangster Roddy Wringer (Jon Finch) murdered nightclub waitress Anna Dubrovski following Wringer's overturned life sentence. The investigation begins with a forensic report informing them that microscopic blood particles belonging to a woman have been found under Dubrovski's fingernails, and that traces of an unidentified man's blood have been found on Wringer's shoes. Upon this discovery each detective returns to their desk and sifts through case files long into the evening. Eventually Pullman makes a breakthrough. Sitting at her desk in deep thought, looking forwards into the empty, central office space whilst her computer displays a screensaver behind her, Pullman instructs her detectives to visit the DNA lab in the morning to cross-match the blood discovered on Wringer's shoe with the blood of murder victim Willy Sefton. This instruction leads directly to the revelation that Dubrovski's blood was planted on Wringer's shoe by police during the initial investigation in order to frame him for Dubrovski's murder. In actual fact, it was his wife, Gaynor (Jill Baker), who murdered Dubrovski, and the microscopic blood particles under Dubrovski's fingernails belong to her. Unwittingly, the original investigator, Ian Lovett (Michael Culver), in deciding to plant Dubrovski's blood on Wringer's shoe, had caused traces of Sefton's blood on the same shoe to be overlooked, thus concealing Wringer's part in Sefton's murder. Similarly, in 'Good work rewarded' (22 April 2004), none of the DNA samples extracted from the suspects can be matched with the DNA found on the deceased's body. This is because murderer Stewart Pimley (Jamie Glover) actually has a different father from his brother David (Tim Downie), whose DNA had incorrectly eliminated Stewart from the enquiry. Also, in 'ID parade' (1 April 2004), Philip Sheppard's (Paul Brightwell) fingerprint identified on the uncovered murder weapon that killed twenty-seven-year old WPC Kate Daniels in 1987 proves to be a red herring. Therefore *Waking the Dead*'s unwavering faith in forensics and communication technology is challenged. In *New Tricks*, detectives are successful through their ability to interpret, cross reference, and process scientific evidence together in person.

Analogously, modern intelligence policing often hinders, rather than aids, UCOS's investigations. The team's only intelligence officer, Jon Clarke (Chiké Okonkwo), has the cumbersome job title 'Information Management Resource Compilation and Technology Liaison Officer'. Correspondingly, Clarke is relegated to the background, interrupting the detectives with trivial matters and inconsequential information for the purposes of comic relief. Visually there is a clear divide, as Clarke is often typing in the corner of the office in a separate shot from the detectives whilst they congregate in the middle of the space to share their intelligence.

Often Clarke's interjections, which impinge on the momentum of the investigation, relay directives sent directly from Deputy Assistant Commissioner Donald Bevan (Nicholas Day). In 'ID parade' Standing discovers, through the autopsy report, that the original investigation overlooked WPC Daniels's stomach contents, suggesting she met somebody she knew before her murder. Clarke stalls Standing's line of enquiry with a phone call from Bevan's personal assistant demanding to see Pullman immediately. Unable to think on his feet, Clarke defies Pullman's instructions to tell Bevan that she is out of the office, and instead tells Bevan 'she'll be right up', grinding the case to a halt in favour of a public-relations initiative planned by Bevan. Then, later in the episode, when Lane tries to figure out who could have killed Daniels, Clarke sits on the other side of Lane's desk instructing him on what to tell the newspapers 'about the application of technology in the push towards smart policing' for Bevan's press open day. Frustrated with this management-speak, Lane confiscates Clarke's clipboard and instead asks him questions about Daniels's disabled ex-boyfriend at the time of the murder, Nick Gilbert (Adam Kotz). Following this new line of enquiry, Lane and Clarke come to the immediate conclusion that Gilbert's debilitating injuries, sustained when he abetted an armed robbery at his place of former employment as a security guard, do not necessarily prove his innocence. At the start of the scene the camera is behind Lane's desk, providing an over-the-shoulder shot of Clarke at an angle where Brian's computer takes up a quarter of the frame. However, when Lane takes control of the conversation his computer is moved off frame, permitting Clarke to have agency beyond Bevan's instructions. By contributing to the investigation at the expense of a public-relations exercise focused on the merits of smart policing technology, a new line of enquiry is opened that later proves Gilbert was implicated in Daniels's murder. Compared to *Waking the Dead*, intelligence operatives and the accompanying technological devices that they use are depicted as a support mechanism for management that detracts from real detective work.

In designing a police series for an older audience, many commentators felt *New Tricks* was grounded by an inherent conservatism, given its 'Neanderthal' protagonists (Sutcliffe 2003: 19). The detectives' scepticism towards intelligence gathering coupled by a pace, tone, and style harking back to older studio drama could be considered to adhere to Frederic Jameson's postmodern 'nostalgia mode': the 'formal attachment to the techniques and formulas of the past' as 'a retreat from the modernist challenge of innovating cultural forms adequate to contemporary experience' (Fisher 2014: 11–12). However, it would be unhelpful to label *New Tricks* as a clear-cut rejection of progress. Producer Tom Sherry attributes the programme's success to giving a voice to people who felt 'fed up with the New Labour nanny state' and who want to say 'we can think for ourselves' (Sherry 2009: 10). *New Tricks* suggests intelligence-gathering initiatives do not automatically enhance detectives' capabilities, as they prioritise performance targets over allowing staff to do their jobs the most effectively: a view then held by many detectives and police officers.[2]

Life on Mars

Following the 2003 Broadcasting Act, independent producers were now entitled to retain ownership of programme rights, and so a number of 'super indies' emerged. Having produced espionage thriller *Spooks* (BBC, 2002–2011) and criminal caper *Hustle* (BBC, 2004–2012), Kudos was a super indie with a reputation for drama that was 'fast-paced, stylish, and modern', produced to 'the same standard as feature films' (Chapman 2009: 7). BBC Wales Head of Drama Julie Gardner commissioned Kudos's *Life on Mars* as it fitted with her strategy of producing original ideas with high production values following her successful revival of classic sci-fi *Doctor Who* (BBC, 2005–). Achieving ratings of around 7.5 million viewers, *Life on Mars* won two international Emmy awards. In 2007 it won the audience-voted Pioneer Award at the BAFTAs, Best Drama Series and Best Writer awards at the Broadcasting Press Guild Awards, and Most Popular Drama at the National Television Awards. Coalescing commercial success with critical recognition arose from a conscious attempt to do something different. Co-creator Matthew Graham was keen to avoid 'another bloody cop show' (quoted in Naughton 2006). Consequently the series follows Sam Tyler, who after experiencing a car accident in 2006 wakes up in 1973, unsure whether he is in a coma and experiencing a dreamlike state, or has genuinely travelled back in time. By combining sci-fi with police drama this deliberate hybridisation of genre, a central characteristic of postmodernism, successfully shifts the police series away from 'gritty' social realism to more 'innovative and playful' fare (Piper 2015: 87).

Stopford House

If *Waking the Dead* presents the contemporary station space as a utopian environment, designed to enable the maximum fulfilment of individual human potential through technological innovation, then Greater Manchester Police's Stopford House in 2006 is a dystopian workplace. Now technologies stifle human fulfilment and 'regulate thought, imagination, and behaviour' (Booker and Thomas 2009: 65). Instead of quickening investigations, technological appliances inhibit Tyler. In the opening sequence of the first episode (9 January 2006), Tyler interrogates murder suspect Colin Raimes (Sam Hazeldine), who is accompanied by his social worker, solicitor, and psychiatrist. When Tyler instructs Raimes to state his name, Raimes menacingly scowls at the CCTV camera behind Tyler's head, repeating his name through gritted teeth. As Tyler presents his evidence, linking Raimes to the crime, Raimes's social worker informs Tyler that Raimes has a watertight alibi, meaning he could not have committed the murder. Upon hearing this crushing revelation, the viewer occupies Tyler's approximate POV of Raimes and his legal team sitting on the other side of the table. A slightly low angle reveals that two large televisions displaying Raimes's face have been hanging on the wall behind Raimes and his team throughout the whole interaction. The television monitors and CCTV camera are supposed to unsettle Raimes and afford Tyler greater scrutiny of his suspect. Instead, they emphasise how Tyler and his co-investigator Maya Roy (Archie Panjabi) have been outnumbered by Raimes's support network. From Tyler's figurative perspective the space appears smaller, as the recording equipment enables suspects to compound Tyler's accountability. Immediately following the failed interrogation, Tyler informs Roy that they must re-examine the synthetic fibres under the deceased's fingernails. Tyler refutes Roy's suggestion that they 'lean on Raimes' further, because they will be 'sued for harassment of a schizophrenic'. Throughout this exchange Tyler avoids Roy's gaze to stare at his computer screen displaying photos of the fibres. When Roy suggests Tyler rediscover his 'gut feeling', he retorts, 'what use are feelings in this room?'. The rhetorical question indicates that the sterile working environment, decorated by pastel colours and populated by officers permanently stationed at their computers, has regulated Tyler's thoughts and deadened his feelings. It is only when Tyler travels back to Stopford House in 1973, a station without modern technology that is saturated in 'earthy, lived-in hues of … orange' realised through advanced digital colour grading, that Tyler identifies and apprehends the actual killer for a previous murder (Piper 2015: 89).

Gene Jeanie

Detective Chief Inspector Gene Hunt (Philip Glenister) enables Tyler to rediscover his gut feeling in 1973. Hunt is widely regarded to be reminiscent of John Thaw's Jack Regan in *The Sweeney* (ITV, 1975–1978) owing to his 'rejection of analytical procedures, reliance on instinct, penchant for violence', and 'working class vernacular' (Lamb 2014: 204). Compared to the interrogation of Raimes, which takes place in a purpose-built interrogation suite, Hunt uses a cluttered lost-property room on account of its 'thick walls'. Here Dora Keens (Jane Riley), the last person to see victim Suzi Tripper alive, is interviewed. In this makeshift, darkened space Keens sits on her own and looks isolated in comparison to Hunt and Tyler sitting together conducting the interview, and Detective Inspector Chris Skelton (Marshall Lancaster), who stands behind her noting down the exchange. Following her deliberate evasion of questions Hunt physically intimidates Keens by aggressively shoving the table to the other side of the room, squaring up to her and denying her legal representation before detaining her in a cell. Tyler protests against Hunt's cavalier attitude towards their detainee's human rights. Hunt immediately quashes Tyler's reservations because his methods have resulted in a 'breakthrough', as they now have a time Tripper left the pub and a description of the man she left with. Surrounding and pressuring their prime suspect leads to the eventual arrest of the murderer, Edward Kramer. When arresting Kramer, Tyler sees a younger Raimes living next door to Kramer. Ultimately Roy is proven correct for having suggested they defy oversensitive contemporaneous procedure to lean on Raimes, as this defiance results in an arrest in 1973 and would have led them to the actual killer in 2006.

Hunt's repeated illegal actions can make for a 'reactionary programme when it comes to its attitude and perspective on contemporary policing' (Willis 2012: 61). Following Kramer's arrest Tyler finds a psychiatric report that means Kramer will not go to trial and, according to Hunt, be 'mollycoddled in a high security hospital' before being let out in thirty years when he will kill again. In spite of his principles Tyler chooses to destroy the report, which means Kramer will be incarcerated for life in spite of his mental instability. Furthermore, in Episode 2 (16 January 2006), Hunt's illegal plan to plant stolen jewellery and drugs on known armed robber Kim Trent (Andrew Tiernan) is overruled by Tyler. Tyler is then made to feel guilty when Trent immediately commits an armed robbery and their station cleaner is shot in cold blood. Similarly, in Episode 7 (20 February 2006), whilst the programme recognises that Detective Inspector Ray Carling's (Dean Andrews) unintentional killing of a suspect in custody has exceeded the realms of acceptability, Carling still evades criminal charges. Whilst Tyler lobbies for an end to institutionalised corruption, the episode's conclusion condones Hunt's ideological view that 'we can't change this world' and can 'only survive in it'.

It would, however, be disingenuous to claim that *Life on Mars* flatly rejects all forms of progress, as Tyler's methodical use of forensics, psychological profiling, and intelligence-gathering helps bring cases to satisfactory conclusions. The successful arrest of Kramer in the first episode is not solely due to Hunt's intimidation of suspects. The arrest occurs once Tyler instructs Skelton to sift through the station's records for any mention of a 'Raimes' as a matter of priority. This intelligence-gathering leads them to Raimes's grandmother, whose knowledge of her neighbour Kramer's soundproofing explains where the synthetic fibres from each victim's fingernails come from. Furthermore, Hunt's intimidation of murder suspect Ted Bannister (John Henshaw) in Episode 3 (23 January 2006) leads to a false confession. It is only when Tyler uses WPC Annie Cartwright's (Liz White) expertise as a psychology graduate that they determine Ted's son Derek (Andrew Knott) is the real killer, given the petrified body language displayed by Derek's father and girlfriend when giving statements. Thus, there is an academic consensus that neither character's viewpoint is favoured because conventional shot-reverse-shot sequences frame Tyler's and Hunt's arguments, close-ups are rare, and both men equally share the spotlight though a two-shot (Piper 2015: 95). This cinematography is prominent during the conclusion to each of the aforementioned investigations. When Kramer is arrested, Tyler and Hunt share the limelight as they march their detained man through the station together in a two-shot to receive their colleagues' plaudits. Also, when Derek Bannister is detained, Hunt promises Tyler that he will 'listen to your little tape machine now and again ... so long as you sometimes listen to this', whilst pointing to his own head. Tyler and Hunt are successful when they combine the best intuitive working practices of the 1970s, uninhibited by bureaucracy and a suspect's human rights, with psychological, technological, and intelligence-gathering advancements of the 2000s.

Hauntology

Whilst combining the best practices of both eras is criticised for providing an unachievable 'idealistic, almost utopian, policing method', the concluding scene of the very last episode cannot be ignored (Willis 2012: 65). Revived in his 2006 hospital bed, Tyler immediately returns to his office to record his thoughts into a dictaphone for a psycho-evaluation. Filmed from behind, in a long shot, Tyler is nothing more than a quietly spoken, darkened silhouette overlooking the colourless skyline of a 'concrete, glass and chrome plated Manchester metropolis', unable to talk to a fellow human being about his experiences (Holdsworth 2011: 108). This scene is interspersed with scenes of Tyler sat pensively alone outside the station, passed by swathes of individuals transfixed by their smartphones. By later jumping from the roof of the station, Tyler is able to return to 1973 to socialise with colleagues, passionately kiss Cartwright, and substitute his bland shirt and tie for his trademark leather jacket. These brightly colour-graded scenes bathe Tyler in orange as David Bowie's 'Changes' plays at a loud volume. Such a soundtrack contrasts sharply with Israel Kamakawiwo'ole's 1990 melancholic version of 'Over the rainbow', a song about passing on, which quietly accompanies Tyler's reawakening into the achromatic décors of the 2000s. As Tyler basks in a nostalgic simulation of the 1970s, the final word of the series is that contemporary policing is in drastic need of the 1970s' warmth, colour, and feeling. *Life on Mars*' station scenes ultimately subscribe to 'hauntology' theory as derived from Jameson's postmodern nostalgia mode. In an identical manner to hauntology, a 'ghostly presence-absence' dictates contemporary life, as personalised technological appliances characteristic of the 2000s appear to be dislocating people from reality (Gallix 2011: n.p.).

At the start of the 2000s, intelligence-led policing is enthusiastically embraced by *Waking the Dead*. The flamboyant station scenes are visually fixated by technological advancements to create a utopian working environment where experts work cohesively to maximise the fulfilment of their individual potential and obtain an accurate understanding of the past. *New Tricks*, however, is wary of such an outlook, as the incorporation of technology into UCOS's offices has a less domineering presence and encourages detectives to channel their personal knowledge, expertise, and intuition to overcome the increased complications intelligence-gathering and forensics create. Such data, whilst vital, need to be interpreted and discussed in person with one another, given a managerial inability to integrate intelligence operations with traditional detective work, as was occurring in the real British police force. Following this scepticism, *Life on Mars* provides a dystopian vision of what policing in 2006 has become. Greater Manchester Police's reliance on technology has created an oppressive working environment that stifles human fulfilment whilst regulating thought and behaviour to dislocate detectives from their gut instinct. This development from utopia to dystopia partially replicates growing criticisms of New Labour's law-and-order policy, which was often characterised as being too soft on offenders and inhibiting law enforcers. Home Secretary David Blunkett's 2003 National Policing Plan in particular was criticised for increasing health-and-safety legislation, regulation, bureaucracy, and centralisation. Throughout the 2000s, plans such as this fuelled beliefs that new national crime-recording practices were obstructing the police from engaging in fieldwork actively to combat crime, and that 'central intervention does not deliver' (Loveday and Reid 2003: 7). Assessing station scenes in isolation reveals how an enthusiasm towards the utopian possibilities of technological innovations in policing, pertinent throughout the public sphere, developed into scepticisms surrounding how such advancements were being inhibited by associative regulations.

CCTV

This interest in how technology was changing the nature of police work also underscores representations of civilian life. Closed-circuit TV systems feature prominently in each series, alluding to how one-fifth of the globe's operational CCTV units were in the UK (Lyon 2007: 39). Following rising crime rates in 1994, the Conservative Government announced an expansion of open-street, city-centre CCTV systems. This strategy continued under New Labour, whose ring-fencing of Home Office budgets funded further units. *Waking the Dead* endorses the widespread use of CCTV in public and, like the official Government line, presents this new technology as a 'utopian solution to complex social problems surrounding crime and disorder' (McCahill 2002: xiv). In 'The blind beggar', CCTV images of James Bowen's (James Hayes) van place him at the scene of Sebastian Stewart's (Barry Morse) murder, proving his guilt. Similarly, in 'Every breath you take', CCTV images recorded during the re-enactment of Debbie Britten's murder lead to the identification of Britten's stalker, Chris Redford (Lee Ross), who reveals Britten was pregnant. Subsequent CCTV footage of Steven Maitland rowing with Britten provides evidence that Maitland was the father of her unborn baby. Extracting key pieces of information from CCTV cameras leads to the arrest of the actual murderer, Maitland's daughter. This omnipresence of CCTV enables the detectives to identify, pursue, and arrest criminals to maintain the public's safety.

Sousveillance

In response to increased Government surveillance, the term 'sousveillance', coined by Steve Mann, was gaining greater currency. Mobile phone cameras, digital video cameras, and various other portable recording devices were becoming increasingly ubiquitous among the general public. This spread of affordable communication technologies was advocated by Mann and others for recalibrating the power equation between State surveillance and ordinary citizens. Where surveillance (deriving from the French for 'watching over') refers to the monitoring of people by some higher authority, sousveillance (French for 'to watch from below') refers to the monitoring of the State's excesses of power by informal networks of citizens (Mann 2013: 3). Martin Willis argues that Boyd's forensic humanism is sousveillance because it counters 'the dehumanising procedures of archival surveillance' (Willis 2016: 49). However, examining the programme's representation of criminal antagonists reveals that this covert form of recording, from 'first person' perspectives, is presented as a dehumanising, subversive, and psychotic activity (Ali and Mann 2013: 248).

Any civilian employing sousveillance to monitor the police is depicted as a dangerous individual who threatens State institutions. In the very first scene of the pilot episode, Boyd assembles his Cold Case Unit at a landfill site where the body of the murdered schoolgirl Alice Miller was discovered. Once Boyd finishes his briefing the next shot of him and his team is framed by a wobbly camera with a low-resolution image and very pale colour palette. Immediately, and for an eerily disquieting fifteen seconds, the non-diegetic soundtrack ceases. It later transpires that this shot was Marshall's first-person view of events when recording detectives through his own digital camera. When Marshall agrees to exchange his recent captive for money, he deliberately sabotages Whitemoor's release to record the detectives in a state of panic. He later plays his recorded video to Whitemoor, revelling with childish glee that the officers are 'running around like headless chickens'. Enveloping the episode with the first-person view of Marshall's unsteady, low-resolution, and eerily silent camera implies that the detectives have been his playthings throughout the whole episode. Despite his comparatively cheaper and primitive technological resources, Marshall has dictated events. Thus, sousveillance is an activity that repeatedly represents intelligence-led policing's greatest challenge.

However, rather than holding those in positions of power to account for malpractice, *Waking the Dead* equates sousveillance with psychologically unstable individuals harbouring twisted scores to settle. When arrested, Marshall reveals he kidnapped girls to sabotage Boyd's career as a form of revenge. Marshall blames Boyd for his previous prison sentence, obtained for beating up a WPC, because during a strip search Boyd left Marshall alone with the officer, who commented on Marshall's scars obtained from childhood abuse. Whilst station scenes have drawn attention to the spectacle of technology, this mysticism is recast as having a sinister quality when used by psychotic individuals. In 'A simple sacrifice', for example, the audience repeatedly witnesses an unidentified, naked, middle-aged man operating a desktop computer in a dark bedroom. Here the man maintains his website campaigning to free convicted child killer Annie Keel, and sends the police emails threatening 'terminal justice' if Keel is not released. Later it emerges that the man operating this makeshift technological hub is Annie Keel's solicitor, Reese Dickson (Nicholas Woodeson). When Boyd uncovers Dickson's centre of operations in his basement, Dickson stabs Boyd and broadcasts the assault through his webcam, confessing that he is the one who killed Keel's husband, as well as the neighbour's son who witnessed this initial murder, as a means of satisfying his infatuation with Keel. Dickson believed that this action would lead to a chain of events where Keel would fall in love with him. This action of monitoring the police from below – literally, as Dickson challenges the authorities from his basement – exists to satisfy Dickson's personal fantasy. This is also true of Redford in 'Every breath you take', who records all broadcast news footage concerning the discovery of murdered WPC Britten's body over a number of simultaneously broadcasting television sets. Although innocent of Britten's murder, Redford kills traffic warden Michael Skinner (Andrew Buckley) for lying to the press about an alleged affair with Britten. Despite the anarchic power sousveillance can inflict on society, for Marshall, Redford, and Dickson it represents nothing more than a means of actualising their 'erotomania': a psychotic condition where a stalker is so infatuated with their victim that they harm those they see as enemies of their 'beloved' (McGuire and Wraith 2000: 320).

The unpredictable nature of *Waking the Dead*'s sousveillance replicates emerging criminological discussions surrounding cybercrime, as the majority of antagonists engage in 'computer-mediated activities ... conducted through global electronic networks' (Thomas and Loader 2000b: 3). When introduced to a criminal the camera spends long tranches of time assimilating the antagonist's approximate POV of their technological devices (through either over-the-shoulder shots or POV shots) as they record images, operate devices, and access the internet. By defining a person's existence and personality through their technological interactions, *Waking the Dead* suggests computer-mediated activities within the home have a power to dehumanise subjects and turn petty criminals, law-abiding citizens, or unstable individuals into dangerous offenders. Little effort is undertaken to explore the 'underlying causes behind law-breaking behaviour' or to 'locate the forces that propel or incline people toward transgressing society's rules' within terrestrial settings and situations (Yar 2013: 17). Instead, *Waking the Dead* replicates the growing view in criminology that the 'existing "stock" of empirical assumptions and explanatory concepts' cannot always be transposed onto cyberspace (Yar 2013: 19). A need for considerable theoretical innovation is echoed, as kidnap, blackmail, murder, stalking, theft, and identity fraud can now be committed by anyone relatively easily, regardless of their class, background, or status, be they taxi driver, solicitor, war photographer, building contractor, or conçierge. Like leading cybercrime criminologists Kovacich (1999), Dowland *et al.* (1999), and Voiskounsky *et al.* (2000), the series portrays cybercriminals undertaking illicit activities for a wide range of personal reasons that are 'as old as human society, including greed, lust, revenge and curiosity' (Grabosky and Smith 2001: 35).

Overall, a dichotomy between public and private spaces is reinforced by *Waking the Dead*'s focus on technology. Ignoring the attitudinal markers of characters to marvel at devices in the station portrays a sophisticated police force overseeing the beginnings of a technological utopia. In civilian spaces, however, the camera being drawn into the gazes of criminals who are transfixed by the bright screens of their sousveillance command-centres serves to heighten fears. Such scenes highlight the challenges cybercrime poses to understanding a criminal's reasoning, the relationship this motivation has to the offender's socio-economic background, and how police could best deter this supposedly new crime wave.

New Labour/*New Tricks*

Following *Waking the Dead*'s interest in the challenges cybercrime put to traditional criminology, *New Tricks*' depiction of civilian life examines criminal activity in the context of New Labour social policy. Through the 2000s the Labour Government implemented its 'third way' philosophy: a doctrine that offsets the supply and demand of a global neoliberal economy with an increased investment in a public sector committed to social cohesion delivered through public–private partnerships. New Labour tried to distance itself from Thatcherism by implementing Keynesian initiatives, including a minimum wage and working tax credits to redistribute income to disadvantaged families. Such strategies helped oversee ten years of modest growth and a steady fall in unemployment, and caused the poorest 20 per cent of the population to experience a 12 per cent rise in income and improvement in living standards (Pugh 2017: 464). With a sustained fall in crime amounting to 39 per cent from 1995 to 2004, a buoyant economy dependent on goods and services, greater supposed egalitarianism between the poorest and middle-income families, and a third of all young people at university, the onus was very much on the individual to achieve success and contribute to society (Pugh 2017: 467). With Prime Minister Tony Blair proclaiming an 'expanded middle class' and Chancellor Gordon Brown guaranteeing 'no return to boom and bust', anybody who committed crime was characterised as a rational actor who had irresponsibly chosen to do so (Blair 1999: n.p.; Brown 2006: n.p.). Out-of-work single mothers and 'chavs', defined as 'a young lower-class person who behaves in a brash or loutish way', were often stigmatised for debasing the country's moral backbone and work ethic (*Oxford English Dictionary* 2011). This was a view propagated by law-and-order policy that issued 1,117 anti-social behaviour orders to disadvantaged children as young as eleven from 2000 to 2004 (Pugh 2017: 467).

On an immediate narrative level, *New Tricks* appears aligned with this Blairite agenda, as all guilty parties have rationally decided to commit crime rather than having been pressured through predestined circumstances. Sometimes crimes are committed for financial gain. In 'ID parade', WPC Daniels was killed for confronting a criminal gang who did not compensate her ex-boyfriend Nick Gilbert following his injuries sustained from assisting them with an armed robbery.

Similarly, in 'Talking to the dead' (8 May 2004), seventeen-year-old Caroline Stillman's body was found in a shipping container in 1982 because her ploy to feign a kidnapping for ransom money went horribly wrong. In other instances, however, crimes are committed to settle personal scores. In 'The Chinese job', the wife of businessman and gangster Roddy Wringer killed Anna Dubrovski because she thought they were having an affair. Then, in '1984' (15 April 2004), peace protestor Josh Livesey was not killed by Special Branch for demonstrating at a nuclear base, as initially believed, but by friend Colin Dobie (Jonny Phillips) because Livesey was having an affair with his wife.

Where *New Tricks* differs from New Labour philosophy, however, is that lower-class victims of crime, who are often immigrants living in council accommodation, are juxtaposed against members of the establishment who pose a greater threat to law and order. 'Painting on loan' (8 April 2004) reveals the horrific consequences of curator Sir Timothy's (Anthony Head) counterfeiting of Buckingham Palace's art. The long shots used to frame Sir Timothy showcasing the palace's bright red, plush, and opulent galleries stand in stark contrast to the small, dark council flat occupied by Sangita (Nita Mistry), with her facial scars obtained from a fire ignited by Sir Timothy's buyer. Similarly, in 'Good work rewarded', Pullman agrees to re-examine the death of Jimmy Spencer because Derek Rodger (Frank Mills), who is dying of emphysema alone in his small council flat, feels his dead son was incorrectly blamed. In contrast, the golf club, where Rodger's son's body was found, is framed by long shots that capture its grand interiors, decorated by oil paintings, trophies, and honours boards. Here the members threaten to use their 'influence' to stop UCOS's investigation. Furthermore, in the pilot, when Dubrovski's murder is being investigated, her widowed mother (Zena Walker) is interviewed at the Polski Club, where she works as a cleaner. A succession of close-ups focus on Mrs Dubrovksi's anguished expressions and her defined wrinkles within the darkened space. In comparison, the Wringers, responsible for the murders of Dubrovski and Sefton, reside in a mansion decorated by cream upholstery, lit by bright white spotlights. *New Tricks* redresses criminological, political, and journalistic discourse, increasingly obsessed with a supposed decline in shared moral values instigated by a rising tide of criminal and anti-social behaviour enacted by a 'chav' culture. A visual contrast is repeatedly drawn between criminals living and working in radiantly coloured and brightly lit grandiose surroundings, and victims of crime who are isolated by close-ups within smaller, darkened dwellings. This dissimilarity draws attention to the increasing gulf between the poorest in society and the emerging super-rich.[3]

Rather than holding the police to account for abuses of power, sousveillance is now exclusively a plaything of the super-rich, used to exert their authority over the police. When Standing visits the Wringers' home to gain further information on Dubrovski's murder, Gaynor Wringer purposefully tries to photograph them together with her digital camera to sabotage the investigation. Later, Roddy Wringer uses his mobile phone to call Standing as Standing leaves the cinema with his daughter. Roddy informs Standing he is being watched and that Roddy can hurt his family at any time. Whereas *Waking the Dead* frames CCTV as an essential means of combating anarchic sousveillance, in *New Tricks* the use of personal CCTV signifies paranoid and corrupt members of the establishment protecting their interests from legal scrutiny. In '1984', Lane observes that the home owned by the CEO of a successful public-relations firm and the head of the Labour Party's Central Policy Planning Unit, both implicated in Livesey's murder, has CCTV cameras outside. Likewise, when Halford and Pullman visit the clairvoyant Martin Lombard (Robert Bathurst), who was complicit in Stillman's manslaughter, a revolving CCTV camera surveys the space in anticipation of UCOS's visit. As a rich individual with access to such technologies, Lombard evades prosecution because UCOS's decision to lock him in a dark shipping container until he confesses is recorded by his solicitor, whom, it transpires, Lombard secretly called on his mobile phone during the ordeal. Compared to *Waking the Dead*, surveillance is Orwellian in nature because it maintains power through its divisive character. Detectives are scrutinised by surveillance equipment belonging to people above them on the social ladder, just as it is used to control the actions of middle-class professionals and party members in George Orwell's 1984 (2008 [1949]). In contrast, the Dubrovskis, Rodgers, and Sangitas stand in as Orwell's proles, excluded to their ghettoes free from such scrutiny to do the 'working, breeding and dying' (Orwell 2008 [1949]: 60). Ultimately, then, in contrast to the Blairite 'we're all middle class now' rhetoric, the civilian scenes of *New Tricks* depict a UK that is beginning to experience a vast wealth gap between those at the very top and those at the very bottom of society: a gap intensified by the inherently divisive nature of surveillance technology used for sousveillance purposes.

Life on Mars

In response to *New Tricks*' divisive surveillance, *Life on Mars* nostalgically longs for simpler times where the collective identity of harmonious working-class communities is remembered for providing a comforting sense of camaraderie and enrichment to its constituent members.

A large degree of narrative unfolds in outdoor, public locations, with washing lines hanging across roads, children playing in cobbled streets, and kitchen chairs parked outside properties to evoke the lost everyday rituals of previous generations. Consistently bright sunlight basks most civilian life in an idyllic brightness appealing to people's collective memories of a 'shared, working class culture' (Piper 2015: 91). Those who commit crime in 1973 are depicted with a degree of sympathy as they misguidedly act to preserve their disappearing way of life. Derek Bannister steals wages from Crester's textile factory because he wants to provide for his family, given the looming threat of job losses following increased automation and a harder-working immigrant workforce who are cheaper to employ. In another instance, Reg Cole (Paul Copley) takes workers from the *Manchester Gazette* hostage because he wants his work as the firm's handyman acknowledged and appreciated in a world that is, in his words, becoming increasingly 'profane' and indulged by the 'sanctity of the self'. Taken together, Bannister's and Cole's alienation derives from fears of their working-class identity being superseded by the onset of neoliberal individualism.

The extent of *Life on Mars*' longing for a communal, working-class way of life is revealed through a direct comparison with Tyler's 2006 home. When the body of loom operator Jimmy Saunders is first discovered on the floor of Crester's textile factory in 1973, Tyler realises that the body is lying on the exact spot where his future apartment will be. Looking at the body Tyler endures a disorienting flash-forward that focuses on his empty, ultramodern kitchen. The camera then focuses on his glass dining table. In the middle of the table is a bowl containing Tyler's car keys, mobile phone, and wallet. Directly underneath the table is a bright red pool of Saunders's blood. Over four seconds the camera cuts eleven times to produce nine different shots of the kitchen table interspersed with two shots of Saunders's body. Tyler recoils from what appears to be, given the disorienting rapidity of cuts, a post-traumatic episode where he struggles to comprehend how the industrial struggles of the past have paved the way for the luxurious domestic spaces of his unappreciative generation. For a moment's respite Tyler walks outside to touch one of the factory's chimneys, of which foreman Ted Bannister explains that the heat bleeds through the brick, making it 'a living thing'. Tyler concurs that once the inside stops working the building becomes 'a shell', implying that previous industrial buildings were living, breathing entities that provided lifelines to communities. This whole scene argues through its sophisticatedly flamboyant style and sharp contrast in colour gradient that a new generation of middle-class professionals who live alone in their isolated flats are devoid of feeling, having placed greater value on their material worth and consumption of food and gadgets: i.e. Cole's 'profane ... sanctity of the self'. In comparison to this isolating existence, whenever the police call on Ted Bannister he is always found using his kitchen table to play board games with his family and children. This juxtaposition invites viewers to hold greater admiration for working-class patriarchs of the 1970s over middle-class professionals of the 2000s. Essentially the series argues through visual means that expunging the distinction between working-class workplaces and middle-class residences through deindustrialisation and gentrification has been a key factor in producing a hauntological milieu. The admirable wholesomeness of Bannister's family life has been replaced by fractured individuals like Tyler, who are guided by a vacuous materialism, exemplified by the disorienting visuals that frame the achromatic mod cons and personal possessions contained within his 2006 apartment.

Just like the stations of every series examined from the 2000s, the homes of civilians are populated by various technologies that provide a character's environment with a distinct agency over their person. Rather than the home being a safe haven removed from the public world of work, technology has made home environments a direct threat towards the institutions that uphold society. In *Waking the Dead*, sousveillant technologies echo cybercrime scholarship, as they can sinisterly awaken criminality in people from a range of classes who might otherwise pose no real threat. This creates a new challenge for the authorities, who require theoretical intervention to understand new forms of criminal behaviour better. Conversely, sousveillant technologies in *New Tricks* are recast as playthings of a corrupt establishment that employs such devices to protect its own interests. This exclusivity of technology to a certain class of people highlights an emerging wealth gap between the super-rich and the underclass, in the form of poor pensioners or immigrant characters, who have seemingly evaded the 'we're all middle class now' rhetoric. Lastly, *Life on Mars* nostalgically accesses memories of seemingly simpler times, where working-class men were apparently able to preside over a wholesome family unit removed from the cut and thrust of the professional world of work.

Overall, civilian scenes from police series produced in the 2000s utilise the advanced colourisation, heightened editing tempo, and manoeuvrability of digital cameras to provide clear contrasts. A sharp distinction is drawn between the basic technologies of cybercriminals and the sophisticated technologies of the Cold Case Unit in *Waking the Dead*. There is a disparity between the expansive, brightly lit, and colourful environments of the super-rich and the impoverished, immigrant underclass in *New Tricks*. *Life on Mars* presents glowing memories of wholesome, working-class family life in the 1970s, compared

The 2000s 143

to the isolated, middle-class professionals of the 2000s. These stark visual differences largely concur with criminologists Barry *et al.* (1996), Bauman (1997), and Reiner *et al.* (2001), who believe that the uprooting of the postwar consensus to rely on individual responsibility has led to a 'universally shared and overwhelming sensation of insecurity' (Bauman 1997: 204). In police series this insecurity is flavoured by postmodernism, whereby a widespread use of the internet and corresponding technologies aggravates existing, and generates new social divisions and internal conflicts.

Home on Mars

This postmodernism, distinctive to police series of the 2000s, repeatedly depicts the individuality of detectives as being inherently fractured. This is because *New Tricks* and *Life on Mars* explore the notion that an individual's home is not a consistently stable entity that permanently grounds a person's identity. Home transforms throughout a person's life as they move house, their personality develops, and their memories of previous accommodation alters. In addition to his 2006 flat, Tyler also rents a flat in 1973 and revisits his childhood home from the same year. In this respect, the series mirrors the growing scholarly interest of Wheeler (1994), Tannock (1995), Boym (2001), Grainge (2002), and Pickering and Keightley (2006), who challenge widespread assumptions that nostalgia is simply an inauthentic, ahistorical, regressive, and sentimental longing for an idealised past. The interplay among Tyler's three different homes, as identified by Amy Holdsworth (2011), replicates Boym's 'reflective' nostalgia because such scenes 'narrate the relationship between past, present and future' that is 'inconclusive and fragmentary' (Boym 2001: 50).

To navigate this postmodern idea that the perception of one's home changes throughout a person's lifetime, each of Tyler's home scenes engages with Freud's 'uncanny'. According to Freud, the uncanny is an experience that awakens our unconscious, forbidden, animalistic impulses that have been repressed by societal conventions. As etymological proof of his psychoanalytic hypothesis Freud bases his term on the semantic study of the German adjective *heimlich* – meaning 'familiar', 'native', and 'belonging to the home' – and its antonym *unheimlich* – meaning 'unfamiliar', 'unknown', and 'unhomely' (Freud 2003 [1919]: 124–125). The uncanny is frightening precisely because the strange emanates from the familiar.

When Tyler first visits his mother (Joanne Froggatt) in his 1973 childhood home, it is a *heimlich* setting. When he visits the sun-drenched streets of his former working-class neighbourhood he beams with delight upon recognising the local rag-and-bone man, Alfie, and the family cat, Ivanhoe, sat on their doorstep. When his mother answers the door Tyler is momentarily lost for words, as he is in awe of her angelic yet matriarchal quality: she is dressed in an apron, yet her make-up is applied and her blonde hair glistens in the sunshine as she smiles. Once Tyler's mother invites him inside for a cup of tea she repeatedly stresses that she is 'surprised' to hear that there have been robberies (which Tyler has fabricated as an excuse to see her), as the house is the 'safest place we've ever been'. Tyler's home is practically identical to his childhood memories, functioning as a regressive form of nostalgia.

However, as Peter Jachimiak argues, time travel transforms Tyler's childhood home, which he remembers as being 'familiar and comforting (*Heimlich*)', into an 'unfamiliar and uncomforting (*Unheimlich*)' experience (Jachimiak 2012: 101). This transformation materialises once Tyler's unconscious processes this revisiting of his childhood memories in his 1973 flat. After visiting his childhood home, he uses his 1973 flat as a safe house for nightclub dancer Joni (Kelly Wenham), who is scared that her employer, Stephen Warren (Tom Mannion), will kill her. Once Tyler falls asleep in his armchair he enters a semi-comatose state where images from his unconscious interplay with his conscious self having sex with Joni. Tyler's uncanny experience begins with his front door opening to reveal his mother standing to the entranceway of his flat in a warm, orange glow as she smiles and calls her son's name. When he calls back she is replaced by a gigantic version of their cat, Ivanhoe, who is so large Tyler hides his face in his pillow in terror. Then, as he finds himself handcuffed to his bed having sex with Joni, his mother looks on ashamed. This view is then undercut by the eight-year-old Carole Hersee, the girl whose face was broadcast on the BBC test card from 1967 to 1998 when no programmes were being broadcast, who escapes from the television and informs Tyler that he has nothing to be ashamed of. He then experiences a childhood memory of walking through the woods, lost and alone.

The way in which this scene distorts Tyler's idyllic childhood memories and juxtaposes them with his being drugged by Joni in a nightmarish setting directly correlates with Freud's uncanny theory. According to Freud, an uncanny experience is where 'the boundary between imagination and reality is blurred' (Freud 2003: 150). Within this omnipotence of thought 'inanimate objects...come to life' (Carol Hersee escaping the TV) (Freud 2003 [1919]: 153). Another principal uncanny sensation is the dominance of 'a compulsion to repeat', whereby an individual experiences repetition of an incident in which one becomes lost and accidentally has to retrace one's steps (Tyler's childhood memories of being lost in the woods). Lastly, Freud asserts that the uncanny awakens Oedipal desires and the corresponding 'fears of castration' (Tyler's unconscious conjures images of his disapproving mother watching his conscious self having sex) (Freud 2003 [1919]: 140). Following this nightmarish experience, Tyler is repeatedly revisited by these essential components of the uncanny within his 1973 flat. Often he revisits his childhood memory of being lost in the woods, or sees Hersee leaving the television set to remind him of his loneliness. Like the uncanny, Tyler's repressed infantile complexes are revived to express his unconscious fear of mortality.

Because of these uncanny experiences Tyler is able to locate and confront the unfamiliar and unsettling (*unheimlich*) elements of his comforting and familiar (*heimlich*) childhood memories, work through his repressed trauma, and rebuild his fractured individuality. In the final episode of the first series, Tyler is ordered to search his childhood home following his father's (Lee Ingleby) connection to an armed robbery. Initially Tyler clings to what is familiar and comforting, trying desperately to preserve his childhood memory of his father as a loving patriarch. He touches the clock in the living room, identifying that the big hand always sticks at twelve. Then, instead of searching for evidence, he sniffs his father's jacket in the hallway to relive the childhood sensation associated with experiencing his father's returning home from work. Also, when talking to his father, Tyler sits in front of a framed painting of a fictional unicorn. Taken together, these aspects of the space signify that his memory has become a fantasy locked in time, stilting his emotional maturity.

However, once Tyler leaves his childhood home for the last time he is able to evaluate his memories from an adult perspective. Upon leaving, Hunt reveals that he found a bookmaker's receipt concealed in Tyler's childhood copy of *Alice's Adventures in Wonderland*, which his father used to read to him as a child. Therefore, concealed beneath the surface of Tyler's comforting and familiar (*heimlich*) memories of his childhood resides sobering, unsettling, and unfamiliar (*unheimlich*) proof that his father robbed the betting shop. Accordingly, by the end of the series finale Tyler concedes that his father was a criminal. Therefore, ideologically, the series is not necessarily advocating nostalgia as a literal retreat to the way things were. Instead, it recognises that 'aspects of the past represent the basis for renewal and satisfaction in the future', as nostalgia is seen as a 'means of taking one's bearings for the road ahead in uncertainties of the present' (Pickering and Keightley 2006: 921). Tyler's processing of his childhood memories in a private, uncanny capacity, within varying iterations of his home, challenges the ideology of station scenes and civilian scenes because the complexities of an individual's past need to be worked through and overcome rather than romanticised.

'You can't teach an old dog a brand new trick'

One of the great appeals of *New Tricks* is how the lead characters collectively present a myriad of different possibilities and problems about ageing, to which the target audience might relate. As Phil Wickham argues, the baby boomer generation had a 'promise of liberation, of a leisure society, but with grounding in community and shared values' (Wickham 2010: 78). Yet the detectives negotiate a world that is 'both increasingly chaotic in some areas and more regulated in others' (Wickham 2010: 79). Again, as a form of reflective nostalgia, each retired detective's home is used as a space to access the past in relation to the present to assess the future. The first time the viewer is introduced to Jack Halford is when Pullman recruits him to UCOS. Here, Halford is shot in the same manner as Dubrovski's grieving mother. As he sits in his front room on a rainy day, the interior is darkly lit and shot through a grey filter that provides a pallid space devoid of colour. In contrast, when Halford spends time in his garden by his wife's grave the scenes are much brighter in the way they are colourised, through post-production digital editing, to provide his rich, green lawn with a distinct and unnatural shimmer. In his garden, Halford finds the comforting solace he needs to make breakthroughs. In the pilot, when speaking to Mary Halford's grave, he realises that Dubrovski's blood was planted on Roddy Wringer's shoe, and in another instance he comes to the realisation that Gilbert was implicated in Britten's murder. Halford's serene garden, representing his idealised memories of his previous married life, provides solutions to the predicaments that come with his currently isolated existence.

In contrast, Brian Lane's private life does not long for the past but draws attention to his wife Esther Lane's (Susan Jameson) sobering acceptance of her missed opportunities in life. When investigating art fraud, Brian asks Esther whether he's ever been a passionate man, to which she affirms he is not. He then asks whether that bothers her, for what seems like the first time in their marriage, to which she replies 'not any more', suggesting that it used to be an issue but that she has since learnt to accept her lot in life over time. Similarly, when watching film footage from the 1970s of a missing woman, Esther recalls the publication of Germaine Greer's *The Female Eunuch* and how she had to queue to buy copy. What begins as a longing for a time when women were liberated from 'buying into our own oppression' is soon cut short, as Esther confesses she never read the whole book because she had to look after the children and her frail mother whilst Brian was working seventy-hour shifts. She maintains she will never read Greer, as it will read like an 'exotic brochure' for somewhere she has 'never lived'. Just like *Life on Mars*, then, it is primarily through the private lives of detectives that *New Tricks* admits not everything was necessarily better in times gone by, despite the team's longing for simpler times in the station. For all Brian's ability to cross-examine evidence, an audience sees the human cost of the time required to produce the breakthroughs that policing intelligence and forensics cannot. Esther is forever wary of her husband's becoming the 'empty shell' he used to be as a younger man, when he was neglectful of her needs and of his own wellbeing.

Sandra Pullman is going through a similar predicament to that experienced by Esther in her earlier life as she cares for her mother, Grace Pullman (Sheila Hancock). As an indicator of progress, the series becomes less interested in 'furnishing' Sandra with a love life, whether 'fulfilling or failed like Tennison' in *Prime Suspect*, as she is 'allowed to exist as a successful older woman without comment on her single status' (Wickham 2010: 74). This advocating of progress in terms of gender relations is also present in *Waking the Dead*, as Boyd's temperament becomes increasingly problematic when struggling to cope with his son's unsolved abduction. In Series 4, Boyd agrees to be psychologically assessed by Foley so that, in a reversal of familiar crime-drama stereotypes, the 'feminised apparatus of professional knowledge' scrutinises the 'masculine subjectivity' of the team's lead investigator (Ridgman 2012: 11). However, Boyd's trauma is not depicted within his private life, as the series ignores the postmodern view that one's fraught relationship with one's past in a private capacity can have an impact upon one's public identity. In *New Tricks* and *Life on Mars*, Pickering and Keightley's nostalgia is applied to a person's perception of their past to overcome trauma and be a more effective, collected professional in the public sphere. Conversely, aligned to technological utopianism, *Waking the Dead* negates the private realm to suggest there is nothing that cannot be solved by innovation and professional expertise.

Conclusion

The explosion in information technology, and the developments in digital camera effects, imbued police series of the 2000s with a new, flamboyant visual style that used sci-fi imagery to reflect on the direction of British society. At the start of the decade, *Waking the Dead*'s Cold Case Unit is a beacon of technological utopianism, as a mobile camera enthusiastically embraces the capabilities of communication technology and its apparent ability to fuse scientists with intelligence operatives and detectives to rectify past miscarriages of justice whilst quashing cybercrime. The UCOS offices in *New Tricks* are more sceptical of technological developments, as the series' slower pace suggests forensic developments have to be skilfully decoded because intelligence-led policing can be a political smokescreen detracting from intuitive policing. Despite its scaled-back station aesthetic, however, *New Tricks* makes use of colour grading, lens filters, and the number of shot scales to reveal a gulf in lifestyle appearing between the super-rich and the poorest in society, uncovering the insecurity lying just beneath the surface of a Blairite political economy. Then *Life on Mars* largely rejects technological developments, as the technologies populating Stopford House station and civilian life in the 2000s make for a chilling dystopia. Instead, the series utilises digital production techniques to bask in the warmth of the past and rekindle the collective identity provided by working-class communities. However, when these advancements in digital camerawork capture the private lives of detectives, contrasts emerge within their identity to complicate a seemingly rose-tinted view of the past. Tyler's disorientated processing of his repressed childhood trauma from an adult perspective, and Esther Lane's sobering acceptance of her missed life-opportunities, suggest Pickering and Keightley's critical form of nostalgia can assist individuals in managing the private traumas underpinning their fractured identities. Such individualities are portrayed as requiring reunification so that a person can navigate a public existence that is increasingly susceptible to postmodern and neoliberal uncertainties. In each police series from the 2000s, unlocking a particular understanding of the past, through a mixture of professional expertise and self-reflection, is central to successfully balancing one's private and public personas within an overarching, cohesive identity.

Notes

1. Other prominent examples of fast-paced police series with a high-tech *mise-en-scène*, accompanied by a highly stylised cinematography to refract the capabilities of forensic detection and contribute to a hyperreal milieu, include: *CSI: Crime Scene Investigation* (Channel 5, 2000–2015), *Criminal Minds* (Sky Living, 2005–), *NCIS* (Channel 5, 2003–), *Law & Order* (Channel 5, 1997–), *Law & Order: UK* (ITV1, 2009–2014), *Silent Witness*, and the later editions of *Prime Suspect*.
2. Again, see John and Maguire (2004), James (2013).
3. In 2001 executives' pay rose 28 per cent at a time when inflation was 2.5 per cent and average earnings were growing by 3.7 per cent (Pugh 2017: 468).

The 2010s: looking to pastures new

6

> The landscape had to feel present everywhere.
> *Broadchurch* creator Steve Chibnall (Graham 2013: n.p.)

As the 2000s unfolded, police series became more and more immersed in the past. From 2010 onwards, however, the genre has begun to cast an eye over the present to ask searching questions of the future. In the face of greater competition from streaming services police series with the most successful viewing figures have marketed themselves as quality television. They feature high-profile actors, make use of high-definition cameras and aerial drone photography, and are narratively designed so that one complex investigation unfolds over six-to-eight episodes. This concluding chapter analyses how *Broadchurch* (ITV, 2013–2017) and *Happy Valley* (BBC, 2014–) typify the genre's latest direction in narrative and style. It specifically considers how the use of HD aerial cameras in both series ideologically navigates the growing socio-economic inequalities of their specific localities in relation to gendered identities deriving from austerity politics.

Digital TV

The UK television industry's switchover from an analogue to a digital service was completed in 2012. The opposition between terrestrial and digital television became anachronistic, as Freeview provided all households with thirty-five additional channels, and the availability of BBC iPlayer (launched 2007), ITVhub, and All4 allowed content to be watched on demand up to thirty days after broadcast. Competition from a global digital marketplace meant that police drama became compelled to devote an entire series to one investigation to sustain prolonged hours of binge-watching. This viewing practice demands closer cognitive involvement of its viewers to make sense of complex and nuanced plot developments (Perks 2015: 66). Jed Mecurio's *Line of Duty* (BBC 2012–) represents how the narrative design of police series has been affected by digital consumption. In the first series, Detective Chief Inspector Tony Gates (Lennie James) sees his life fall apart as a result of fraudulently doctoring his own crime figures and adulterously courting Jackie Laverty (Gina McKee). Narratively, the viewer's 'structure of allegiance is divided by dual systems of spatial alignment' between Gates and Detective Sergeant Steve Arnott (Martin Compston), the officer investigating Gates for anti-corruption unit AC-12, weaving together 'multiple plotlines' too intricate to repeat in full (Piper 2015: 134). Rather than the series neatly concluding episodic crimes on a weekly basis, as presented by police series broadcast in the 2000s, viewers now follow one complicated investigation from varying perspectives in order to discern gradually a number of characters' multifaceted motives.

Digital police series

Luther (BBC 2010–) was the first police series of the decade to navigate this digital landscape. Created and written by Neil Cross, the drama revolves around the eponymous Detective Chief Inspector John Luther (Idris Elba), making use of a highly sensational primary plot alongside parallel storylines concerning Luther's disintegrating marriage and battle of wits against villain Alice Morgan (Ruth Wilson). According to Piper, the series is 'ostensibly cinematic', as the London depicted is 'a city of extremes' with 'exportable postcard views' of the Thames and its skyline counterbalanced by 'backdrops of suspiciously underpopulated council estates' to reveal a 'global city ... untouched by everyday operational realism' (Piper 2015: 128). In direct response, *Scott & Bailey* (ITV, 2011–2016) centres on female detective constables Janet Scott (Lesley sharp) and Rachel Bailey (Suranne Jones) working under Detective Chief Inspector Gill Murray (Amelia Bullmore) of the Greater Manchester Police's Major Incident Team. In marked contrast to *Luther*, creator Sally Wainwright professed that her series was 'the antithesis of something macho like Luther ... [that] procedurally is rubbish' (quoted in McLean 2012: 11). This statement illustrates how *Scott & Bailey*'s 'realist counter claim' is based on its capturing of mundane 'procedural detail'. This is also true of the series' close affinity to the soap opera, given the tightly framed close-ups of faces used to capture events, and the long-running personal storylines that exist in tension with the shorter investigations resolved over one or two episodes (Piper 2015: 130). These two series represent the state of the police series at the start of the decade. *Luther* is an overblown cinematic thriller starring a Hollywood A-lister that is sold internationally through Netflix. Concurrently, at the other end of the spectrum, lies *Scott & Bailey*: a domestic success that relied on episodically resolved investigations and the iconography of the soap opera to retain weekly audiences of 5.8 million (Piper 2015: 133).

Nordic noir

This emerging binary was soon broken by subtitled Scandinavian crime drama: Nordic noir. The success of *The Killing* (BBC, 2007–2011) and *The Bridge* (BBC, 2008–2011) provided a formula that would impact subsequent British police series. There are three components to a Nordic noir drama. First, it must be a long-form whodunnit, whereby a central enigma 'sustains an audience's interest over a surprisingly large number of episodes' (Creeber 2015a: 21). Second, there is 'double storytelling' at work that weaves 'a number of intricate narrative strands' (Creeber 2015a: 21). In *The Killing*, for example, there are 'the crime plot', involving the brutal rape and murder of a young girl; 'the political plot', set in motion when a local politician becomes a major suspect; and 'the family plot', focusing on the murdered girl's friends and family. Lastly, a 'theory of interdependence' philosophically underpins the genre. Coined by producer Sven Clausen, 'interdependence' refers to the belief that increasing societal divisions can only be 'healed through a combination of tolerance and cooperation' (Creeber 2015a: 22). In response to fears that the power of the State and the compassion of the welfare state have been subsumed by neoliberal global capitalism, the interdependence of Nordic noir implicitly reveals that society *does* exist. Its society consists of individuals who are all intimately connected and who must work together because 'one incident has an impact on many different layers of people in society' (cited by Redvall 2013: 230). In response, a crop of UK police series set in rural communities utilised a whodunnit narrative to explore interdependence through double storytelling, including *Southcliffe* (Channel 4, 2013), *The Tunnel* (Sky Atlantic, 2013–), and *Hinterland* (BBC, 2013–2016).

Broadchurch and Happy Valley

Of these Nordic noir-inspired police series, *Broadchurch* and *Happy Valley* proved to be the most popular. The former received an average, consolidated viewing figure of 9.4 million per episode, the highest figure for a new weekday drama series on ITV since 2004. The latter achieved 7.2 million viewers across the whole series (BBC Media Centre 2014: n.p.). Chris Chibnall's first series of *Broadchurch* is an eight-episode investigation into the murder of eleven-year-old Daniel Latimer (Oskar McNamara). Set within the eponymous Dorset seaside town (in reality West Bay and Clevedon), *Broadchurch* examines the ripple effect a murder has on a wider community. Whilst Chibnall does not cite Nordic noir as a direct influence, he claims 'what *The Killing* did was that when we got to conversations with commissioners they were more open to it than they might have been five years ago' (quoted in Gilbert 2013: n.p.). For Chibnall personally, his writing 'DNA' owes a greater debt to American series *Murder One* (1995–1997) and *Twin Peaks* (Channel 4, 1990–1992) (Gilbert 2013: n.p.). However, both series were also progenitors of Nordic noir, given that Søren Sveistrup (creator of *The Killing*) cites the exact same American series as informing his approach to sustaining an audience's interest over many episodes (Chipping 2012: n.p.). For many commentators the success of *Broadchurch*, including its four BAFTAs, indicates UK audiences' 'demand for high-quality drama' (Turnbull 2015: 706). In response to *Broadchurch*'s success, the BBC's *Happy Valley*, which won the 2015 Best Drama BAFTA, interweaves storylines around Sergeant Catherine Cawood (Sarah Lancashire), responsible for the day-to-day policing of her town (Hebden Bridge, Sowerby Bridge, and Halifax) in the Calder Valley of West Yorkshire. When aggrieved accountant Kevin Weatherill (Steve Pemberton) masterminds the kidnapping of his boss's daughter for a hefty ransom, wider significance emanates from the crime. In particular, Cawood holds one of the hired kidnappers, convicted rapist Tommy Lee Royce (James Norton), responsible for her daughter's suicide.

Austerity and policing

By examining how crime can ripple through a community, both *Broadchurch* and *Happy Valley* address how austerity has impacted policing. In 2008 the UK experienced an economic recession unprecedented in recent times. Since 1997, New Labour had based their management of the economy on the same principles as the neoliberal fiscal policies of the USA, including financial deregulation of the banks, expanding consumer credit, allowing property prices to rise, and a growing service sector. This meant ignoring rising personal debt, a dwindling manufacturing sector, and the decline of house building, while the financial sector enjoyed inflated profits. The bubble burst when Northern Rock, Bradford and Bingley, HBOS, and the Royal Bank of Scotland were all bought by the Government, as these institutions' imminent collapse, after they had aggressively lent 125 per cent mortgages to people who could not afford them, threatened national economic stability (Pugh 2017: 486). Such events mirrored the reckless lending policies of major US banks and the resultant 2008 Global Financial Crisis. Following the 2010 general election, a coalition government headed by the Conservatives, alongside the Liberal Democrats, introduced austerity measures to tackle the country's financial deficit. Chancellor George Osborne claimed the financial crisis had been caused by excessive State expenditure under thirteen years of New Labour, and so shrank the State accordingly by adopting drastic reductions in spending. He imposed an average 19 per cent cut across Government department budgets, resulting in the loss of 600,000 public-sector jobs and 700,000 private-sector positions. Council services also suffered from 40 per cent cuts to their budgets (Pugh 2017: 489).

This ongoing austerity package had a considerable effect on policing. Home Secretary Theresa May was booed by police staff when announcing 20 per cent budget cuts to the Police Federation on 16 May 2012, demonstrating a rift between Government and police for the first time in recent memory. In 2018, recorded crime continued to skyrocket at a 14 per cent year-on-year increase as the number of police officers in England and Wales fell to 121,929, the lowest level since records began (Travis 2018: n.p.). Home Office figures also revealed that 91 per cent of recorded crimes did not result in a conviction, as the 'charge/summons rate for offences recorded in the year to March 2018 currently stands at 9 per cent' (Home Office 2018: 17). On the one hand, police management can be criticised for failing to prioritise certain crimes in light of their diminished resources. In particular, the Metropolitan Police's slow response to the national rioting of 2011, following the shooting of Mark Duggan, was met with a large public outcry, as was the South Yorkshire Police's failure to deal with the widespread sexual grooming of children by gangs in Rotherham up until 2014. Furthermore, the introduction of Police and Crime Commissioner elections in 2012, a move designed to replace 'invisible and unaccountable Police Authorities', was met with widespread public apathy, the average voter-turnout of each constituency being 14.5 per cent, and has been dismissed as a 'superficial public relations exercise' (HAC 2016: 3; McDaniel 2018: 45). Simultaneously, however, there has been a renewed public sympathy for frontline officers facing increasingly dangerous circumstances in light of their lessened manpower, such as during the 2017 Manchester Arena bombing. Thousands witnessed the funerals of PC Nicola Hughes and PC Fiona Bone, who were shot dead during a routine call on 18 September 2012. Hundreds also attended the funeral of PC David Rathband, who was blinded by gunman Roal Moat on 4 July 2010 and committed suicide on 29 February 2012. This renewed support for uniformed officers is evidenced by a report carried out for Her Majesty's Inspectorate of Constabulary and Fire & Rescue Services on *Public Perceptions of Policing*, which states that the majority of people (53 per cent) 'are satisfied with the police' (Ipsos MORI Social Research Institute 2017: 1).

Broadchurch station

This apparent disparity between the working practices of managers and frontline officers in light of austerity is addressed by *Broadchurch*'s and *Happy Valley*'s station scenes. Both constabularies are small-scale operations with their crime-fighting abilities dictated by costs, leaving them underequipped to deal with their respective murder and kidnapping cases. Initially, *Broadchurch*'s dialogue appears to criticise the ramifications of austerity for Wessex Police, as a lack of funding and resources inhibits Detective Inspector Alec Hardy (David Tennant) and Detective Sergeant Ellie Miller (Olivia Colman) at key points of their murder investigation. When Hardy first enters Broadchurch station, Miller informs him they have only committed five officers to their initial house-to-house enquiries, including two inexperienced probationers; one cannot drive and the other has 'never taken a statement before'. Despite having been this understaffed from the start, Hardy informs Miller at the beginning of the sixth episode (8 April 2013) that their already-low staffing levels are 'being pulled back' by the Chief Superintendent because 'we've reached our budget ceiling'. Although in agreement with Miller's frustrations, Hardy explains that 'when a case drags on … bosses panic about explaining it to the accountants'. Compared to previous series, where a range of factors have been taken into consideration when resourcing enquiries, cold, hard finances are now the principal concern of authority figures, and are the deciding factor in committing to investigations.

Despite being pressured by a shoestring budget and below-par resources, *Broadchurch*'s station scenes reject Nordic noir's interdependence philosophy. Glen Creeber feels *Broadchurch* advocates interdependence through 'two diametrically opposed detectives' and their 'vastly contrasting personalities' (Creeber 2015a: 28). Creeber rightly characterises Hardy as an 'outsider who is withdrawn, rather tetchy and no-nonsense', compared to Miller, who is 'married, warmhearted and trusting, as well as a long-standing pillar of the community' (Creeber 2015a: 28). However, a visual analysis of the station scenes does not necessarily provide the 'formidable team' Creeber talks of, where Miller's 'closeness to the community' enables Hardy to 'gain access to places and people he may have missed, while his distance from the community gives a much needed injection of objectivity' (Creeber 2015a: 28). To succeed in Wessex Police one must be dissociated from one's community. Miller's trusting of others is depicted as weakening her professional capabilities, and through the course of the series she learns to operate like Hardy, whose professional perspective and methods remain unchanged.

Aerial shots of West Bay beach are prominent throughout the series. From the start Chibnall made clear that 'the landscape had to feel present everywhere. Even in the police station'. So, 'the big windows with all of that light' that feature prominently are a key factor in visually working through the programme's ideology (quoted in Graham 2013: n.p.). The darkly lit stations of *The Killing* and *The Bridge* signify, through their ominous atmosphere, that the humanity and compassion of civil society are being engulfed by an impersonal and uncaring neoliberal individualism that detectives must work together to overcome. In *Broadchurch*, however, the bright yellow sunlight that percolates throughout the station represents the trusting interdependence of the town's close-knit community, which Miller must shun.

When returning from her holiday in the first episode (4 March 2013) Miller walks into the communal area of the station beaming with joy to her applauding colleagues. As she proceeds to dispense personalised gifts to members of the team, the windows filling the feature wall of the communal working area come into view. This grid of fifteen small windows overlooks the team's desks, ensuring they are all lit by natural sunlight. Miller basks in the warm, yellow glow provided by these windows and stands in the centre of the room to ask for the latest 'gossip' (see Figure 4). Before anyone can answer, Chief Superintendent Elaine Jenkinson (Tracy Childs) appears in Miller's eye-line at the edge of the space untouched by the sunlight to ask for 'a word'. In the following scene, in Jenkinson's office, Miller learns she will not be receiving her promotion to Detective Inspector despite having been promised so by Jenkinson. The scene begins with a close-up of Miller's face as her smiling expression immediately drops to a frown. The camera then cuts to a long shot of both characters, as Jenkinson sits down and invites Miller to do the same. This second shot (see Figure 5) is viewed from outside the glass wall of Jenkinson's office, adding a distant, removed, and unsympathetic angle to proceedings. In this shot the top row of five yellow windows,

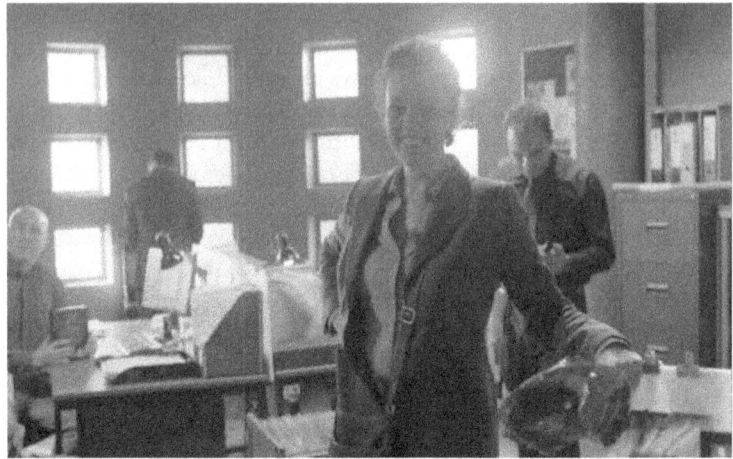

Figure 4

Figure 5

Figures 4 and 5 Miller must learn to shun the warm sunlight and the corresponding interdependence it represents in order to thrive as a successful detective worthy of promotion.

from the communal area's grid of windows, are reflected in the glass wall above both characters' heads, clashing with the drab, grey décor of Jenkinson's office. The visual composition implies that Miller's close emotional ties to her community do not provide her with the withdrawn objectivity required for promotion. This is confirmed later in the episode, when Miller is berated for disclosing the identity of murder victim Daniel Latimer to her journalist nephew, resulting in the news breaking via Twitter before the police have issued a public statement. Storming past the bright yellow windows, Hardy opts to stand outside the light by the darker greys of his office door as he demands to know who told the journalist. Miller, sitting centrally in the brightly lit communal space, sheepishly stands up from her desk as if a school pupil awaiting punishment. An unwavering trust in verbal promises from Miller's extended family or colleagues is presented as naïve.

Instead, Miller learns to embrace the darker recesses of the station space that, comparative to Nordic noir, instil Miller with the autonomy required to succeed. Here Miller is able, in accordance with Hardy's advice, to 'learn not to trust' and 'look at [her] community from the outside'. When initially separated from her colleagues Miller finds it difficult to adjust. Upon delivering her first briefing, her performance is tentative and hesitant. Introducing herself as 'Ellie', Miller swiftly reintroduces herself as 'err DS Miller'. Then, whilst she issues vague and unclear instructions an unsteady handheld camera occupies her approximate POV as it pulls in and out of focus in a disorienting manner. This shot is interspersed with a long shot of Miller standing in front of a blue wall far removed from the yellow light seeping in through the station windows. Here she stretches her arms out from both sides, looking uncomfortable (see Figure 6). However, by the end of the series, once Miller has embraced Hardy's worldview, her character becomes far more confident and assured. When she delivers a similar briefing in the penultimate episode (15 April 2013), the establishing shot frames Miller through the doorframe of Hardy's office. With the camera inside Hardy's dark and empty office this framing suggests Miller herself has now embraced Hardy's isolationism enough to warrant promotion. This is confirmed by the rest of the briefing, as when framed alone in a mid-shot Miller points authoritatively at officers and issues clear, direct, and specific instructions because time is running out (see Figure 7). Visually Miller no longer appears out of her depth, and this time the shot from behind puts her head in the middle of the frame, with a steady camera that remains in focus and depicts officers sat around her attentively hanging on to her every word. She is now confident enough to thrive with the limited timescale and diminished resources austerity has created.

Figure 6 Miller's first briefing is tentative and hesitant.

Figure 7 Miller grows with confidence and stature as she learns how to operate independently from her colleagues.

Norland Road police station

In contrast to *Broadchurch*, *Happy Valley* has an anti-austerity agenda. Instead of reduced spending being used as a means of assessing characters' professional capabilities, direct connections are drawn among austerity, death, and trauma. When Councillor Marcus

Gascoigne (Steven Hartley) is caught drink-driving, PC Kirsten McAskill (Sophie Rundle) is too intimidated by his status to arrest him, and so calls in Sergeant Cawood to do it. Then, despite Cawood's persevering to have Gascoigne charged for his drink-driving and drug possession, her efforts are blocked by District Commander Praveen Badal (Ramon Tikaram). Badal tells Cawood that Gascoigne 'does a lot for us on the council' and to consider the 'implications before taking it further': i.e. cuts to public spending have left the West Yorkshire police at the mercy of certain councillors who have the power to vote through policies and secure resources that will help them. Tragedy then emanates from this austerity because, having been disciplined by Cawood for her mishandling of Gascoigne, McAskill dies trying to impress Cawood by stopping a speeding white van, driven by Royce. McAskill is murdered by Royce for her efforts, as he does not want her finding the kidnapped Ann Gallagher (Charlie Murphy) captive in the back of his vehicle. Thus, austerity results in McAskill's death because there is a lack of manpower required to carry out routine two-person patrols. Furthermore, McAskill's death can be linked to austerity because she cannot navigate between Cawood's view of policing, where 'nobody is above the law', and Badal's fiscal priorities as District Commander. This failure to satisfy such contradictory guidance when arresting Gascoigne results in McAskill's attempt to impress Cawood by apprehending Royce's van. Badal is shown to be ignorant of this correlation between austerity and tragedy, because after consoling McAskill's bereaved family personally he immediately instructs Cawood in private to drop Gascoigne's charges as if they are a separate matter. Badal is unaware that this rift between his priorities and Cawood's instructions, arising from austerity, led to McAskill's death, and that he is actively worsening this disjuncture, which could threaten the safety of further officers.

A link between austerity and trauma is articulated visually when Cawood experiences bouts of post-traumatic stress disorder (PTSD) exclusively within the station. When Badal briefs all the uniformed officers about McAskill's death he informs them that 'my door is always open', despite his being permanently stationed at Leeds, and reminds officers of the station's chaplain and doctor, should they require professional help. Whilst Badal continues to deliver his speech the camera zooms into Cawood's face as a loud ringing muffles Badal's dialogue. A POV shot then reveals that Cawood is looking at what appears to be her daughter's pale corpse at the back of the room, which causes Cawood to tense up and clench her fists. Then, later in the episode, when clearing McAskill's locker, Cawood is interrupted from itemising

McAskill's personal effects when she looks up to see her daughter's corpse hanging in the back of the room. This causes Cawood's ears to ring again as she struggles for breath. Cawood's first attack is triggered by an outlining of the limited resources available to counsel officers. Then her second attack is prompted by her looking at a newspaper photo of McAskill surrounded by primary schoolchildren holding a placard reading 'people who help us'. These triggers are significant because they are reminders that the professional apparatus available to maintain community relations (the local newspaper has moved online permanently), support officers (they have limited counselling services), and generally engender compassion as well as interdependence, is becoming increasingly scarce as a result of austerity. This is directly detrimental to Cawood's mental and physical health.

The abject returns

As Hardy suffers from similar physiological attacks to Cawood, the abject once again becomes a central component of the station. Compared to 1990s series, where bloody images of murder victims decorate incident rooms, the abject is now something that officers have internalised. In several instances, when suffering from his heart arrhythmia, Hardy develops the same symptoms as Cawood, including blurred vision, a ringing in his ears, and clenched fists. This first occurs when chatting with Miller in the station canteen, where she protests that Broadchurch is not the sort of community that hides dark secrets. Later, at the end of Episode 6, after all the detectives have gone home, Hardy calls his estranged daughter and leaves a message on her answerphone in a bid to reconnect with her. He then searches through officers' desks for evidence before falling to the floor incapacitated with pain. In the next, penultimate, episode Hardy's attacks become so severe that he is admitted to hospital. Swiftly, however, Hardy discharges himself to resume his leadership of the investigation. It is revealed that his arrhythmia is a condition caused by the stress he has experienced from a previous assignment – the Sandbrook case – where he was publicly and professionally disgraced for not charging a suspect. It transpires that the Sandbrook case was not solved because the detective sergeant (Hardy's wife) lost the only clear forensic evidence linked to the guilty party whilst having an affair with another detective sergeant on the same case. Hardy then decided to take the blame to preserve his wife's reputation and his daughter's close relationship with her mother. Misjudged decisions are to blame for Hardy's condition, rather than austerity. The only way he can cure himself is to channel his ambition, determination, and independence into solving the murder case. It is as if he is punished for reaching out to his daughter before the case is complete and momentarily entertaining Miller's view that Broadchurch may not have secrets. The series largely subscribes to a neoliberal ideology: any sign of dependency or opening oneself to the need for others is reviled, as 'any attempt to do this produces, as a consequence, a visceral and abject reflex of rejection' (Dave 2017: 133).

In contrast, *Happy Valley*'s Cawood operates as the matriarch of Norwood Road station, helping officers through their trauma with coping mechanisms she has personally developed and refined through her working life. Cawood's care for the community rejects the fierce independence and scepticism promoted by Hardy to solve cases in times of austerity. Instead, Cawood's leadership fosters interdependence to help police workers overcome the trauma and difficulties austerity creates. When she tells PC Shafiq Shah (Shane Zaza) that McAskell was crushed to death Shah sits back in his chair, rubs his face, and undoes the top of his zip, gasping for breath. Recognising these symptoms of an oncoming panic attack, Cawood instructs Shah to 'put your head between your knees' as she gently pushes on his back to ensure he assumes the position. Similarly, when uniformed police constables are out on patrol, Cawood speaks to them through her radio in her office whilst they are facing testing circumstances, in order to provide her staff with reassurance, companionship, and advice. This helps McAskill to conduct arrests, and 'Twiggy' (Amer Nazir) to gain legal entry into a tower-block flat. Cawood's active care for her staff's welfare enables her to succeed professionally.

Compared to Miller of *Broadchurch*, Cawood retains her role as a pillar of her community. Cawood's knowledge of, and relationship with, specific members of the town provide her with the key information required to learn of Ann Gallagher's kidnapping, locate where Gallagher is being held captive, and then arrest and charge Royce. This interdependence is reciprocated by the public, given that following McAskill's death the station becomes filled with flowers sent in by a grieving public. These moments demonstrate a renewed sympathy for those whose job has become more dangerous and traumatic in light of austerity. In contrast, Badal's financial prioritising makes him a distant, isolated, and incompetent figure who upon his infrequent visits to the station is comically clueless about the status of ongoing investigations. Instead, Cawood's close relationship with her community enables her informally to bypass these official, incompetent, and financially obsessed channels. Through its station scenes, *Happy Valley* champions an interdependent working environment and close community-relations to overcome the challenges of austerity and solve the case. In contrast, *Broadchurch* adopts a more neoliberal view, as austerity is part and parcel of the pressures a senior detective must learn to thrive under. Separating oneself from one's community, as symbolised by Miller's and Hardy's active avoidance of the warmth and camaraderie emanating from the bright sunlight illuminating Broadchurch station, is what leads to professional success.

Austerity and social inequality

In addition to exploring the effects austerity has had on the police service, both *Broadchurch*'s and *Happy Valley*'s civilian scenes acknowledge the social implications of austerity. The sharp increase in wealth inequality and the fall in living standards feature prominently. From 2008 to 2014 real wages fell by 9.2 per cent, representing the largest decline since the 1860s (Pugh 2017: 497). By 2007 the ratio of bosses' pay to that of their employees had risen to 98:1 (Pugh 2017: 496). Meanwhile, widespread prejudice against the welfare state, as an insupportably high burden on tax payers, had been exacerbated by Government policy. Cuts to the welfare budget of £16 billion helped increase the number of food banks run by the Trussell Trust from 56 in 2009 to 445 by 2015, when 1 million emergency food parcels were distributed (Pugh 2017: 498). Furthermore 2,380 people died between 2011 and 2014 after their claim for Employment and Support Allowance ended because a Work Capability Assessment found they were fit for work (Pugh 2017: 497). In response, United Nations special investigator Phillip Alston entered the UK on 12 November 2018 to conduct his two-week inquiry into the UK's alleged breaching of international human rights, including the rights to food, housing, and adequate living standards.

Landscape television

Broadchurch and *Happy Valley* consider the impact austerity has had on communities through the way in which each series captures its surrounding landscape. With the advent of high-definition simulcasting in 2010, major broadcasters could now use a higher resolution of up to 1920 × 1080 pixels, compared to the 720 × 480 of standard television. With a sharper clarity of image on much larger screens, viewers were increasingly invited to scrutinise the visuals of drama in more detail. In a similar manner to cinema and Nordic noir, then, shots of West Yorkshire townscapes and the Jurassic Coast provide 'natural space freed from any emphasis on the representation of figures and eventhood' (Lefebvre 2011: 63). This framing of landscapes in both series navigates between the visual discourse of British social realism and the recent spate of landscape television documentaries. On one hand, like British New Wave cinema, landscape shots are 'never quite fully contained by narrative' to provide 'pleasurable voyeuristic spectacle' of working-class squalor (Higson 1996b: 134). Then, on the other hand, they also borrow elements from recent landscape programming documentaries, including *A Picture of Britain* (BBC, 2005), *Coast* (BBC, 2005–), and *Wainwright Walks* (BBC, 2007–2009), to invite a contemplative mode of viewing that creates a nostalgic, 'heritage' image of an 'unspoilt Britain' entirely devoid of urban space (Wheatley 2016: 125). The way in which this balance is achieved reveals each programme's predominant disposition towards austerity.

Jurassic Coast

In *Broadchurch*, unnerving shots of West Bay beach's East Cliff, accompanied by Ólafur Arnalds's haunting score, envelop civilian scenes to provide the landscape with an oppressive agency over its ensnared, middle-class, seaside community. In the first episode, East Cliff is viewed from a low-angle shot that draws attention to the imposing nature of the 46-foot-high Bridport Sand Formation. For six seconds the audience is able to scrutinise the intricate, fossilised patterns embedded in its golden yellow limestone structure, dating back to Lower Jurassic times, whilst the cliff is encircled by flying seagulls. Then the camera cuts to a bird's-eye view of the beach from above the cliff. This shot sequence occurs after local journalist Olly Stephens (Jonathan Bailey) finds his application to the *Daily Mail* has been rejected, having applied for jobs at all the national newspapers. In another instance, Episode 2 (11 March 2013) opens with a seven-second medium shot of onshore sea-waves pulling in with the tide, focusing on the foam patterns of the crashing whitewater, before transitioning into shots of Beth Latimer (Jodie Whittaker) in her deceased son's bedroom, folding his clothes. Also, when Chloe Latimer (Charlotte Beaumont) disappears, the scene begins by zooming out from a side profile of East Cliff before cutting to Beth, distressed that her daughter has gone missing. Using contemplative imagery of the coast devoid of narrative purpose at these moments suggests that the physical location of the beach and its erosive nature are the source of the residents' entrapment. The long duration spent viewing the landscape's structures emphasises the powerlessness and insignificance of characters who lack the agency needed to evade their fates as unsuccessful journalist, bereaved mother, or 'dead boy's sister'.

These landscape shots subscribe to a neo-environmental, determinist view that, through the work of geographers Eric Jones (2003), Jared Diamond (2005), Jeffrey Sachs (2008), and Betty Meggers (2010) believes the environment is predominantly responsible for 'shaping the traits of individual human beings' (Meyer and Guss 2017: 7). For these theorists it is environmental factors, over social factors, that account for the 'present-day world pattern of wealth, power, and well-being' (Meyer and Guss 2017: 40). Like the most extreme incarnations of neo-environmental determinism, where humans are considered to be 'passive pawns at the mercy of natural phenomena', *Broadchurch* downplays the recession in relation to the physical features of the town's surrounding landscape (Erickson 1999: 634). A low-angle shot of East Cliff at night is followed by drunk business owner Laurie (Bill Fellows) abruptly silenced by hotel owner Becca Fisher (Simone McAullay) and the Revd Paul Coates (Arthur Darvill) in the Trader's Hotel pub for suggesting that the murder will economically 'cripple the rest of us' following the 'recession' and 'weeks of rain'. The implication here is that being trapped by the seasonal nature of the tourism economy is a larger problem to overcome that pales in comparison to the temporality of the recession.

Whilst it has been argued that *Broadchurch*'s landscape shots succumb to 'the functional mechanics of setting', the duration of these shots freed from eventhood provides the landscape with the agency emerging in neo-environmental, determinist thought (Roberts 2016: 377). Cowering at the imposing nature of the seaside is a marked contrast from the city-dwelling protagonists of social-realist films *A Taste of Honey* (1961), *This Sporting Life* (1963), *A Room for Romeo Brass* (1999), and *London to Brighton* (2006). In each case, the 'calm sea ... operating independently of narrative' provides freedom to the spectator 'from the chaos of the characters' lives' (Hockenhull 2009: 73). *Broadchurch* challenges the heritage of seaside imagery throughout British social-realist cinema by recasting the coast as an entrapping environment responsible for alienating its middle-class residents. Therefore, in keeping with the neoliberalism of its station scenes, any mention of austerity and its potential ramifications is trivialised.

Calder Valley

Broadchurch utilises the visual discourse associated with landscape documentaries to invert British social realism's iconography of seaside locations and to downplay austerity. *Happy Valley*, however, combines the visual discourse of both genres to stigmatise the underclasses of West Yorkshire. According to Andrew Higson, the New Wave iteration of British social realism consistently provides 'that long shot of our town from that hill' to lure 'the eye across the vast empty space of a townscape' independently from the narrative (Higson 1996b: 138). Such aerial images of working-class housing are presented as both beautiful and dangerously strange because the viewer is invited 'to identify with a position outside and above the city', thus replicating the 'voyeurism' of the middle-class filmmakers looking down on the working classes (Higson 1996b: 152). This is the tradition of social realism that *Z Cars* (BBC, 1962–1978) sought to break away from by employing writers, producers, directors, and actors from such communities to provide an authentic view of working-class life. *Happy Valley*'s utilisation of landscape shots familiar to British New Wave cinema and landscape documentaries, however, provides the British police series with a distanced, middle-class view of lower-class subjects.

In several instances a camera contemplatively admires the townscapes of West Yorkshire from a high vantage point before having to divert its gaze towards a disturbance unfolding in an impoverished area of the town populated with social housing. Regularly, Victorian architecture and rural features of the town are juxtaposed against underclass characters who are dislocated from, and unappreciative of, their surroundings. The first episode (29 April 2014) commences with an aerial view of Sowerby Bridge. A Victorian railway bridge is centre-frame, and a third of the frame is filled with green hills and a blue open sky. The calming, four-second shot is only accompanied by the diegetic sounds of distant, off-screen motorway traffic and wind, inviting viewers to marvel simultaneously at the industrial heritage and at the peacefulness of its rurality. However, this peace is interrupted by Cawood's speeding police car, which the camera has to pan downwards to capture. In panning down, it omits the green hills and railway bridge from view as the narrative unfolds. Cawood then deters twenty-three-year-old 'unemployed smack-head' Liam Hughes (James Burrows) from setting himself on fire following the breakdown of his relationship. Hughes stands in a children's play area in the centre of a council estate, drinking alcohol and holding a lighter, having taken drugs and dowsed himself in oil. He is only ever framed by an over-the-shoulder shot assimilating Cawood's perspective, which maintains a tentative distance from Hughes and exaggerates his jittery, drug-induced gestures. Hughes appears infantile compared to the assured actions of Cawood, as the series literally and figuratively looks down on a person who chooses to indulge in excessive behaviours that clash with the wider environment's tranquillity.

Later in the same episode, Jason Tindall (Jason Varley) and his girlfriend (Lily Jane Stead) are found lying amongst household rubbish whilst playing a videogame and taking heroin in their council-flat bedroom. Tindall's girlfriend explains the videogame controller was dropped by accident, which caused her to scream, prompting a neighbour to dial 999. Once Tindall is apprehended and the police car drives off, the camera cuts to an aerial shot of the high-rise flat's location. Two-thirds of the concluding shot provides an aerial view of Victorian millworkers' cottages and the green rural fields they are located on. However, the tall, council-flat structure fills a third of the shot on the right-hand side of the frame in the immediate foreground, obstructing and spoiling the picturesque view as an intrusive eyesore. A similar shot is used to commence the second episode (6 May 2014), again contrasting the high-rise flats against the old workers' cottages, before Cawood fails to apprehend two men selling drugs from an ice-cream van. Each of these young underclass adults feeds into the rhetoric espoused by education minister Michael Gove, who felt such deviants grow up with a 'poverty of ambition ... discipline ... and soul' (quoted in Porter 2011: n.p.). Locating these scenes in a play area, ice-cream van, and a bedroom codifies the underclass condition as a childish 'lifestyle choice' (Biressi and Nunn 2013: 64).

Rather than acknowledging criminology that criticised law-and-order policy for managing and controlling 'undesirable' populations, *Happy Valley* sides with modern political discourse, as young underclass men are depicted as rational actors. The young men actively ruin the tranquil beauty of the rural landscape (captured in the same visual manner as landscape documentaries) and rustic charm of Victorian working-class houses (viewed from the same voyeuristic vantage point as the British New Wave).[1] *Broadchurch*'s landscape shots downplay austerity in relation to the stranglehold that natural phenomena have over middle-class residents dependent on a seaside economy. *Happy Valley* draws attention to an underclass actively blemishing their landscape. However, unlike West Yorkshire's overworked frontline police officers, the residents whom Cawood classifies as 'scrotes' and 'dropouts' are portrayed as deserving of their circumstances, worsened by austerity's wealth gap, for deciding to ruin their peaceful town.

The squeezed middle

In relation to these brief scenes of underclass characters, *Happy Valley* is more devoted to the plight of middle-class characters. Understanding the perspective and motives of accountant and kidnapping-mastermind Kevin Wetherill, seeing through caravan-park owner Ashley Cowgill's (Joe

Armstrong) execution of the kidnapping, and witnessing the suffering endured by business owner Nevison Gallagher (George Costigan) as his daughter is taken, provide the audience's reoccurring point of focus. Each of these characters represents what sociology refers to as the 'squeezed middle'. Originally coined in the USA, the term has been applied to British workers coping with the 'sharp rise in economic inequality', 'limited social mobility', and the 'squeeze on middle class living standards' (Parker 2013a: 1). Wetherill and Cowgill turn to crime because they fear for their millennial children failing to maintain the same socio-economic position as themselves. Two-fifths of the workforce in 2011 identified as middle-class, compared to before the Second World War, when fewer than 15 per cent of the population were in professions or management positions, which has led to 'career congestion' (Roberts 2011: 134). These diminishing opportunities for career progression, higher house prices and living costs, continued austerity, and increased student debt mean that millennials are the first generation to face 'generational pay stagnation', as they will, on average, earn less than the generation before them over the course of their working lives (Intergenerational Commission 2018: 11). As empirical evidence shows, 'family economic resources are crucial to the reproduction of middle class advantage' (Devine 2004: 178). Therefore Weatherill masterminds the kidnapping of his boss's daughter to fund the private education of his own daughters, whilst Cowgill facilitates the lucrative supply chain of drugs into the valley to provide for his sons. Thus, *Happy Valley* is a series predominantly interested in the intra-class conflict of the squeezed middle.

Toxic masculinity

A dark consequence of this middle-class conflict is Weatherill's, Cowgill's, and Gallagher's regular displays of Terry Kupers's 'toxic masculinity', a term used in psychological studies of abusive male behaviour following Raewyn Connell's (2005) analysis of hegemonic masculinity. The kidnapping, for example, demonstrates a 'readiness to resort to violence' and a 'lack of consideration of the experiences and feelings of others' (Kupers 2005: 717). Among the men there is also a distinct 'incapacity to nurture' their children (Kupers 2005: 717). The only time Weatherill interacts with his daughter is when he makes her a tuna mayo sandwich, on which she reminds him that she 'hates' tuna and he 'never listens' (Kupers 2005: 717). Similarly, the only scene Nevison Gallagher and his daughter Ann share is when he claims that he 'pissed' the money he spent on her private education 'up the wall'. Furthermore, a 'dread of dependency' on others motivates all the men (Kupers

2005: 717). Gallagher's refusing to ask the police for help worsens his daughter's fate, whilst Weatherill plots the kidnapping having felt humiliated after initially being refused a requested pay rise. The 'stigmatization and subjugation of women and gays' is also a common trait (Kupers 2005: 717). Cowgill refers to Weatherill, when first demanding a ransom from Gallagher, as 'that irritating little twat of an accountant'. Weatherill also tells his wife he deserves a pay rise because work is akin to 'taking it up the arse' every day, given that Gallagher's business was once co-owned by Weatherill's father. Regularly, this sexually abusive language is used as a means of attempting to maintain power, dominance, and control over other men in public by belittling them as effeminate. Therefore, the toxic masculinity emanating from *Happy Valley*'s principal crime-plot comes from male characters attempting to maintain or better the public socio-economic standing of their family name. The toxic masculinity does not come from a desire to provide for their children's personal needs, as is often implied by sociological discussions of the squeezed middle.

In contrast, the wives of Nevison Gallagher and Kevin Weatherill are much more level-headed, as it is their calm discussions in private domestic spaces that offer solutions to the problems created by the men in public environments. Having been refused a pay rise, Kevin Weatherill explains the day's events to his wife, Jenny (Julia Ford) in their opulent conservatory. Repeatedly, Kevin undercuts his wife's view that securing a pay rise does 'not really matter' in light of their 'nice house' and 'two lovely daughters'. Jenny's view is underlined by the establishing aerial shots of their home. In comparison to the disorder experienced on the council estates, the Weatherills' large and peaceful suburban house is comfortably nestled at the foot of a hill on the edge of the greenbelt. Instead of being comforted by such picturesque and idyllic surroundings, Kevin draws the camera into darkened close-ups of his face as he sternly dismisses his wife's advice and aggressively punches the kitchen table in a moment of catharsis. In contrast, the Gallagher household provides a more democratic atmosphere, where Nevison's wife Helen (Jill Baker) and daughter Ann convince him to grant Kevin Weatherill his previously requested pay rise. The Gallaghers share the space on equal terms as discussions over the round dining table are framed through a medium shot. Here, Nevison looks to his wife and daughter for reassurance, perspective, and advice. Like the publications of Grayson Perry (2016), Jack Urwin (2016), and Robert Webb (2018), *Happy Valley*'s domestic scenes assert the importance of men being able to talk 'without fear or judgement' whilst looking at what can be learnt 'from women to better ourselves', without

Figure 8 Kevin Weatherill draws the camera into a darkened close-up as he expresses hatred of his boss to his wife Jenny Weatherill in their conservatory.

succumbing to toxic masculinity and further harmful action (Urwin 2016: 228, 229).² Had Kevin Weatherill listened to his wife, and not continued to disconnect himself from his environment, then he would have received his raise without having to resort to a kidnapping. *Happy Valley* suggests interdependence of the genders within middle-class families can enable citizens to be satisfied with their public status, helping to find civil and constructive ways to overcome austerity's continued effects on a growing wealth gap, and intergenerational pay stagnation.

Maternal solutions

Broadchurch's civilian scenes revolve around the squeezed middle-class and grieving Latimer family. Mark Latimer (Andrew Buchan) is the owner of a small plumbing business who cannot afford to take compassionate leave as his wife Beth works part-time. At home the Latimers work out how to balance the seaside economy's alienating and determinist expectations of them alongside asserting a sense of agency over their lives. Initially, abiding by Detective Inspector Alec Hardy's independent and neoliberal worldview espoused from the station makes for a claustrophobic existence. In communal areas of the Latimers' household a window's reflection features prominently when they are reluctant openly to discuss their emotional problems. This makes for an inward-looking family environment. Regularly the camera cuts to a window, which fills the shot with a reflection of the back garden, blocking one's view of the unfolding scene. At the start of Episode 1, for example, Beth argues with her daughter Chloe because she is not convinced by Chloe's repeated assertions that she is ill and should not go to school. Beth seeks support from her husband, who states 'I'm not getting involved' as the camera cuts to frame Beth through a shot of the window, which fills the camera's frame with a blurred reflection of the back garden and obstructs the view of her. Then, later in the series, when Mark tries to discuss Beth's pregnancy in the kitchen, she tells him 'not today', as the camera focuses on the window to look again at a reflection of the garden. Reflections of the outside environment are used when the family fails to open up, which makes the interiors of their home appear smaller than they are and so produces a reclusive, dissonant, and emotionally obstructive environment.

Compared to Broadchurch station, a rewarding life is achieved once Beth Latimer stops pursuing Hardy's brand of independence. Initially she is an alienated family figure, who seeks refuge in the bathroom secretly to admire her pregnant stomach in the mirror, or locks her daughter in the bathroom to demand allegiance when her husband Mark, Chloe's father, is suspected of the murder. At this time Beth grows frustrated with her family for not letting her leave the house alone without explanation, and grows increasingly frustrated, panicked, and even paranoid. When Beth accepts her role as mother in the image of David Cameron's pro-social conservatism, however, she acquires a more fulfilling and stable existence. At this time the Prime Minister repeatedly emphasised the importance of two-parent families by supporting proposals for 'tax and benefit reforms to ... make it financially easier for one spouse to stay at home to care for their children' (Bryson and Heppell 2010: 37). This change in perspective occurs when Mark Latimer proposes that he and Beth both look through their murdered son's baby photos and possessions, instead of continuing to bicker about Mark's affair or Beth's pregnancy. Together, both parents look through Daniel's first shoes and certificates, and Beth fondly strokes her son's hospital wristband. When flicking through baby photographs both parents maintain eye contact, lovingly embrace, and laugh together as part of a tender exchange. When the camera cuts to its signature shot of both characters through the window no reflection is produced, as for once the parents appear comfortable together and content in their home. In previous scenes a view of the back garden's reflection, through a shot of the window, would coincide with Beth's and Mark's reluctance to vocalise their true feelings. Here, the lack of reflection coincides with a moment of contentment that serves to '*naturalize* Beth's decision to have the child to significantly lessen her "emotional turmoil"' (Greer 2017: 338).

Correspondingly, once Beth Latimer decides to be a stay-at-home mother, the secretive, inward, and emotionally stilted family setting is replaced by a more wholesome family environment. On the morning of Daniel's funeral Beth affirms she is happy to give up work and live as a stay-at-home mother and housewife because there is 'plenty to do'. She no longer feels a need to return to her part-time work at the tourist information centre because she realises 'nobody wants to hear a dead boy's mum give directions'. Beth becomes the show's 'heroically maternal figure, exposing motherhood as a woman's primary identity', and complies with the 'new traditionalism' of postfeminism (Greer 2017: 338). In sync with Anne Kingston's (2004) analysis of Nigella Lawson and Kirstie Allsopp, Stephanie Genz's (2009) examination of *Desperate Housewives*, and Diane Negra's (2009) study of romantic comedies, Beth is a figure who also provides 'a vision of the home to which women have "freely" chosen to return' as a site of fulfilment (Probyn 1990: 149). Severing 'previous associations of drudgery and confinement' of domesticity (see Chapter 2 on *Hunter's Walk*), the domestic sphere is now 'redesigned and resignified as a domain of female autonomy and independence' (Genz and Brabon 2018: 94). Contradictorily, in following this postfeminist logic, the home is also a comforting 'fortress' where Beth can 'escape economic/national/social insecurities and threats' that have arisen from the Government's austerity programme (Genz and Brabon 2018: 102). Both Latimers now appear comfortable in each other's company as they are able to discuss their feelings candidly and openly. Succumbing to a pro-social conservative outlook of her own accord provides Beth with the rewarding level of autonomy and purpose in life she requires, whilst protecting her from the challenges of neo-environmental determinism and austerity.

Overall, where *Happy Valley* previously endorsed interdependence in the police station to overcome the challenges of austerity, *Broadchurch* instead opted for isolationism to make detectives more effective in light of such budgetary challenges. These ideologies are given a new dimension by civilian scenes. *Broadchurch* further downplays the severity of austerity and uses HD aerial cameras to provide the Jurassic Coast with an oppressive, neodeterminist agency over its residents. This agency inverts the heritage of social-realist film, which has consistently viewed the seaside as a place of freedom and escape. *Happy Valley*, however, uses the same technology to adopt 'that long shot of our town from that hill' from British New Wave social realism to stigmatise the underclass residents who are demonised for childishly making lifestyle choices that ruin West Yorkshire's tranquillity and industrial heritage. Helen Wheatley argues that further debate is required to work out what 'this contemplation' provided by drone-mounted aerial HD cameras 'might distract us from' politically (Wheatley 2016: 148). In this instance, the interdependence that *Happy Valley* advocates between genders within families, as advocated in police-station scenes, prevents toxic masculinity from manifesting. However, this focus overlooks the underclass because overcoming generational pay stagnation is depicted as a solely middle-class pursuit. Then, *Broadchurch* encourages women to succumb to a domestic idyll as part of a pro-social conservative and neoliberal postfeminist agenda. Thus, the outside world and the difficulties associated with it are visually presented as having an emotionally stifling presence when reflected into the home. As such, the noble struggle of asserting one's autonomy over a determinist environment is portrayed as an exclusively male and middle-class endeavour.

Private lives of officers

Overlooking an underclass perspective in *Happy Valley* and dictating middle-class femininity through the limitations of the domestic sphere in *Broadchurch* are offered some recompense by the private lives of Sergeant Catherine Cawood and Detective Inspector Ellie Miller. For the first time in the police-series genre, crime does not just exist in the homes of police officials; it has the potential to thrive in an uncontrollable manner. Catherine Cawood cares for her grandson Ryan Cawood (Rhys Connah) because her daughter Rebecca killed herself, unable to cope with the fact her son was conceived from a rape enacted by Tommy Lee Royce. Ryan's bad behaviour requires frequent disciplining at school and concerns Catherine, afraid that Ryan is a 'potential monster' who has genetically inherited the violent temperament of one of the most prolific offenders in the valley (Greer 2017: 342). In *Broadchurch*, the killer of eight-year-old Daniel Latimer is revealed to be Ellie Miller's husband, Joe. Ellie is distraught that she has been oblivious to the predatory relationship her own husband has been conducting with their son's best friend under her nose. Officers and detectives having to combat the same pressures as their community within their own homes has been a central tenet of the British police series. The home of a police officer has been far from a safe haven since 1962, when PC Bob Steele of *Z Cars* subjected his wife to domestic violence. Now, however, an unexplainable form of sinister criminality underpins police officials' homes, over which they have little control. In finding a solution to deal with this criminality both series briefly complicate the ideology of their civilian scenes to some extent. Where Cawood offers an intermediary value system to guide the petulant middle classes and irresponsible lower classes of her community, Miller is not wholly defined by her domestic identity.

Common Valley culture

The design of Catherine Cawood's home is 'decidedly ordinary in lifestyle and status', compared to those of Nevison Gallagher, Ashley Cowgill, and Kevin Weatherill, who enjoy comparative 'economic leverage' in their spacious suburban homes (Piper 2017: 192). Cawood lives in a Victorian former millworker's terraced house. In addition to her grandson, Cawood cares for her sister Clare Cartwright (Siobhan Finneran), who is a recovering heroin addict seeking work. Compared to the 'muted chrome palettes and minimalist designs' of the other middle-class civilian characters' houses, Cawood's home is 'steeped in bright colour, surrounded by pleasant clutter', and the kitchen is 'replete with bold tomato red walls' that garishly clash with the turquoise cupboards (Piper 2017: 192). Thus, the house is a space for living in, rather than to display one's wealth like 'the ideal bourgeois home advocated by leisure programming and magazines' (Piper 2017: 192). Cawood is of a middle-class status, in that she can afford regularly to 'eat out' (Roberts 2011: 146). Correspondingly Cawood is not, strictly speaking, a working-class character, because she is not subject to 'low-level', 'part-time', or 'casual' work (Roberts 2011: 89). Instead, Cawood, with her 'display of lower middle class ordinariness', articulates a set of moral values that are at odds with the ideology of 'the ever enterprising middle class discourses of self-improvement' (Piper 2017: 192). Her private life comparatively tempers the greedy lifestyles of the middle-class characters whilst offering guidance to the feckless underclass by emphasising the importance of 'a strong work ethic, respect, collective values, and reciprocal support' (Beider 2011). These values, Harris Beider's ethnographic research argues, are integral to contemporary working-class communities, and are communicated visually. Aerial shots are not used to establish Cawood's home. Instead of voyeuristically assessing the material worth of her house before a scene unfolds, as occurs in underclass and upper-middle-class locations, viewers are encouraged to assess Cawood's character on the values she abides by, removed from the underclass/upper-middle-class binary of the town.

The relationship shared between Cawood and her sister is markedly different from the other middle-class family relationships of *Happy*

Figure 9 Cawood and Cartwright share the frame in a two-shot when conducting their responsive conversations whilst overlooking the neighbourhood. This starkly contrasts with the darkened close-ups of Weatherill whose enraged jealousy of Nevison Gallagher exponentially worsens when conversing with his wife Jenny in their isolated conservatory.

Valley. Unlike the Cowgills and Weatherills, the sisters do not draw one another into darkened close-ups to isolate themselves from their surroundings and mull over their jealousy towards those of a higher economic standing. Instead both sisters share brightly lit, medium two-shots, offering advice to one other regarding their personal affairs and working lives on an equal basis. A significant proportion of discussions takes place outside Catherine's back door, overlooking the alley shared between themselves and their neighbours' terraced houses (see Figure 9). Having conversations in this space suggests, visually, that the sisters are part of their community, as they reflect on their actions and gain perspective when overlooking their neighbourhood. Kevin Weatherill grows increasingly paranoid, delusional, and jealous of the Gallaghers' wealth, being isolated from his community within his own conservatory. However, Cawood's family spend sufficient time with their neighbours to the point that clothes and personal possessions can be left in the street without being stolen; Ryan Cawood can play football in the street at night; and he can also take pride in feeding their neighbour's cat, believing the cat 'likes me the best'. By being more firmly rooted to their community, Cawood and Cartwright prevent petty jealousies and actions, that could detrimentally affect themselves and others, from aggressively materialising. For example, Cartwright is able to talk

Cawood down from acting rashly against Royce on the day of his prison release. Initially referring to Royce as 'that subhuman rotting piece of excrement', Cartwright tempers her sister's hasty plans by asserting that she is concerned Cawood will make herself ill again. Cartwright has the final say in the conversation, stating 'You worry about me staying on the wagon. I worry about you. You're the only sister I've got.' The final close-up shot of Cawood looking into Cartwright's eyes without a comeback suggests she has taken on board her sister's advice. It is not Cartwright's pleading with her sister to 'act rationally' that calms Cawood down. Instead Cartwright equates Cawood's worries about her staying clear of drug abuse with her own concerns that Cawood's bloodlust towards Royce will destroy their family. This enables Cawood to assess her thirst for revenge from a different and markedly selfless perspective.

Catherine Cawood's open, frank, and tender exchanges with her sister replicate the nature of her conversations with other women in the town, thus creating an informal community of citizens who are collectively grounded by their respect and reciprocal support for one another. It is Helen Gallagher who approaches Cartwright about the kidnapping of her daughter at the charity soup kitchen where they both volunteer. Cartwright is all too happy to arrange a meeting between Helen and her sister, given the support Helen gave Cartwright to overcome her drug addiction. By breaking Nevison Gallagher's orders and speaking to Cawood in a personal capacity, Helen enables Cawood to bring in specialist expertise and prevent Ann Gallagher from being murdered. Then, when Ann is rescued, Cawood sits outside the back door of her house with Ann, in the same manner she does with her own sister, to offer her the support and confidence that Ann's own education and family life have failed to provide. Essentially, what Cawood oversees throughout the community is what Raymond Williams refers to as a 'common culture'. Writing in postwar Britain, Williams argued that culture should 'not be confined to an educated minority', as it 'exists in a hierarchy of levels down to the everyday tastes and practices of the masses' (McGuigan, 2013: 93). Cawood presides over what Williams sees as the need for a 'free contributing and common process of participation in the creation of meanings and values' as part of a 'participating democracy', as the women provide a network of support to one another guided by their own humanitarian values to counter the destructive effects of toxic masculinity arising from middle-class materialism (Williams 2013: 99, 100). These scenes between Cawood and other members of the community echo the calls in contemporary social science to incorporate the public into a participatory democracy. The school of 'democratic criminology', for example, argues for an approach that takes into account the public's 'concerns and beliefs ... on their own terms', communicates the results of research to the public, and synthesises 'public opinion and criminological research ... to policy-makers' (Fichtelberg and Kupchik 2011: 69, 75). Overall, it is Cawood's private life that provides the Calder Valley with a common culture, guided by the humanitarian values of its citizens, that strives to achieve reciprocal respect and support-networks. Such interdependence challenges a divisive political climate of austerity, where leading social scientists have discerned 'the only thing almost everyone strives for is to better their own position – as individuals' (Pickett and Wilkinson 2010: 4).

Crucially, the final scene of *Happy Valley* sees Cawood overlooking the valley (Halifax) to reclaim 'that shot of our town from the hill' as something that belongs to a native maternal figure, rather than a middle-class outsider and voyeur. Once Cawood makes peace with her son following a dispute, she walks to the top of a hill to survey the landscape in the same way the aerial camera has done throughout the series. Once she reaches the top of the hill the camera sweeps around to assimilate her eye-line of the town and view it from over her shoulder. She then closes her eyes in a close-up as she processes her memories of her violent confrontations with Royce and loving embraces of her sister and grandson. Then she opens her eyes slowly whilst smiling as the music reaches a triumphant crescendo, and she walks away from the vista having purged her memories and put her community at peace. Viewers are taken on a journey that 'begins with the anger and injustice resonant with the male protagonists of social realism, but as women, this anger and injustice is worked through', in a manner, similar to the contemporary social-realist films *Morvern Callar* (2002), *Red Road* (2006), *Fish Tank* (2009), and *The Arbor* (2010), that 'leads to a greater sense of commitment to her community' (Gorton 2016: 73).

A *Broadchurch* of gender?

In contrast to Cawood, who is the maternal pillar of her community, Hardy is clearly an outsider. The personal struggles Hardy experiences, however, suggest *Broadchurch* may not be as all-embracing of the independent and neoliberal outlook that he espouses at the station. Compared to Cawood, who reclaims 'that shot of our town on the hill' as a means of strengthening her connection to her locale, Hardy consistently occupies an outsider's voyeuristic disdain for *Broadchurch* and its people. When receiving the news he has a heart arrhythmia Hardy confesses to his former colleague, whilst his eye-line occupies 'that shot of our town from the hill', that he 'hates' the 'air', 'sand', 'stupid bloody people', and 'never ending sky', and has taken the job as 'penance' for failing to solve the previous Sandbrook case. Hardy is unhappy with his troubled private life, as he regularly has night terrors, frequently endures bouts of pain from his heart arrhythmia, and often becomes discombobulated when taking his prescribed pain relief. In one instance it is by chance that Hardy happens to be found by Becca Fisher, passed out and bleeding on the floor of his hotel room, before she escorts him to hospital posing as his wife. Longing for human contact Hardy subsequently misreads Fisher's signals when caring for him and clumsily makes a pass at her that she swiftly declines.

Miller, on the other hand, presides over a more wholesome family life of the sort that Hardy longs for. Compared to the Latimers' home the interiors of the Millers' house glow with a warm, yellow hue that does not produce reflections of the outside, suggesting they are already a content family. Ellie is a nurturing and doting mother who helps her son Tom (Adam Wilson) come to terms with his friend's death by explaining to him 'its ok to be sad' and encouraging him to 'cry', teaching him the emotional articulation required to avoid the destructive effects of toxic masculinity. Joe Miller is continually framed as a comfortable and competent stay-at-home father as he provides Ellie with the confidence and support she needs by hugging her and cheering her up whilst simultaneously caring for their children. When Hardy is invited for a meal at their home, he is reluctant to discuss the personal circumstances that have led to his daughter living with her mother. Hardy is markedly isolated on the other side of the dining table, sitting alone as he confirms his personal arrangements are 'hard' and that the 'job does it to you'. In response Joe exclaims, 'not to us', as he tenderly strokes his wife's back. At this moment it would appear Ellie has succeeded in treating 'work and home' as 'two different things', serving as a model to which Hardy can aspire in making peace with himself.

The ideological binary underpinning Hardy's and Miller's private lives, however, is undone by Joe Miller's admission that he killed Daniel Latimer. Joe's role as a stay-at-home father becomes instantaneously 'pathologized rather than celebrated' (Greer 2017: 336). Ellie, by extension, becomes the 'oblivious – even neglectful – mother', as previously innocent and tender exchanges 'take on new meanings' (Greer 2017: 336). In Episode 1, for instance, Joe gently rubs his son's hand to comfort him over Daniel's death. Then, in Episode 2, Ellie returns home from work to look lovingly at Joe and Tom, who have fallen asleep together in the same bed. Before Joe's confession these scenes appear relatively innocuous and typical of a loving family. Through these new revelations, however, Ellie is criticised 'for being oblivious to the dysfunction in her own house' (Greer 2017: 340). Her character learns to become more successful in the workplace by not keeping her work and private life as two separate entities. By shunning postfeminist, new traditionalist notions that her home is a safe sanctuary from the world's ills, Ellie learns to treat her family members as potential suspects. Abandoning her previous moral compass permits her to rifle through her son's bedroom at 2.30 a.m., whilst he sleeps, to locate his computer, which may contain vital evidence. According to *Broadchurch*'s logic, Miller's maternal instincts have indeed negated her capabilities as a detective. She only learns the extent of her professional failings when Joe confesses and she, like Hardy, has to use a hotel room as her home because her house is cordoned off into a crime scene. Ellie concludes the series believing 'a brilliant copper' would have known they were 'lying next to the murder', succumbing to Hardy's advice of 'don't trust'. There is a clear message here that, in direct contrast to *Happy Valley*, one must remain wary of individuals in their family and wider community. Rather than striving to produce a common culture, detectives must estrange themselves from their community to be successful, and recognise signs of abuse within their own homes. However, this cold message is partially measured by Ellie's final scenes with her family. In her hotel room she embraces her son Tom and young baby Fred, suggesting she does not need to sacrifice her 'nurturing maternalism' to become a successful 'career woman' as argued by Greer (2017: 336). Essentially, what differentiates the women of *Happy Valley* from the women of *Broadchurch* is that in *Broadchurch* 'new momism', the widespread postfeminist insistence in modern culture that 'no woman is truly complete or fulfilled unless she has kids', is used as a yardstick to gauge to what extent women are successful in a private and professional capacity (Douglas and Michaels 2004: 4).

Conclusion

What marks police series of the 2010s as distinctive is the way they employ HD aerial cameras, often with the assistance of drone technology, to capture the landscapes free from eventhood to envelop scenes. From the police station to the private homes of police officials, each type of setting maintains a different relationship to the surrounding landscape to provide both of the series discussed with a very different, and multifaceted, ideological view of class, gender, and crime within an era of austerity. The way in which the bright, coastal sunshine can be seen and felt within Broadchurch station means the programme advocates a solitary detective who is resilient enough to be undeterred by the resource implications of austerity and can evade community pressures. Alternatively, *Happy Valley* draws clear connections among austerity, tragedy, and trauma to call for an interdependent working environment where frontline officers can work together to mitigate the lack of support austerity has created. These views are given a gendered dimension when examining civilian scenes. The eerie, neo-environmental determinist hold the Jurassic Coast has over the middle-class inhabitants of Broadchurch encourages women to return autonomously to the domestic sphere as a safe haven from real-world problems, of which the recession is just one. Alternatively, *Happy Valley*'s shots of the Calder Valley in West Yorkshire suggest that the underclasses are ruining the tranquil landscape, and that interdependence can only be achieved by middle-class families to prevent toxic masculinity threatening such peace. Then, when turning to the private lives of officers, Cawood's lower-middle-class lifestyle and traditional working-class values serve as a guide for the petulant middle classes and irresponsible underclasses. Her common culture encourages residents to be part of a participatory democracy, as advocated by the social sciences, that is increasingly keen to incorporate the public's views. By not framing Cawood's home in relation to the surrounding landscape, greater attention is placed on these collective values and her community of reciprocal support. In contrast, whilst Hardy experiences difficulty and trauma at home, Miller's ultimate lesson is to estrange herself from her community in order to achieve the delicate balance required between 'nurturing maternalism' and 'career woman' –something that both series recognise as being difficult, but that *Happy Valley* portrays as being realistically, if imperfectly, achievable (Greer 2017: 336).

In summary, both *Broadchurch* and *Happy Valley* represent how 'quality' texts 'seek to appeal to the structures of taste of a middle-class 'quality demographic', relying on audiences who can afford to renew their video-on-demand subscriptions and 'own the technology needed to consume it' (Jenner 2017: 312, 313). Being increasingly geared towards 'younger, educated, metropolitan and wealthy brackets of the audience', it is important to remember that whilst online streaming and viewing by other devices are manifestly growing, at time of writing 98.5 per cent of viewing is still via a conventional television set and almost 88 per cent of British viewing is actually of 'live'-broadcast programmes (Logan 2016: 149; Piper 2016: 172). Nevertheless, police series of the 2010s are predominantly dealing with social, political, and economic concerns of the middle-class population. Whereas *Z Cars* founded the modern British police series as a means of providing an authentic, working-class perspective of society, the equivalent 'underclass' are now no more than an omnipresent plot device used to ratchet up middle-class anxieties. It would appear that the British police series has lost its social-realist desire to extend a viewer's social perspective. With the genre now ridiculing vulnerable characters with an underclass standing or disposition, it will be interesting to see how future police series will navigate public socio-economic concerns and portray changing class identities. These issues are all likely to be part of an era of increased division, anxiety, and hardship as the UK attempts to exit the European Union.

Notes

1. For further information see Bell (2011), Cavadino and Dignan (2006), Reiner (2007), and Wacquant (2009).
2. Swathes of empirical research have proven suicide is currently the biggest killer of men under forty-five, as they are often more inclined to avoid openly 'talking about emotions' to 'manage stress' (Wyllie *et al.* 2012: 2).

Conclusion: good evening, all

> Times change and so do genres.
> Charlotte Brunsdon, scholar (Brunsdon 2016: 30)

Since Robert Barr produced his instructional series of *Telecrimes* (BBC, 1946) police series have become a staple of British television drama. Over the last seventy years, the genre has undergone so many changes that its iconography would be largely unrecognisable to audiences who witnessed its inception. Therefore it is challenging to provide an accurate account of the genre's development that honours the specificities of television as an audiovisual medium. Texts from other media, particularly literature and film, have a 'greater tendency to draw upon their own predecessors thus keeping generic boundaries relatively distinct' (Feuer 1992: 158). In comparison, television genres have 'a greater tendency to recombine across genre lines' as a means of assuring 'the delivery of the weekly audience' (Feuer 1992: 158). Furthermore, 'television has adopted and adapted formats and forms' from radio, film, literature, theatre, journalism, and others that have all 'played an important part in television and its history' (Neale 2015: 4). With television genre's fluidity in mind, I will demonstrate how this study's research aims have been achieved.

A new genre history

The first objective of this book was to provide a narrative of British police series that charts how the relationship among production practices, visual style, and ideology developed and collectively had an impact on changing definitions of the genre. Concentrating on the depiction of stations in each series is a particularly useful way of determining how this relationship among production, style, and ideology has developed through the genre's history. The 1960s begin with the conservative visuals and ideology of *Dixon of Dock Green* (BBC, 1955–1976). Being tied to the BBC Light Entertainment Department's standard practice of using three immobile video cameras over three different sets was a key factor that influenced the series' reassuringly patriarchal depictions of law and order in accordance with the police force and Government. However, Michael Barry stepping down as BBC Head of Drama in 1961 provided the opportunity for dramatists and documentarians to work together and implement the series *Z Cars* (BBC, 1962–1978). Combining working-class practitioners from two previously separate BBC departments instigated a documentary approach to researching character alongside a high-octane pace and the use of six mobile cameras over fourteen different sets per episode. This stylistic practice shook televisual social realism out of the nostalgic register employed by *Dixon* and various soaps to provide a refreshingly candid view of the competing priorities between detectives and police constables when protecting vulnerable citizens. Then, in the 1970s, ITV's *The Sweeney* (1975–1978) recast the police series as an action series. Producer Ted Childs's insistence on using a documentary crew and a 16 mm-film camera to emulate the verisimilitude of American films *Dirty Harry* (1971) and *The French Connection* (1971) ensures audiences formulate a close identification with protagonist Detective Inspector Jack Regan (John Thaw). Like Harry Callaghan (Clint Eastwood) and Jimmy 'Popeye' Doyle (Gene Hackman), Regan's renegade persona reduces the politics surrounding Commissioner Robert Mark's shake-up of the Metropolitan Police to petty squabbles between a heroic protagonist and his stuffy, 'pencil pushing' superiors. Meanwhile, the observational, studio-based approach of the often forgotten *Hunter's Walk* (ITV, 1973–1976) scrutinises the social shortcomings of law-and-order policy unable to protect female victims of crime. The way in which laws are debated conversely presents Broadstone station as a forum for debating citizens' rights.

The most popular police series of the 1980s are often overlooked by television scholarship due to not using film cameras in real locations, as the most prestigious dramas of the time were doing. Nevertheless, the sharper definition of video cameras, accompanying the rhetoric of melodrama, and the studio technique associated with soap operas mean that *Juliet Bravo* (BBC, 1980–1985) and *The Gentle Touch* (ITV, 1980–1984) scrutinise the police force's working methods from a woman protagonist's perspective. Not having humanitarian concerns resigned to the domestic sphere means that a benevolent image of policing is promoted in direct contrast to the increasingly militaristic practices of the police force used to clamp down on civil unrest at the time. Contrarily,

Conclusion 183

The Bill's (ITV, 1984–2010) use of handheld video cameras portrays Sun Hill station as such a high-pressure environment populated by an overworked ensemble of police officials that the humanitarian and feminist concerns directed at the police have to be pragmatically sidelined.

As rates of violent crime continued to climb through the 1990s, *Prime Suspect* (ITV, 1991–2006), *A Touch of Frost* (ITV, 1992–2010), and *Cracker* (ITV, 1993–2006) all use a 35 mm-film camera over feature-length episodes to have the style of the horror film reassess 'the boundaries between the human and the non-human' (Creed 2003: 14). In each instance an outsider is required to circumnavigate the increasingly privatised nature of police work to achieve real justice. In *Prime Suspect* Detective Chief Inspector Jane Tennison's (Helen Mirren) adoption of the monstrous feminine figure forces her male colleagues to confront the abject and the suffering endured by victims. Detective inspector and pensioner Jack Frost (David Jason) traverses trivial modern protocols to acknowledge the abject. Lastly, Dr Edward 'Fitz' Fitzgerald's (Robbie Coltrane) psychological expertise makes him better equipped to undertake interrogations and improve the efficiency of Greater Manchester Police's Senior Incident Team. By the decade's end, however, producer Tony Garnett aligns *The Cops* (BBC, 1998–2001) with the pessimism underpinning 1990s British social-realist cinema, as inhabitants of a deindustrialised town reluctantly accept their lot. This outlook is mediated by digital betacams and their close affinity to the emotional realism of docudramas. Now raw emotion principally dictates characters' actions, making for a petty and bickering police force operating in a manner largely identical to the people they police, thus contravening the 1998 Human Rights Act.

Incorporating the iconography associated with sci-fi provides police series of the 2000s with a splash of colour and playful visuals. The decade begins with *Waking the Dead*'s (BBC, 2000–2011) Cold Case Unit operating as a beacon of technological utopianism, as mobile cameras enthusiastically embrace the capabilities of communication technology and its apparent ability to fuse scientists with intelligence operatives and detectives. But, following the sceptical *New Tricks* (BBC, 2003–2015), *Life on Mars* (BBC, 2006–2007) largely rejects technological developments, as the technologies populating 2006's Stopford House station make for a regulatory dystopia. Then, with the regularisation of HD cameras and drone technology, series of the 2010s increasingly capture landscapes. The way in which the bright coastal sunshine can be seen within the station in *Broadchurch* (ITV, 2013–2017) means the programme advocates a solitary detective who is resilient enough to reject the warmth and camaraderie of his community whilst thriving under the resource implications of austerity. Alternatively, *Happy Valley* (BBC, 2014–) draws clear connections among austerity, tragedy, and trauma to engender an interdependent working community to overcome austerity.

Ideological developments

The second objective of this study is to examine how representations of social class and gender in domestic civilian settings engage with wider socio-political debate, and whether such depictions endorse, debate, or challenge the dichotomy traditionally demarcated between private and public spaces. *Z Cars*' domestic scenes are informed by socio-economic anxieties of the 1960s, including the buoyancy of unskilled youth labour and the infirm types of men likely to retreat from society. Here the boundary between the public and private is blurred, as traditional social realism's sentimental view of the home is superseded by a domestic space where men's frustrations manifest in response to challenges from the public world of work. Being concerned with particularly vulnerable working-class men falling through the cracks of the postwar social contract aligns *Z Cars*' civilian scenes with criminology's deviant subculture theories, which sought to determine what societal elements predispose poorer people to criminality. In contrast, in the 1970s *The Sweeney* equates lawbreaking with villainy in accordance with criminology's influential deterrence doctrine, where society is exonerated of blame as individuals are understood to be solely responsible for their criminality. This view is challenged by *Hunter's Walk*'s regular depictions of domesticity that draw the viewer's attention to the physical and emotional toll that domestic labour has on women to reveal the social consequences of a police force prioritising public, over private, crime. In the 1980s, studio productions *Juliet Bravo* and *The Gentle Touch* continue this precedent set by *Hunter's Walk*, by presenting the domestic as a political space where the isolating psychosocial effects of Thatcherite attempts to reassert the Victorian model of the two-parent family are revealed. Both challenge the social effects Thatcherism has on the private sphere but assimilate with the rationale underpinning its law-and-order policy in the public sphere as, in line with rational choice theory, each series identifies a reoccurring subgroup of offenders; determines why the characteristics of offences are differentially attractive to these subgroups; and then finds pragmatic solutions, having recognised that crime arises from a mixture of individual choices and environmental factors. Then *The Bill*, in its repeated visits to the Clayview council estate, depoliticises the domestic sphere, as predatory crimes within poorer communities are portrayed as inevitable. Corresponding with routine-activity theory, the job of the police is only to arrest offenders without concerning itself with troublesome 'domestics' and social initiatives.

The 1990s begin with regular depictions of violent crimes in private settings that threaten the stability of wider society. The gruesome injuries inflicted represent the fears of social collapse being espoused by prominent journalists and politicians in light of the recession and rising crime rates. *Prime Suspect* utilises slasher-film iconography to depict a highly polarised country where the irresponsible lifestyles of the underclass threaten to infect the responsible middle-class citizenry who uphold society. Meanwhile, *Frost*'s utilisation of the gothic-television tradition of horror suggests the sexual transgressions of middle-class women aggravate recessionary gloom. *Cracker*, however, uses the assaultive gaze of the slasher film to understand why marginalised, working-class men in crisis feel the need to seek agency over middle-class professionals. In each instance, what occurs in the private, domestic settings of irresponsible individuals is no longer arbitrary, as depicted in *The Bill*, but has the potential to threaten public security and engender societal collapse. *The Cops*, however, makes a concerted effort to step back from sensationalising the gruesome crimes of disturbed individuals to return to a social-realist agenda. The viewer's social outlook is extended by depicting the daily tribulations of a working-class-turned-underclass community in crisis. The regular vandalism, theft, prostitution, drug dealing, and domestic violence committed by Skeetsmore residents reveal New Labour's law-and-order policy to be segregationist, rather than interventionist as left-realist criminology had planned. The boundaries between public and private become irrelevant, as most of the police officials hail from the same area and conduct themselves in the same manner as the Skeetsmore residents when on duty.

Following the pessimism of the 1990s, civilian scenes of the 2000s utilise the advanced colourisation, editing tempo, and moveability of digital cameras to provide clear contrasts. In *Waking the Dead*, a sharp distinction is drawn between the basic technologies privately owned in the dark basements of unhinged cybercriminals and the Cold Case Unit's sophisticated apparatus that oversees public security. *New Tricks* reveals a gulf in lifestyle appearing between the super-rich and poorest, despite Blairite assertions of economic prosperity and middle-class egalitarianism. *Life on Mars* then basks in comforting memories of working-class communities from the 1970s and the collective identity they provided. Retreating to memories of the past to solve modern-day problems, particularly in the latter two series, harnesses postmodern thought to suggest what defines a person's home, and that what constitutes the role, purpose, and responsibilities of the State is not fixed and is in regular flux. In comparison, civilian scenes of series in the 2010s largely re-establish a clearer dichotomy by agreeing with socio-economic elements of neoliberal ideology through the way in which HD aerial cameras capture picturesque locations. *Happy Valley* adopts 'that long shot of our town from that hill' from British New Wave social-realist cinema alongside the contemplation of landscape documentaries to demonise underclass residents for childishly opting to ruin West Yorkshire's tranquillity and industrial heritage. The eerie, neo-environmental, determinist hold the Jurassic Coast has over the middle-class inhabitants of *Broadchurch* encourages women to return autonomously to the domestic sphere as a safe haven from real-world problems. Thus a dichotomy is reaffirmed, because the difficulties associated with the public world of work are visually presented as having an emotionally stifling presence when imposed on the home. *Happy Valley* does, however, suggest that a crossover between the private and public spheres can mitigate certain excesses of neoliberalism. The way women openly discuss their feelings in domestic spaces rectifies the destructive effects of toxic masculinity emerging in the local businesses community.

A new framework for television genre analysis

The third promise made in the introduction of this study is to provide a new methodological framework for studying television genre. The most seismic scholarly developments in television genre criticism since the turn of the century have called on studies to focus on wider cultural discourses. Jason Mittel asserts, 'we need to look beyond the text … and instead locate genres within the complex interrelations among texts, industries, audiences, and historical contexts' (Mittel 2008: 173). Similarly, Julie D'Acci's (2004) work on television representation and gender suggests that genre analysis must examine production, reception, programming, and social/historical contexts. Also, Simon Frith stipulates that 'technological, political, economic, managerial, professional and aesthetic issues are intermingled' and need to be unpicked (Frith 2000: 35). However, in analysing wider discourses it is important not to lose sight of the ideological complexity of the text in question, as ideology is not a fixed set of beliefs but 'an arena of representational practice (and therefore a site of struggle and contestation)', as affirmed by Newcomb and Hirsch (2000; White 1992: 179).

Conclusion 187

Therefore, my approach to analysing television genre is to examine the reoccurring types of public and private settings, which are a central fixture of the genre being examined, in each text. This enables the study to become more attuned to the multifaceted ideologies operating through a programme, and to how the nuanced relationship among production, style, and ideology develops over time. This is a form of analysis that can be applied to genres unique to television, including the sitcom, soap opera, and medical drama, and the series of stock settings they return, to be it the family home, pub, or hospital, to name but a few. Charting a genre's visual and ideological development means placing the types of space that reappear at the forefront of an analysis. Examining sets is a burgeoning field of academic enquiry, from Helen Wheatley's (2005) spatial analysis of *Upstairs Downstairs* (ITV, 1973–1976) to Geraint D'Arcy's (2018) study of how production design impacts a viewer's reading of television. By analysing the stylistic and ideological make-up of the station, domestic spaces, and then the private homes of police officials, in a semiotic method attuned to the relationship shared between a character's attitudinal markers (gesturing) and their illocutionary markers (dialogue), I have unearthed some contradictions that complicate dominant understandings of key texts, the police series, and its development.

Whilst the civilian scenes of *Z Cars* largely softened the boundary between public and private spaces to politicise the home as an environment of male struggle, witnessing PC Bob Steele's (Jeremy Kemp) character in a private capacity recognises that a boundary still exists. Compared to *Dixon*, a person's conduct and behaviour are revealed as susceptible to change in correspondence to their surrounding environment. In his home, Steele has committed domestic violence by giving his wife a black eye, despite arresting those who have committed similar offences, and offering support to women who have suffered such attacks. Similarly, Regan's relationships with middle-class women in private provide glimpses of a sophisticated, debonair, and cultured character, contastring sharply with his professional persona, who swears, drinks heavily, and dresses scruffily to war against middle-class careerists. Also, Tennison's repudiation of the male gaze and associative misogynist working practices of the metropolitan police, in *Prime Suspect*, is challenged by her domestic scenes, when the audience is encouraged to share the terrified reactions of her partner as her obsessive and monstrous behaviour threatens bourgeois patriarchal capitalism. Furthermore, despite Detective Inspector Alec Hardy's (David Tennant) teaching Detective Sergeant Ellie Miller (Olivia Colman) to estrange herself from the Broadchurch community, he privately suffers from trauma in choosing to live alone.

188 Conclusion

As well as complicating the ideology of station and civilian scenes, the private homes of officers also offer criminological solutions to the problems posed in the station and homes of others. *Cracker* suggests that domesticity, as the realm of femininity and leisure, can provide a moral compass and comforting sanctuary for those who are amidst the throes of masculinity in crisis and are increasingly tempted by criminality. Also, Detective Inspector Sam Tyler's (John Simm) private scenes as a civilian in *Life on Mars* add a degree of constructive criticality to what often appears to be a seemingly rose-tinted, nostalgic view of the 1970s. Processing his repressed childhood trauma from an adult perspective unearths the key to reunifying his identity, which has been fractured by postmodern and neoliberal uncertainties.

Can television change the world?

Bearing in mind these new, multifaceted ideological readings of each programme, the final promise of this study is to discern to what extent television programmes can be considered evidence of social change. It is challenging to quantify how a programme can provoke a change in the general public's consciousness. Sometimes a particular broadcast is directly referenced in a parliamentary speech; it causes a twitterstorm; it occupies newspaper column inches; or, in the case of *Cathy Come Home* (BBC, 1966), it helps establish a new charity or form of civil action. It is even more difficult to conceptualise the impact a text can have on the wider socio-political context that has informed the postwar settlement's disassembly. As Stuart Hall states, the potential 'effect' of a programme has to be meaningfully decoded by enough viewers to 'influence, entertain, instruct, or persuade', with very 'complex perceptual, cognitive, emotional, ideological or behavioural consequences' (Hall 1973: n.p.). Although it can be 'wrong to see television as an originator of social change', John Fiske is keen to assert that 'television is part of this movement' when ideological values shift and social changes occur (Fiske 2003: 45). Therefore, in alignment with Fiske's view, my analysis of each programme has been situated in relation to the metadiscourse of dominant ideologies at the time, as well as to the prominent discourses of social change.

When analysing the station space, civilian domestic spaces, and then the private settings of police officials, it becomes clear that the police series is a genre that can reflect, refract, or challenge mainstream politics, public opinion, journalistic discourse, criminological thought, and Government policy. As a series predominantly interested in the social anxieties of vulnerable, working-class men, *Z Cars* was part and parcel of the public appetite and resultant political will to have a 'relative' definition of poverty, based on people's ability participate in the 'conventional and customary' norms of society, replacing Seebohm Rowntree's 'physical efficiency' model (Abel-Smith and Townsend 1965: 63). *Hunter's Walk* engages with second-wave feminism's concerns, as the domestic sphere is a political space where the concerns of housewives, whose domestic labour is not recognised, are aired, thus contributing to the campaign for women's equal rights. Similarly, the refusal of Inspector Jean Darblay (Stephanie Turner) of *Juliet Bravo* and Detective Chief Inspector Maggie Forbes (Jill Gascoine) of *The Gentle Touch* to conform to the housewife role expected of them challenges increasing Thatcherite pressures to adhere to a Victorian ideology of gendered spheres. Darblay is unfairly expected to be a doting partner and housewife in relation to the demands of her career, whilst Forbes asserts single mothers can effectively balance their maternal responsibilities with career success. Both series contribute to public debate surrounding second-wave feminism by informing press discussion. Mary Kenny was adamant that *The Gentle Touch* was 'not in the least bit women's libbish' and was a 'feminine fantasy' about 'being an attractive, glamorous, sexy yet respected woman surrounded by male admirers' (Kenny 1981: 18). However, Geoffrey Hobbes was of the opinion that *The Gentle Touch* is 'a realistic series' when 'handling the problems of a woman working at a high level in a man's world' (Hobbes 1980: 27). Similarly, Stephanie Turner's press interviews reaffirm her view that the importance of *Juliet Bravo* lies in subverting the established practice of exclusively casting women in supporting roles, and challenging 'the prejudice in real life against women in the police' (Phillips 1980: 9). Turner also uses her interviews to campaign for women actors to receive 'equal pay' in relation to men, and to assert that 'more women writers are needed' (Beauman 1982: 74).

There are also series that are less aligned with social change and serve the meta-discourse of dominant ideologies by skewing and refracting aspects of socio-political debate. *The Sweeney*, for example, clearly exacerbated fears surrounding an organised-crime epidemic. It agreed with the belief of the public, press, and judiciary that 'the rate of violent crime was on the increase', as was expressed by numerous 'crime reports, features, editorials, statements by representatives of the police, judges, the Home Secretary, politicians and various prominent public spokesmen' in the press (Hall *et al.* 1978: 9, 7). *The Sweeney* endorses the discourse underlying Prime Minister Edward Heath's successful 1970 law-and-order general election campaign, as the stifling violent crime, professional crime, gang warfare, and the spread of criminal empires is achieved by reverting to traditional ' "get-tough" policies' (Hall *et al.* 1978: 9). Similarly, *Prime Suspect*'s and *Frost*'s horror-film aesthetic confirmed fears espoused by the press, politicians, and certain social scientists that British society in the 1990s was regressing morally as well as economically. Whilst trying to make sense of the psychological reasoning for committing such violent crimes, *Cracker* has also received much criticism for its 'misleading impression of what offender profiling can achieve' (Ainsworth 2013: 6).

Lastly, *Life on Mars* is a particularly influential text for having established an identifiable strategy for twenty-first-century television crime drama. Series including *Ashes to Ashes* (BBC, 2008–2010), *Ripper Street* (BBC, 2012–2016), *Inspector George Gently* (BBC, 2007–2017), *Endeavour* (ITV 2012–), and *Whitechapel* (ITV, 2009–2013) turn to pre-twenty-first-century policing to permit a 'range of anachronistic and often rather smug forms of retrospective political correctness' (Brunsdon 2016: 34). But it was the Gene Hunt (Philip Glennister) character who managed to infiltrate social, cultural, and political discourses. Hunt and his Audi Quattro car, from *Life on Mars* spin-off *Ashes to Ashes*, appeared in a poster supporting the Labour Party during its 2010 general election campaign. The poster was launched on 2 April 2010 to correspond with the day the first episode of Series 3 of *Ashes to Ashes* was transmitted. Having been designed by a member of the public for the purposes of a competition, the poster superimposed the face of the Conservative Party leader and prime minister to be, David Cameron, over Hunt's face, with the words 'don't let him take Britain back to the 1980s'. Cameron responded by recognising Hunt's robust approach to policing as indicative of his own political party, stating 'I think there will be ... millions of people in the country who wish it was the 1980s and that the police were out there feeling collars and nicking people instead of filling in forms' (Hennessy 2010: n.p.). Conservatives then hurriedly produced a different version of the poster, complete with the new slogan 'Fire up the Quattro. It's time for change.' Therefore, even when a police series is directly referenced by political discourse, it can be decoded as having different ideological meanings to different audiences. Nevertheless, the ability of the British police series to contribute inadvertently to its socio-political climate, through the ways particular texts criticise ineffective law-and-order policy and the State's inability to protect the vulnerable, is evident.

The end of (television) history?

Television drama scholarship is largely locked into three prominent schools of thought. One strand comprises the academics Robert

Conclusion 191

J. Thompson (1997), Glen Creeber (2004), James Lyons and Mark Jancovich (2003), Robin Nelson (2007), Lisa Glebatis Perks (2015), and Elliott Logan (2016), who are invested in quality television drama. Each author appreciates how high-end dramas require 'close scrutiny not only as artefacts of popular culture but also rich complex artworks' (Cardwell 2007: 33). Then there is the work exploring fandom by Matt Hills (2002), Henry Jenkins (2012), Lucy Bennett and Paul Booth (2016), and many others that examine how television with a cult following promotes inter-textuality. Lastly, the work of Francis Bonner (2003) and Su Holmes (2008) and others is continuously making a convincing case for analysing the form and cultural impact of ordinary television such as game shows, light entertainment, current affairs, chat shows, and lifestyle-programming as a recognised field of academic enquiry.

I propose a new approach that challenges this three-way split by analysing texts that are not classified as either 'quality', 'cult', or 'ordinary television'. I am referring to television programmes such as *Hunter's Walk*, *Juliet Bravo*, *The Gentle Touch*, and *Waking the Dead*, which were successful, popular, and occupied peak broadcasting hours but are not continuously broadcast like soaps; they are not considered quality television or ordinary television, nor do they have a cult following. These are the overlooked texts that either have evaded cultural memory and academic scrutiny for not fitting into a television-studies development narrative (i.e. not utilising technologies that were going against the grain of regular television output), or are overlooked in relation to 'quality' texts thought to be more representative of their era. Why *The Bill* creator Geoff McQueen or Terence Feeley of *The Gentle Touch* are not names that are as instantly recognisable as the Kennedy Martin brothers suggests that the type of texts valued by television scholarship have had a problematic impact on studies of television authorship. These are not dramas that have been lost, forgotten, or wiped, but they are texts still in commercial circulation that have been culturally sidelined whilst hiding in plain sight. Examining further drama that adheres to this host of criteria should make for a more accurate and nuanced understanding of developments to television genre, its style, and its resultant ideologies.

In terms of the British police series, then, the biggest change the genre has undergone since becoming a popular television genre in the early 1960s is the loss of its desire to use police characters as an incidental means of learning about people's lives and wider British society. From the 1960s until the late 1990s, police series were often synonymous with the social-realist form, as they looked socially to extend a viewer's outlook and impact national class-consciousness. Since 2000, however, British police series have increasingly become postmodern in nature, as they revel in the complexity of their own interlocking narratives and polished visual sheen. As a result, the police series genre has dropped its clear political consciousness and so has lost its social connection to the real world. Television police series have largely capitulated to Francis Fukuyama's postmodern view that with the end of the cold war came the end of history: that is, 'the end point of mankind's ideological evolution and the universalization of Western liberal democracy as the final form of human government' (Fukuyama 1989: 1). Be it *Waking the Dead*, *Luther*, *Line of Duty*, *Broadchurch*, or *Happy Valley*, British police series now contribute to the neoliberal 'pervasive rhetoric of responsibility, flexibility and self-improvement that has come to dominate life domains from employment and education to health, consumption, and leisure' at the expense of working-class characters (Walker and Roberts 2017a: 3). The repeated practice of pathologising the working class for being inherently backward within the social, political, and cultural discourse of western democracy heavily contributed to the Brexit vote, and Donald Trump's presidential campaign across the Atlantic, as people had begun to feel left behind by globalism without a political voice representing their interests. Ignoring elements of the UK population to cater for middle-class tastes in a global broadcasting marketplace has made the contemporary police series a key contributor to a divided nation. Welder, trade unionist, and Labour Party supporter-turned-skinhead anarchist Albie Kinsella's (Robert Carlyle) prophesy that 'the despised and the betrayed' will 'light the fuse and this country's gonna blow' is now finally materialising. Little did *Cracker* audiences know at the time that they were in fact, as Kinsella states, 'looking at the future': a future where the socially marginalised would indeed turn to explosive, populist, far-right political movements to have their voices heard.

Postscript: Jed Mercurio thrillers, pandemic policing, and populism

What has happened to us? When did we stop caring about honesty and integrity?

Superintendent Ted Hastings, *Line of Duty*

Since 2020, Jed Mercurio's *Line of Duty* (BBC, 2012–2021) has had an unprecedented impact on British television police series. Employing the principal conventions of the thriller genre, Mercurio has his detectives navigate an ever-growing complex external threat whilst the limits of their physical and mental endurance are tested (Glover 2003: 135–154). This postscript considers how *Line of Duty*, *Vigil* (BBC, 2021), *Trigger Point* (ITV, 2022), and *The Responder* (BBC, 2022) utilise the thriller genre to explore how the COVID-19 pandemic has changed policing. I ask how each series adheres to a model of 'normative compliance', whereby compliance with the law emerges because people deem the 'directions of authority to be morally appropriate' and fairly enforced (Stott *et al.* 2020: 575). Then I consider to what extent each series adopts a model of instrumental compliance, where adherence revolves around 'fear of authority's capacity to impose punishment' (Stott *et al.* 2020: 575). I discover which model of policing is preferred in a manner akin to enquiries that criminologists are conducting into police forces worldwide, by assessing how the fictional police operate across stations, civilian settings, and in private. Employing this spatial model of textual analysis helps us better understand the political cut-through that Mercurio's series have experienced in an era of populism.

Context

When *You're Nicked* was first released in January 2020, no one knew that the 'pneumonia of an unknown cause' spreading through Wuhan, China would soon escalate into a global pandemic (Kantis *et al.* 2022).

194 Postscript

Monday 23 March 2020 saw Britons experience the strictest laws imposed on their freedoms since the Second World War. Prime Minister Boris Johnson instructed the nation they could only leave home once a day, either to buy food, exercise, or go to work if a 'key worker'. Citizens who failed to comply were fined. Following a phased reopening of schools and non-essential businesses the following June, the UK went on to experience two further lockdowns. A month-long national circuit breaker on 31 October 2020 closed pubs, restaurants, and non-essential retail, and on 4 January 2021 England entered its third national lockdown, with schools closing again and citizens only allowed to leave their homes once a day for exercise or essential shopping.

Through these lockdowns, the 2020 Coronavirus Act granted government discretionary power to limit or suspend public gatherings, detain individuals infected by COVID-19, and intervene in different sectors to limit transmission of the disease. Crest (2020), Hogarth (2020), and Stott (2020) have uncovered the impact these unclear legislative changes and fast-changing guidance had on frontline police officers. Collectively, criminologists have called for a new social contract that balances instrumental compliance alongside normative compliance, as a state power 'too forceful could erode public trust in policing and government' (Stott *et al.* 2020: 576). Following the lifting of facemask regulations and the introduction of COVID-19 vaccination passes on 27 January 2022, opinion remains divided on how our new, insecure COVID reality is policed.

Rationale

I am grateful to everyone who purchased my book amidst this tumultuous period and the overwhelmingly positive critical reception it received. This postscript responds to Lez Cooke, who found my decision not to discuss *Line of Duty* in detail 'curious given its popularity and critical profile' as a series 'primarily concerned with the operational practices of the police' (Cooke 2020: 657). To be clear, when I submitted the final draft of my manuscript to Manchester University Press in November 2018 the series was not yet a flagship drama smashing television viewing records. In 2012, *Line of Duty*'s first series attracted 3.76 million viewers on average (Soen 2021). In 2014, series 2, episode 1 was watched by 2.74 million people, roughly a million fewer than the programme's debut episode. When I signed my publishing contract in 2016, series 3 was receiving an average of 5.42 million viewers, half the number of the *Broadchurch* (ITV, 2013–2017) finale broadcast a year later. It was in 2017, having completed my first draft, that *Line of Duty* series 4 rose in popularity following a move to BBC One. Whilst the average viewership almost doubled to 9.55 million, a complete overhaul of Chapter 6 did not seem warranted at this stage. In 2019, six months after submitting my final draft to the publisher, series 5 intensified the hunt for criminal mastermind 'H' to receive average viewing figures of 12.85 million. The consolidated viewing figures for the 2021 series six finale were 15.21 million, making *Line of Duty* the most watched drama (excluding soaps) since a 1999 episode of *A Touch of Frost*. Attracting 56.2 per cent of the UK TV audience made *Line of Duty* the 'most watched TV drama of the 21st Century' (Chilton 2021). I explore the series here because the 2020s is the decade it is most associated with, after the BBC released the entire boxset on iPlayer as a lockdown tonic to build an audience for its finale.

The Mercurio effect

Staffordshire-raised Jed Mercurio began his career as an RAF officer before working as a hospital doctor. Upon answering an advert in the *British Medical Journal* for a TV medical adviser, he went on to write the acclaimed BBC drama *Cardiac Arrest* (BBC, 1993) and pursue a full-time writing career. Mercurio's series are predominantly interested in how institutions close ranks and spin narratives to defend themselves following malpractice. For Mercurio, *Line of Duty* represented an opportunity to apply his craft to policing. Simon Heath of World Productions permitted Mercurio to write every episode and oversee the whole process from casting to the edit. Now, 60 per cent of audiences regularly binge-watch television (Trouleau *et al.* 2016) – the practice of seeing two or more consecutive episodes in one sitting (Walton-Pattison 2018: 19). Mercurio purposefully rewards his attentive audiences by adding more detail to his scripts, something he was initially discouraged from doing (Mercurio and McClure 2017). Correspondingly, *Line of Duty* captures how the UK has changed. The debut episode was aired the day after the 2012 Olympic opening ceremony, an event that exuded a national feeling of pride and unity. Since then, Mercurio has used his nuanced writing to document the UK's transition into a divided society accustomed to senior politicians profiting from corrupt enterprise (quoted in Mahase 2021: 375).

Authoritarian police stations

Through each *Line of Duty* series, the fictional AC-12 unit are assigned to a different police station to investigate suspected corruption. Overseen

196 Postscript

by Superintendent Ted Hastings (Adrian Dunbar), Detective Sergeant Steve Arnott (Martin Compston) seizes records, gathers intelligence, and conducts interrogations, whilst Detective Inspector Kate Fleming (Vicky McClure) goes undercover. As the series draws closer to 2020 and viewing figures increase, each unit under investigation exhibits an increasingly authoritarian approach to policing. In line with leading definitions of authoritarianism, each station strongly centralises political and economic power while exhibiting minimal accountability and transparency. Technology and science are also used for control and manipulation (Koestler 2015 [1941]: 162–163). Authoritarianism is a criticism increasingly levelled at the UK government for, among other things, policing citizen's movements, mandating vaccine passports, and securing PPE contracts with business contacts instead of adhering to the due tender process. Whilst Mercurio did not write COVID into the final series, he feels questionable government conduct during the pandemic is indicative of the political culture his series has explored (Bernstein 2021). Since series 4 and the hunt for criminal mastermind 'H', viewers have witnessed the murder of DI Matthew 'Dot' Cottan (Craig Parkinson), ACC Derek Hilton (Paul Higgins), and the arrest of the PCC's Legal Counsel Gill Biggeloe (Polly Walker). Between series 5 and 6, with these three corrupt senior police officials out of the frame, the inept DS Ian Buckells (Nigel Boyle) has since become the 'fourth man' to feed information to the Organised Crime Group (OCG). As a thriller, the final *Line of Duty* series ideologically exposes the complex and external threat to a functioning police force as a network of below-par police personnel open to corruption for financial gain. Buckells is exposed through AC-12's investigation of DCI Joanne Davidson (Kelly MacDonald) of Hillside Lane station. Davidson is the Senior Investigating Officer of Operation Lighthouse, inspecting the murder of journalist Gail Vella. Through series 6, Davidson believes she is receiving instructions via encrypted laptop messages from retired DCI Marcus Thurwell (James Nesbitt) to obstruct the investigation. However, her colleague Buckells is revealed to have been messaging her all along to protect Chief Constable Philip Osborne (Owen Teale) from the evidence Vella found implicating him in covering up the police's racially motived murder of Lawrence Christopher.

As in an authoritarian regime, the logic underlying senior ranking officers' decisions is shrouded in secrecy. There is no transparent process in place to disseminate the reasoning behind key decisions to rank and file operatives. Decisions are made behind closed doors before being dictated downwards by a select number of officers with power and influence. Getting entry to Hillside Lane station's briefing room

Postscript 197

for crucial conversations requires gaining Davidson's trust to enter her inner circle, as she claims 'the fewer cops in the loop the better'. Despite being assigned to Operation Lighthouse, Sergeant Farida Jatri (Anneika Rose) is excluded from this process. Viewers are first introduced to Hillside Lane through a close-up of Jatri's concerned face as she takes a deep breath. The camera then cuts to an over-the-shoulder shot of the briefing room. In the distance, Jatri's perspective reveals three officers talking inaudibly by the 'Operation Lighthouse' whiteboard in the briefing room on the other side of the glass panel. As the camera cuts to inside the room, viewers learn about suspects being processed for Vella's murder. The camera then cuts back to its original establishing shot as foreboding music begins and Jatri leaves the shot and her desk to knock on Buckells's office door and request a transfer. The station design instils paranoia among its workers, as the soundproofed glass partitions enable detectives to observe important decisions being made behind closed doors as a chilling reminder of their subordinate status. Many work in fear and suspicion of one another. In episode 3, Fleming instructs DS Chris Lomax (Perry Fitzpatrick) alone in the briefing room to do a background check on their witness, due to the lack of CCTV footage of Vella's murder. Haunting music begins to play as the camera cuts to a shot of Davidson watching them both from her office, unable to hear. As with Jatri's transfer request, Davidson sees conversations unfolding out of the corner of her eye through the interior glass wall of her office. The scene begins and ends with close-ups of her concerned face, concluding with unsettling music in order to suggest that everyone is suspicious and fearful of the conversations taking place.

The interior glass partitioning of Hillside Lane that separates the briefing room, Davidson's office, and Buckells's office from the communal desks of their team gives the illusion of a transparent process. Conversely, this increased visibility is used to threaten punishment – another essential component of authoritarianism. After Buckells is sent to prison, Davidson announces she is now the Acting Detective Superintendent during a briefing. Following this, she walks outside the station and looks up to see PC Ryan Pilkington (Gregory Piper), an OCG plant, standing at a window, frowning at her and looking over her head, signalling the real power dynamic at play despite her formal promotion. Similarly, when Davidson, Fleming, and Lomax work through possible sites for the armed robbery rendezvous point, which obscured their arrest of Vella's suspected murderer, the scene is bookended by Pilkington watching their conversation from outside the briefing room. In a low-angle close-up, Pilkington's angry but assured focus signals to Davidson who is really in charge. Compared to series 1, where DCI Tony

Gates was a lone rotten apple with a position of influence, now the level of corruption has increased to the point where corrupt foot soldiers are using the station space to threaten punishment. Making key decisions in a soundproofed briefing room, in full view of other officers, not only enables Davidson to prevent officers like Jatri being able to inform AC-12 with reliable intelligence, but it also keeps Davidson in a vulnerable position, reminding her of who she works for and keeping all her movements under OCG surveillance. Hillside station is subject to a tiered model of instrumental compliance, where detectives and officers operate under fear of reprisals from Davidson and Davidson is fearful of OCG operatives.

Another means by which Hillside Lane engenders compliance through fear is the authoritarian way technology is used as an instrument of control, manipulation, and intimidation. Personal technology use is regulated and prohibited to control officers. When Operation Lighthouse's covert human intelligence source (CHIS) Bothroyd is found dead, Jatri runs outside the station panicked and repeatedly looks around before calling Arnott to withdraw her assistance from AC-12's enquiry, petrified she will be murdered by Davidson. When sitting at her desk, Jatri looks around the room before checking her call history. Seeing a spate of missed calls from Arnott prompts her to leave the station to call him. Regulating workers' use of personal technology is a means of determining where a person's allegiance lies. When Fleming is granted permission to lead an operation, she instructs all officers to surrender their phones and not to leave the room without permission. As all staff search possible locations for the armed robbers' rendezvous base, Pilkington is spotted by Arnott's covert surveillance using a secret phone to warn his OCG employers that the investigators are close to finding them. Personal smartphones, then, are a means of leaking information to AC-12 or to the OCG. However, the open-plan design of Hillside station with interior glass partitioning means a person's use of their smartphone is controlled as a means of intimidation.

The final component of authoritarianism at play within stations under AC-12's investigation, alongside obfuscated transparency, fear of punishment, and harnessing technology to manipulate, control, and intimidate workers, comes from how power is centralised to forestall accountability for the most senior of ranking officers. Series 4 is the most illustrative of this working practice, particularly the way DCI Roseanne 'Roz' Huntley (Thandie Newton) runs Polk Avenue station. Under political pressure from ACC Derek Hilton to charge the innocent Richard Farmer (Scott Reid) for the attempted murder of Hana Reznikova (Gaite Jansen), Huntley deliberately ignores Forensic

Coordinator Tim Ifield's (Jason Watkins) proof that the crime scene has been tampered with so she can close Operation Trapdoor for the ACC. When Huntley confronts Ifield unannounced in his flat, a row breaks out over the guilt of Farmer that escalates into Huntley murdering Ifield. After disposing of his body Huntley deposits his blood onto submitted forensic evidence, to implicate Ifield in Leoni Collersdale's murder, a murder Farmer has already been charged with. Huntley then persistently orders her officers to find links between Ifield and Farmer in order to divert suspicion from herself over Ifield's murder and successfully close Operation Trapdoor.

Huntley centralises power in an authoritarian manner within Polk Avenue by micromanaging every aspect of the investigation, particularly interrogations. When Farmer is first interviewed under suspicion of kidnapping Reznikova, the camera never enters the interview suite itself. The audience only sees Huntley's facial reactions as she stands in the observation room or her point of view of the camera monitors filming it. During key moments in the interrogation, a viewer's focus is drawn to Huntley's reactions rather than being invited to scrutinise Farmer's replies. As Farmer answers each question, the camera focuses on Huntley's response to the information being dispensed rather than giving Farmer screen time and permitting an audience to scrutinise his body language and draw judgements on the authenticity of his claims. Once questions have been fielded, the camera cuts from Huntley's view of the blurry screen to a close-up of Huntley's face so that the audience can process how well Farmer's answers sit in relation to the narrative Huntley wants to impose on events. First Huntley nervously gulps down a bottle of water whilst Farmer tells the officers the time he left his grandma's house. Huntley then groans in close-up as Farmer's solicitor informs the investigating officers that Farmer's phone is not a smartphone, meaning it will be difficult to deduce his exact whereabouts at the specific time of the murder. Despite officers' assurances that triangulation can be conducted on all active sim cards, Huntley's reactions undercut their confidence.

From her privileged position alone in the observation room, Huntley is constantly poised to steer interrogations towards her narrative. When Melanie (Lucie Shorthouse) refuses to testify in connection with Farmer's previous sexual assault, Huntley writes a text stating 'I'm coming in' and prepares to send it to Fleming, who is conducting the interrogation. The camera focuses on Huntley's thumb in close-up whilst Melanie gives her reasons for refusing to identify Farmer in an identity parade. However, Huntley refrains from sending the message, as Fleming convinces Melanie to take part. Similarly, during

Reznikova's interview, Huntley is compelled to enter the interview suite unannounced from the observation room in order to arrest Reznikova for not letting them search her flat. Then, during Reznikova's next interview, Huntley is initially pensive, standing in her usual observation room location to dictate proceedings. However, Reznikova admits Ifield is one of her clients and that she has been contacting him through her unregistered burner phone for prostitution. As the information is confessed, the camera zooms out of Huntley's point of view of the monitor, pulls out of focus, and then cuts to a close-up of Huntley's face in which she leans back, closes her eyes, and smiles, relieved that she has finally drawn a concrete link between Ifield and Reznikova and can frame her for Ifield's murder. The camera pulling out of focus and then cutting to Huntley leaning back embodies her dizzying relief. The camera either focusing on, or simulating, Huntley's emotions during interrogations in the observation room ensures viewers process the outcome of interrogations through her emotions.

Huntley also concentrates power by micromanaging Operation Trapdoor's administration. Polk Avenue station is first revealed when Huntley enters the briefing room. Huntley takes a file from Jodie Taylor (Claudia Jessie) and pins each item from the file to the noticeboard herself, whilst the camera focuses on her face in close-up as she explains each photograph's significance. Again, Huntley's frustrations are expressed by the camera privileging her facial emotions over the evidence itself. Later, Huntley discovers Fleming has been allowed into the briefing room unsupervised to read witness transcripts. Upon hearing this, Huntley storms through the communal office, types in the security code on the briefing room door, and marches inside. Here the camera following her judders and shakes in line with the rushed, erratic, and panicked nature of Huntley's movements. Huntley loudly informs Fleming that all requests must go through her, before instructing Fleming to desist. Fleming's polite offer to put the files back where she found them is undercut by the camera whip-panning upwards from the file in Fleming's hand to Huntley's face, in tandem with Huntley snatching the file from Fleming's grasp. Even when the link between Farmer and Ifield is questioned, Huntley forcefully removes a Post-It note displaying question marks from between Farmer's and Ifield's photos on the Operation Trapdoor noticeboard and scrunches the paper in close-up. Huntley centralises power by guiding the camera's movements as she controls interrogations from the observation room, manipulates forensic evidence, and eradicates all transparency by overseeing access to files and briefings from within the locked briefing room to minimise accountability.

AC-12

Compared to Hillside Lane and Polk Avenue's authoritarian model of instrumental compliance, whereby a host of detectives are ruled over through fear of punishment, AC-12's offices adhere to a normative-compliance model of policing. The office design, power structure, work relations, and communication between the anti-corruption officers ensure that staff adhere to authority because they judge their orders to be morally appropriate and fairly enforced. AC-12 officers abide by the seven Nolan Principles of Public Life. In 1995 the first report of the Committee on Standards in Public Life, under the chairmanship of Lord Nolan, stipulated public sector workers must be committed to conducting their work with selflessness, integrity, objectivity, accountability, openness, honesty, and leadership. Since Boris Johnson won the 2019 general election, these seven principles have come under scrutiny from journalists, politicians, and religious leaders, with YouGov polling revealing that 75 per cent of Britons find Johnson untrustworthy (Smith 2022). Conservative commentator Peter Oborne has also claimed that fifty mistruths and falsehoods are made by Johnson a week on average (Oborne 2021).

Compared to the corrupt stations, where superiors are rooted to their offices, conduct chats in private, and accumulate as much power and knowledge as possible in order to protect themselves, AC-12 operates with a distinct **openness.** As this Nolan principle states, 'holders of public office should act and take decisions in an open and transparent manner' and 'information should not be withheld from the public unless there are clear and lawful reasons for so doing' (Nolan 1995: 1.5). In this bright, open-plan space, where officers of all ranks work communally, there is no paranoid secrecy between operatives. Breakthroughs take place in the central communal area of the office as evidence is processed openly using the collective expertise of all staff. In series 5, whilst Arnott is reading armed robber Lisa McQueen's (Rochenda Sandall) social services record on his computer, the camera cuts to PC Maneet Bindra (Maya Sondhi) entering the office. PC Tatleen Sohota (Taj Atwal) then stands over Arnott revealing a document detailing McQueen's call burner phone history. As Sohota passes the file over to Arnott, the camera focuses on it and moves with it in close-up. Bindra then produces a map that she places on top of the list of phone calls with McQueen's recent whereabouts. Rather than the camera being drawn to Arnott's emotional processing of evidence, here it focuses on the classified evidence, as experts disseminate its importance to the viewer. Arnott then jumps up from his desk and goes to liberate trafficked

Eastern European women from a Moss Heath brothel. Similarly, in the following episode, as Fleming enters AC-12 and stands by her desk, she asks 'what's happening?'. Before she has a chance to take off her coat or sit down, Arnott walks over to inform her that DNA evidence proves DCS Lester Hargreaves (Tony Pitts) is not 'H'. Their conversation is interrupted by Sohota and cyber analyst Amanda Yao (Rosa Escoda), who informs them the cybercrime unit have made a 'breakthrough' by linking a computer from the Kingsgate raid to Thurwell's Spanish IP address. All four officers stand in the centre of the communal office processing this evidence and explaining what it means to their investigation. Across all series, the communal office is a safe space where key classified documents are openly shared to develop cases in earshot of fellow operatives.

Alongside openness, Nolan's **objectivity** is repeatedly foregrounded by AC-12's interrogation suite. This Nolan principle states 'holders of public office must take decisions impartially, fairly and on merit, using the best evidence and without discrimination or bias' (Nolan 1995: 1.3). The interrogation suite is central to AC-12's offices, as it is surrounded by glass, directly faces Hastings's office from the other side of the room, and is a focal point for the workforce. For actors 'the glass box scenes are really pivotal', as they know 'it's what people love' (MacDonald 2021). Unlike the dark, murky, and hidden interrogation rooms of Polk Avenue and Hillside Lane used to intimidate suspects into confessing through fear of punishment, objectivity here is key. On the feature wall of the brightly lit interrogation suite is an HD television linked to an iPad. The displaying of evidence dominates the space and is the focal point of the suite, where objective truths can be scrutinised in the cold hard light of day. Whenever a new piece of evidence is formally introduced, the camera pans up from a side profile of the desk to have the screen prominently fill the frame as all characters look up towards it. The evidence has a magnetic pull, commanding the camera's gaze, dominating the room, and occupying the focus of the characters. The rapidity of evidence displayed and its dominance over the space intimidates suspects into confessing. AC-12 use this technology to piece together an objectively coherent narrative compared to other stations, where evidence is found to fit with investigators' established narrative. On average, a new piece of evidence is introduced every minute of an AC-12 interrogation scene, often with suspects instructed to look at documents both in their folders and on screen. In series 6, Davidson's first AC-12 interrogation is sixteen minutes long and she is subjected to fifteen items of evidence. Hastings exposes her weak hypothesis that Ordroyd simply killed Banks and then committed suicide because the wider picture of evidence presents a series of suspicious deaths that have not been properly investigated. Then, in Davidson's final half-hour interrogation, twenty-one items of evidence, including forensic lab reports, messages recovered from her unregistered laptop, and copies of Operation Lighthouse files found in her flat, are disclosed. The weight of evidence is what compels Davidson to stop replying with 'no comment' and confess to having planted Burner phones in Jatri's home.

Following Nolan's openness and objectivity, AC-12's strong culture of **accountability** mitigates corruption. This Nolan Principle states 'holders of public office are required to submit themselves to the scrutiny necessary to ensure they are accountable to the public' (Nolan 1995: 1.4). Through the course of the final series, Arnott has developed an addiction to painkillers following his brutal attack in series 4. The viewer witnesses Arnott deleting four e-mails from occupational health at his desk. In each instance, a viewer is introduced to the scene via a close-up of the top-right corner of Arnott's screen, replicating his point of view as a beep announces the email arriving in his inbox. Each email reads 'urgent: following your recent [drugs] test please make an appointment'. The camera then cuts to Arnott's concerned face in close-up as he sighs, before then cutting back to the previous shot, where he clicks delete. In between discovering the e-mail and clicking delete, however, Arnott looks into Hastings's office and meets his boss's gaze through the glass wall and then looks behind himself before pressing delete. In each instance that an email is deleted, Arnott is then approached by Yao and Chloe with a key piece of evidence. Despite ignoring these warnings through fear of losing his job, Arnott eventually schedules a meeting with Occupational Health. Because Arnott is under the scrutiny of all his surrounding colleagues and cannot look at his emails privately, aside from very short windows of time, he eventually complies with orders. When Arnott finally attends his Occupational Health meeting, he is told their department exists to 'help not judge' and will give him the help required to wean him off drugs. Arnott is relieved to be given assistance rather than immediate disciplinary action. This is underscored by Hastings later telling Arnott 'I'm just happy you're getting help with'. Having developed an addiction problem in the line of duty, Arnott eventually tackles his problem because the rules surrounding substance abuse are morally appropriate and enforced in ways that are fair. Rather than Hastings immediately suspending, transferring, or shunning Arnott – as superiors do in other stations to ensure their workers adhere to law through instrumental compliance – Hastings's surprise drugs test encourages Arnott to face his problems and receive support.

204 Postscript

A major reason Arnott welcomes scrutiny is because Hastings is subjected to the same checks and balances as his staff. Hastings's **leadership** actively promotes and robustly supports openness, objectivity, and accountability through how he respectfully treats others (Nolan 1995: 1.7). In terms of openness, Hastings's office has an open-door policy. Anybody can enter without an appointment, often with his door already open in earshot of others. Officers regularly letting themselves in is a far cry from the Hill Side and Polk Avenue stations, where detectives only enter superiors' offices when summoned. Within his office, Hastings hears out the opinions of his officers to determine what the most appropriate plan of action is objectively. In season 4, after their informant Ifield has been murdered, Arnott strongly asserts that AC-12 'can't sit on our hands' and that they must launch an official investigation using AC-12 as a 'blunt instrument' to seize evidence. Fleming, however, prefers to continue their current subtle undercover approach. After hearing out both officers, Hastings agrees with Arnott that they must go 'back to the coalface'. Then in, series 5, Arnott and Fleming walk into Hastings's office to inform him that Arnott has been receiving intel from the very officer they are investigating, John Corbett (Steven Graham). Initially Hastings rises to his feet, outraged that Arnott has compromised his safety by not receiving authorisation for these undercover meetings. However, following Arnott's assertion that all intelligence relayed to them has been proven correct, keeping his meetings secret has protected Hastings, and maintaining Corbett's confidence is the best means of getting to 'H', Hastings vows to consult with the DCC rather than officially report Arnott. Through careful deliberation and a discussion of the facts, Hastings deduces the most appropriate course of action. Later in the same series, Fleming enters Hastings's office to suggest it is not lawful for Hastings to sanction an undercover operation and then carry it out first-hand without consulting the head of covert unit or independent officer to guarantee his safety. Hastings concedes to Fleming's view. Hastings's detectives are loyal to him because he is accountable to the same protocols and is open to having his views changed when presented with evidence. Adherence to authority is upheld because people judge Hastings to be morally appropriate.

The Nolan principle Hastings is most associated with is **Integrity**, a word he uses often. As the Nolan committee stipulates, 'holders of public office must avoid placing themselves under any obligation to people or organisations that might try inappropriately to influence them in their work' (Nolan 1995: 1.2). Furthermore, 'they should not act or take decisions in order to gain financial or other material benefits for themselves, their family, or their friends' (Nolan 1995: 1.2). When DCS

Patricia Carmichael (Anna Maxwell Martin) is announced as Hastings's imminent replacement, the exchanges both characters have in his office are telling of their motivations for the role. When Carmichael first talks with Hastings in his office she interacts with the set design differently. Asking whether Hastings has been informed of the AC-12 restructure, she stands in front of his trophy cabinet, which is in deep focus behind her. Compared to discussions Hastings has with his team, where his trophy cabinet is edited out of the space, here it is brought into sharp focus and clearly anchors Carmichael's motivations. Carmichael is after the accolades and prestige the Superintendent title brings over the values Hastings works by. Here, Hastings says his team are the 'best' and her turning up is 'a kick in the teeth'. The camera then cuts in closer to Carmichael to reveal a closer view of the trophy cabinet behind her. We can now see four trophies and a plaque in the cabinet, with a further four plaques mounted to an adjacent wall that was previously out of shot. Carmichael walks closer to the cabinet and asks whether their case on Buckells is watertight. When Hastings replies 'no', she informs Hastings, whilst looking at the trophies instead of maintaining eye contact with him, that the charges must be dropped to avoid the humiliation of an unsuccessful trial. For Carmichael the job is about earning accolades, maintaining appearances, and satisfying political targets. This is further emphasised in the penultimate episode, when Carmichael interrupts Hastings and Arnott discussing Fleming's and Davidson's possible whereabouts. As Hastings talks from his desk, he sits in front of a photograph of his police graduation. When Carmichael comes in, she takes pleasure informing Arnott she is now in charge. Again bringing the trophy cabinet into the space, this time through her eyeline of both characters. Carmicheal informs them she has had Fleming put tracking monitors on all AC-12 cars, despite Hastings's protestation of this being a 'flagrant breach of trust'. Whilst Hastings visually aligns himself to unity and trust with his team, Carmichael sacrifices integrity for her career trajectory.

Similarly, in the last ever episode, once Carmichael assumes full control of AC-12, Hastings's former office is introduced through her point of view. Within her exact point of view, an audience watches a news report stating 'city council deny cronyism in sell-off of public land to private developers' on her desktop computer screen. After an audible click the window minimises into the bottom right corner of the screen to display the prominent AC-12 desktop wallpaper. The camera then cuts to a mid-shot of Arnott and Fleming standing over Carmichael's desk and looking at her, to imply both have been present in the room for some time before Carmichael has decided to stop watching the news and address their presence. Visually, the scene demonstrates that Carmichael always has one eye on public perceptions of her AC-12 responsibilities as a matter of priority. An audience has not witnessed Arnott and Fleming entering their superior's office. When the office was occupied by Hastings, he would meet either Fleming's or Arnott's gaze through his glass office wall and let them in to immediately talk about case developments openly whilst subjecting himself to the same accountability. However, before their conversation can continue, the camera cuts back to Carmichael's view of her laptop, to which she states 'the Chief Constable is about to make a statement, do you mind?'. Carmichael then enlarges the previously minimised window to watch the Chief Constable formally launch an enquiry into corruption. Once Carmichael stops playing the news, Hastings has entered the office to protest 'my officers have just caught the last ring leader in a clandestine network of corrupt police officers and the Chief Constable hasn't a blind word to say about it' before eulogising how we've stopped 'standing up for accountability', stopped 'caring about truth' and 'integrity'. Carmichael spends her time gazing at her computer screen, prioritising the media's perception of her work. Hastings as Superintendent, however, sits at his desk with his computer kept to one side so that he can oversee the work of his officers and regularly meet their gaze through his glass office walls, see them entering his room, look through case files, or maintain eye contact during their open discussions to objectively determine the appropriate course of action to charge suspects.

In fact, Hastings's final act in his (former) AC-12 office exudes the last two of the seven Nolan principles: **selflessness** and **honesty**. Just as Hastings has expressed that integrity has been the principal driving factor of his conduct in office and is about to leave, he decides to re-enter Carmichael's office to confess that in the previous series he disclosed to criminal Lee Banks (Alastair Natkiel) there was an informant in the OCG. Hastings hoped this would have prompted undercover Corbett to hand himself in, but instead the OCG got to him first and murdered him. Carmichael asks 'what do you expect me to do with this information' to which Hastings responds 'that's entirely up to you ma'am' before requesting that whatever she does with the information, she do it 'because you care about truth and integrity'. Here Hastings has potentially damaged his professional reputation to maintain honesty as a policing principle before retiring from AC-12. Through his tenure at AC-12, Hastings has overseen a policing model that adheres to all seven of Nolan's principles of public life. In so doing, Hastings has created a system of normative compliance where detectives buy into his hierarchy as it abides by the law fairly and in a morally appropriate manner. In sharp contrast, the corrupt Hillside Lane and Polk Avenue stations are run by an authoritarian overseeing instrumental compliance through the threat of punishment in order to receive personal material reward.

Populism and political impact

As the UK emerges from COVID, *Line of Duty* has enjoyed a new lease of life on social media in satirising the political scandals unfolding within British government. Hastings's increased obsession with honour and integrity is antithetical to populism. In 2007, Cas Mudde coined 'populist' as a term for politicians who characterise society as being divided between hardworking, virtuous and honourable people – a group they portray themselves as belonging to – and a 'corrupt elite' who have held power for too long (Mudde, 2007: 23). Since then, the Philippines' Rodrigo Duterte, Turkey's Recep Erdogan, Brazil's Jair Bolsonaro, President Donald Trump, and Prime Minister Boris Johnson have harnessed this very strategy to secure power and capitalise on the electorate's increasing feelings of marginalisation due to economic and cultural globalisation, increasing levels of immigration, and the decline of ideological class politics (Albertazzi and McDonnell 2008:1). In summary, a populist leader is someone who offers straightforward 'common-sense' solutions to society's complex problems, and in so doing adopts a forceful yet colloquial mode of communication that galvanises those who have lost faith in traditional politics and its representatives. Chief Constable Osborne's speech to the press that Carmichael makes Arnott, Fleming, and Hastings watch in her office emulates the rhetoric of populism. Despite endemic corruption, Osborne claims that 'pressure to launch a criminal investigation into police corruption is not what the public want'. He establishes himself as being in tune with the electorate's general will in seeking short-term and swift action rather than undertaking the methodical negotiation and deliberation of 'slow' politics (Moffit and Tormey 2014). Earlier in the series, when initially denying corruption, Osborne states police 'serve the public not politicians' and so 'it is about time police officers took control over policing' rather than 'unelected bureaucrats'. Through the final series, viewers learn Osborne wants to prevent an enquiry from discovering his covering up of Lawrence Christopher's racially motived murder. Therefore, Osborne spins a narrative that a nefarious elite are simply politicising events to remove him and curb the power of police officers, justifying his cuts to AC-12's power and resources to levels that have 'never been weaker', as the epilogue states.

208 Postscript

Shortly after *Line of Duty*'s broadcast, the UK government began facing pressure from opposition MPs and parts of the press to address circulating rumours that Downing Street had hosted illegal parties through the course of the pandemic, when the strictest lockdown measures, imposed by Johnson's government, were being enforced by the police. On three separate occasions, the Prime Minister dismissed the need for an enquiry, clearly stating there had been no illegal parties and all guidelines had been followed. On 26 June, when the *Mirror* broke news of an alleged 2020 Christmas party, Johnson outright denied the allegations. However, as photos were leaked to the press, an enquiry into 'partygate' was eventually launched. On 8 December, after a video of Downing Street Press Secretary Allegra Stratton was leaked in which she strongly implied Christmas parties had taken place, Johnson announced the commencement of the Civil Service's investigation.

Mercurio himself has played a notable part in the mounting pressure on the Metropolitan Police to investigate partygate. On 17 December 2021, it was announced that Cabinet Secretary Simon Case would no longer lead the partygate inquiry, as a party had been held in his own office around the same time. Two days earlier, something curious had happened. On 15 December, *Line of Duty*'s Adrian Dunbar had purportedly reprised his role as Ted Hastings for a stunt held outside New Scotland Yard. Activist group Led By Donkeys projected a five-minute clip on to the side of a van pulled up outside the Metropolitan Police headquarters. The van, which had a large television attached, hears 'Hastings' point out that the Met's original defence for not undertaking an investigation was due to 'an absence of evidence' before asserting 'the whole purpose of a police enquiry is to gather evidence'. A voice remarkably similar to Dunbar's concludes: 'Who exactly does the Metropolitan Police work for ma'am? Our citizens or Boris Johnson?' Whilst the Met refused to comment on the video directly, a spokesperson issued a statement confirming the Met 'will not commence an investigation at this time' based 'on the absence of evidence' (Hewitt 2021).

Following mounting pressure, however, on 9 February 2022 the Metropolitan Police announced they would contact over fifty people as part of Operation Hillman to probe the partygate row. Operation Hillman would investigate twelve separate gatherings across eight dates by sifting through 500 documents and 300 images from Sue Gray's Civil Service Inquiry. Before this announcement, on 18 January 2022, a video produced by Led By Donkeys was uploaded to twitter and retweeted by Jed Mercurio's account. Boris Johnson's body from previous media appearances is superimposed over the top of an interviewee in an existing *Line of Duty* interrogation scene. Voice artists sounding remarkably similar to Arnott, Fleming, and Hastings deliver dialogue dubbed over the top of extreme close-ups of each corresponding character's eyes. Here Johnson is presented with key documents in the public domain, including an email from private secretary Martin Reynolds, inviting more staff to bring their own booze to an evening party at 10 Downing Street on 20 May 2020. As in *Line of Duty*'s signature interrogation scenes, the AC-12 team reiterate the context of what happened on this date to poke holes in Johnson's public statements. Fleming points out that an hour before the party began, Culture Secretary Oliver Dowden made a televised statement reminding the public of COVID regulations. Arnott then recalls that people at that time were only permitted to meet with one person outside their household in an outdoor public place provided they stay two metres apart. Hastings puts it to Johnson that the gathering described in Reynolds's e-mail would breach 'health and protection regulations in operation at the time as you well know' and that Johnson 'knowingly and intentionally flouted the rules because you believe you're above the law'. The video satisfied the public appetite for holding Johnson to account for his crimes at a time when police officials were not. Obviously, no direct link can be drawn between these videos and the Met's decision to open Operation Hillman. Nor can it be proven with absolute certainty that without the Led By Donkeys videos, produced with Mercurio's approval, a Met investigation would not have been launched. However, these Twitter videos, watched by millions of people across the world, struck a chord with the British public and added to the pressure that would eventually result in the first instance of a sitting PM being issued with a police fine.

Vigil

The British police series in the form of a thriller where senior ranking politicians are held to account has been carried through by subsequent ratings successes. The far-reaching impact of *Line of Duty* has resulted in further series testing the mental endurance of protagonists who are restricted to a limited number of locations. Boundaries between spaces of work and leisure are thoroughly breached, and so speak to the general population, whose experience of transitioning between work and home were inhibited for the first time in generations amidst a spate of COVID-19 lockdowns. *Vigil* is a six-part submarine thriller made by World Productions and marketed as being from 'the makers of *Line of Duty*', despite Mercurio's lack of involvement. According to BARB 28-day consolidated data, *Vigil* has been the highest-rated new drama launch across all UK channels since Mercurio's political thriller *Bodyguard* (BBC 2018), with viewers growing from 10.2 million in episode 1 to 10.9 million by the finale (BBC Media Centre 2021). Based on an original idea by George Aza-Selinger, and written by Tom Edge, the series follows DCI Amy Silva's (Suranne Jones) investigation into the mysterious death of Chief Petty Officer Craig Burke (Martin Compston). Silva is sent to ballistic missile nuclear submarine HMS Vigil, where she uncovers a Russian conspiracy to discredit Britain's Trident nuclear deterrent.

Silva's three-day investigation is extended when the submarine's security is compromised by an undercover Russian spy. On land, Silva's DS and former lover, Kirsten Longacre (Rose Leslie), undertakes a parallel investigation into deceased Burke's final movements and acquaintances. Unable to send messages back to her detective team, Longacre speaks to Silva in code, referencing moments in their private lives together to communicate intel in a way undecipherable to their enemies. Silva finds herself in a claustrophobic situation where workspace, civilian space, and her own private space are not delineated. Silva's every movement is monitored by those in command of the submarine. Ultimately Silva struggles with sleeping, eating, relaxing, and spending all her leisure time in the same place she works, having been instructed on her arrival that 'there's no privacy on this boat'. Much like *Line of Duty*, *Vigil* wrangles with the implications underpinning instrumental-compliance and cultural-compliance models of policing, as Silva regularly clashes with the submarine's hierarchy and protocols and is accordingly disciplined. Lt. Commander Mark Prentice (Adam James) and Captain Commander Neil Newsome (Paterson Joseph) operate according to the navy's strict code of conduct, policing Silva through a constant threat of punishment, right down to her use of language. When Silva seeks free rein of the submarine to continue her murder enquiry she is dogmatically instructed that 'whilst you are on my boat you will obey my orders'. During her work Silva is only given specific windows of time to investigate areas of the submarine, she is specifically told 'your twenty minutes are up' after she tests Gary Walsh's (Daniel Portman) urine for traces of heroin. Every moment of her private life on the submarine is also regulated and controlled. When the coxswain, Elliot Glover (Shuan Evans), first shows Silva to her separate ladies bunk, he instructs her to sleep for four hours, to recover from the headaches she is experiencing from the low oxygen environment. Silva is not even able to carry her own medication, as all dispensed medication must come through the ship's doctor. This discovery is later used against her, as the captain fears she is spreading

Postscript 211

fear and paranoia among the crew and so confines her to quarters. The captain will not free her unless she can convince the doctor she is fit for duty, having shouted her frustrations at the captain in front of his own crew and broken hierarchical protocols.

The physical challenge Silva must face whilst navigating the complex Russian threat is being locked in closed, dark, and confined spaces with her freedoms physically limited and policed. Silva is therefore driven by memories of her previous life on shore, where her movements were not inhibited. Interestingly, the fond daydreams that motivate Silva to complete her task are memories of falling in love with Longacre at the police station they worked at together. When Silva asks to speak to the coxswain, she recalls the first time Longacre caught her eye by wearing makeup at work and buying her a hot chocolate as a means of charming Silva into helping her prepare for a promotion interview. The scene is deliberately shot through with a warm orange filter and underscored by ethereal music. In the next scene, the coxswain confesses to Silva that he was involved in blackmailing Burke. Similarly, during her breakfast on the submarine the following day, the camera focuses on Silva's pale and vacant face as she sits alone in the canteen. The sound of the submarine's engine triggers a memory; as its whirring mechanics transition into the sounds of the wind she remembers standing on the station roof with Longacre after her failed interview. As the camera cuts to this memory, the audience assumes Silva's point of view of Longacre, who a tucks her hair behind her ear and looks up at Silva in a bashful manner. In this memory Silva attempts to console Longacre by telling her nobody gets promoted on their first attempt and advising her that a successful detective 'shuts herself off and focuses on work at the cost of everything else' and therefore must not be 'emotionally involved'. She instructs Longacre not to have a heart, to which Longacre retorts, 'but you're not always at work though are ya?' before the camera cuts back to Silva sitting alone in the canteen. Silva snaps out of the daydream as she notices the chef, overcome with emotion, being congratulated by her colleagues for her son having been let out of prison. This piques Sliva's interest and commences a new line of enquiry that results in her discovering the chef is being bribed with the release of her son to sabotage the mission.

Interestingly all Silva's memories of the workplace to which she no longer has access are nostalgic, happy, and touching moments, whereas memories of her private life are dark, traumatising nightmares of her husband dying or Longacre breaking up with her. The workplace represents a time gone by, replicating the experiences the British public were experiencing through the course of COVID lockdowns, confined to their homes, unable to socialise, and having to work and relax in the same space. For many, memories of working in an office and socialising with colleagues were recalled fondly, as people could no longer have tangible interactions with people outside their household. These memories of work are what propel Silva forward, and accessing them results in breakthroughs. Her cultural compliance to this traditional mode of detection is at odds with the navy's instrumental mode of compliance, which threatens disciplinaries and keeps the truth from the public. At the end, the intelligence service chooses to cover up the Russian conspiracy. This feels increasingly prevalent in an era when Russian donations to senior politicians have fallen under scrutiny following Putin's 2022 invasion of Ukraine.

Trigger Point

Jed Mercurio's latest thriller series also blurs the distinction between home life and work life. *Trigger Point*, produced by Mercurio's HTM Television, follows the deployment of Explosives Officer (EXPO) Lana Washington (Vicky McClure) to suspected bomb sites, where she disarms explosive devices in real time. Whilst the series is executive-produced by Mercurio, it was created and written by Daniel Brierley, and directed by Gilles Bannier and Jennie Darnell. *Trigger Point* quickly became ITV's highest rated drama of 2021/2022, with nearly 10 million viewers watching the launch episode. In this episode, Washington and Joel Nutkins (Adrian Lester) are called in to deal with two improvised explosive devices (IEDs) on a council estate. In between diffusing bombs that surface one at a time, Washington takes refuge in her van, where she listens to hip hop music on full volume and reads holiday magazines, nodding along to the music with her windows shut. Whilst relaxing, Washington is approached by her boss, DI Thom Youngblood (Mark Stanley), who enters the van and sits beside her to discuss whether the bomb was planted by an Islamic fundamentalist. In the same breath, Youngblood reaches over and holds her hand tightly in a close-up and changes his intonation to an intimate level saying 'I'm glad you're OK'. Nutkins interrupts this tender private moment, prompting Youngblood to leave as Nutkins and Washington discuss her relationship with her boss through the car window. Nutkins explains his wife wants him to choose between her and his job, to which Washington replies 'then there is no choice is there', shortly before Nutkins is killed by a bomb. Again, there is a recognition here that the workplace, civilian space, and one's private space have merged into one composite space.

The Responder

BBC One hit *The Responder* is also a series that denies access to the workplace and requires all police characters to work through their personal problems whilst soldiering on with their career in a confined space or series of spaces far removed from the station. Here, PC Chris Carson (Martin Freeman) undertakes night patrols in central Liverpool. His work is interspersed with scenes of him in therapy, sleeping at home during the day, and his mother in a nursing home. Never at the police station itself, Carson is partnered with Rachel Hargreaves (Adelayo Adedayo), an inexperienced and still idealistic officer who wants to play by the rules. Carson begins his counselling by telling his therapist he wants to be a bobby who does 'good things', having been turned into a 'shell' by his job. Working from his car, the aptly named Carson is endlessly firefighting for an understaffed force as he cannot give aid to a man who cannot afford to eat, a girl who has been put in a bin by her schizophrenic mother, or an alcoholic vicar causing a public disturbance struggling with homosexuality. Instead, Carson sees his job as only helping people in immediate danger. Helping drug addict Casey (Emily Fairn) evade the clutches of Carson's childhood friend, the midlevel drug dealer Carl Sweeney (Ian Hart), represents an opportunity to make a meaningful difference. Confused with his own morality and police procedure, Carson drives around the night streets of Liverpool struggling to come to terms with the fact 'I don't know what's right and wrong anymore'. Having saved Casey, he then attempts to keep the stash of drugs for himself so he can pay off his ailing mother's debts. This nightmarish vision of contemporary policing is one that is coming to terms with its moral duty following austerity within a post-pandemic world

Conclusion

As the 2020s progress, the most successful police series continue to explore how cultural compliance can be achieved over heavy-handed instrumental compliance in a post-pandemic world. On balance, each series concurs with the Police Federation's view that, compared to the earlier iterations of the British police series, the forces that shape today's world – globalisation, technology, and market economics – are homogenising. Therefore 'culturally, architecturally, environmentally ... we are being impelled towards geographic sameness' (Higgins 2021: 2). Whilst searching for more and more 'sophisticated, evidence-based and efficient responses to social harms' has pulled policing towards the universal, most uniformed police now find themselves spending every rostered hour blue-lighting between emergency calls, as has been poignantly reflected through thriller genre formula (Higgins 2021:3). What the police service has learned from the pandemic is that 'people follow rules and cooperate with officials, not because they fear the consequences of disobedience, but when they believe that it is the right thing to do' (Higgins 2021: 6). When officials like Hastings behave 'fairly and respectfully', 'listen and allow people to have their say', and 'demonstrate that they are well-intentioned, trustworthy, and aligned with our values, they can generate the legitimacy and authority from which compliance and cooperation then flow' (Higgins 2021: 9). Even within the police force itself, television drama is understood to be an important mechanism for working through this alignment in values between a national police force and its citizens. The Police Federation cites 'Dixon and Morse and Tennison and Luther and the rest' as all having a role to play in helping us 'figure out where we stand in a world that often feels unsafe and insecure and unjust' (Higgins 2021: 8). The British television police series continues to be an important reference point for people making sense of their place in the world now, just as it did in 1955. From this perspective, there is little difference between PC George Dixon and Superintendent Ted Hastings, as both will live long in cultural mythology as they continue to anchor the nation's moral compass for generations to come.

References

Abbott, M. (2003). *Family Affairs: A History of the Family in 20th Century Britain*, London; New York: Routledge.
Abbott, P. and C. Wallace (1992). *The Family and the New Right*, London: Pluto Press.
Abel-Smith, B. and P. Townsend (1965). *The Poor and the Poorest: A New Analysis of the Ministry of Labour's Family Expenditure Surveys of 1953–54 and 1960*, London: G. Bell & Sons.
Ainsworth, P. B. (2013). *Offender Profiling and Crime Analysis*, London: Routledge.
Albertazzi, D. and D. McDonnell (2008). 'Introduction: the sceptre and the spectre', in D. Albertazzi and D. McDonnell (eds), *Twenty-First Century Populism: The Spectre of Western European Democracy*, Basingstoke: Palgrave Macmillan.
Albertazzi, D. and D. McDonnell (eds) (2008). *Twenty-First Century Populism: The Spectre of Western European Democracy*, Basingstoke: Palgrave Macmillan.
Ali, M. R. and S. Mann (2013). 'The inevitability of the transition from a surveillance-society to a veillance-society: Moral and economic grounding for sousveillance', in *2013 IEEE International Symposium on Technology and Society (ISTAS 2013): Social Implications of Wearable Computing and Augmediated Reality in Everyday Life, Toronto, Ontario, Canada, 27–29 June 2013*, Piscataway, NJ: IEEE, pp. 234–254.
Allen, R. C. (ed.) (1992). *Channels of Discourse, Reassembled*, London: Routledge.
Allen, R. C. and A. Hill (eds) (2004). *The Television Studies Reader*, London: Routledge.
Alvarado, M. and J. Stewart (eds) (1985). *Made for Television: Euston Films Ltd*, London: British Film Institute.
Arnell, T. (2008). 'Introduction', *The Gentle Touch Series One*, Network DVD.
Ascoli, D. (1979). *The Queen's Peace: The Origins and Development of the Metropolitan Police 1829–1979*, London: Hamish Hamilton.

References

Askham, J. (1984). *Identity and Stability in Marriage*, Cambridge: Cambridge University Press.

Barnes, T. (2016). '"*Dixon of Dock Green* to Darth Vader": Campaigners slam move to fit 22,000 Met Police officers with body cameras', *East London & West Essex Guardian*, 17 October, www.guardian-series.co.uk/news/14807086._Dixon_of_Dock_Green_to_Darth_Vader___campaigners_slam_move_to_fit_Met_officers_with_bodycams/ (accessed 11 October 2018).

Barry, A., T. Osborne, and N. Rose (1996). *Foucault and Political Reason: Liberalism, Neo-Liberalism and Rationalities of Government*, London: UCL Press.

Baudrillard, J. (1994). *Simulacra and Simulation*, Michigan: University of Michigan Press.

Bauman, Z. (1997). *Postmodernity and Its Discontents*, Cambridge: Polity Press.

Bazalgette, C. (1976). 'Regan and Carter, Kojack and Crocker, Batman and Robin?', *Screen Education*, 20: 54–65.

BBC (1962). 'Audience research report: *Z Cars*', BBC WAC T5/2,444/1.

BBC Media Centre (2014). 'BBC One drama *Happy Valley* closes with 7.8 m viewers', 12 June 2014, www.bbc.co.uk/mediacentre/latestnews/2014/happy-valley-figures (accessed 11 November 2018).

BBC Media Centre (2021). 'BBC's *Vigil* is the UK's most watched new drama in three years', 5 October, www.bbc.co.uk/mediacentre/2021/vigil-ratings (accessed 1 May 2020).

Beauman, S. (1982). 'Inspector Ma'am', *Radio Times* (4–10 September): 9.

Beider, H. (2011). 'White working-class views of neighbourhood, cohesion and change', *Joseph Rowntree Foundation Report*, www.jrf.org.uk/report/white-working-class-views-neighbourhood-cohesion-and-change (accessed 4 May 2016).

Bell, E. (2011). *Criminal Justice and Neoliberalism*, Basingstoke: Palgrave Macmillan.

Bellamy, E. (2000 [1888]). *Looking Backward*, Mineola, NY: Dover.

Bennett, L. and Booth, P. (eds) (2016). *Seeing Fans: Representations of Fandom in Media and Popular Culture*, London: Bloomsbury.

Bernstein, A. (2021). '*Line of Duty*: creator Jed Mercurio on season 6 – exclusive interview', *Assignment X*, 16 June, www.assignmentx.com/2021/line-of-duty-creator-jed-mercurio-on-season-6-exclusive-interview (accessed 1 May 2020).

Bevacqua, M. (2000). *Rape on the Public Agenda: Feminism and the Politics of Sexual Assault*, Boston, MA: Northeastern University Press.

Beveridge, W. (1942). *Social Insurance and Allied Services*, Cmd 6404.

Beynon, J. (2002). *Masculinities and Culture*, Philadelphia: Open University Press.

Beynon, J. and C. Bourn (eds) (1986). *The Police: Powers, Procedures and Proprieties*, Oxford: Pergamon.

Bignell, J. and S. Lacey (eds) (2005a). *Popular Television Drama: Critical Perspectives*. Manchester: Manchester University Press.

References

Bignell, J. and S. Lacey (2005b). 'Editors' introduction', in J. Bignell and S. Lacey (eds), *Popular Television Drama: Critical Perspectives*, Manchester: Manchester University Press, pp. 11–14.
Bignell, J. and S. Lacey (eds) (2014). *British Television Drama: Past, Present and Future*, 2nd edn. Basingstoke: Palgrave.
Bignell, J., S. Lacey and M. MacMurraugh-Kavanagh (eds) (2000). *British Television Drama: Past, Present and Future*, Basingstoke: Palgrave.
Biressi, A. and H. Nunn (2005). *Reality TV: Realism and Revelation*. London: Wallflower Press.
Biressi, A. and H. Nunn (2013). *Class and Contemporary British Culture*, Basingstoke: Palgrave Macmillan.
Blair, T. (1993). 'Tony Blair is tough on crime, tough on the causes of crime', *New Statesman*, 29 January, www.newstatesman.com/2015/12/archive-tony-blair-tough-crime-tough-causes-crime (accessed 25 October 2018).
Blair, T. (1999). Speech to the IPPR, 14 January, IPPR, London.
Blair, T. (2010). *A Journey*, London: Hutchinson.
Blakey, D. (2002). *Under the Microscope – Refocused: A Revisit to the Investigative Use of DNA and Fingerprints*, London: HMIC.
Blandford, S. (2013). *Jimmy McGovern*, Television Series, Manchester: Manchester University Press.
Bonner, F. (2003). *Ordinary Television: Analyzing Popular TV*, London: SAGE.
Booker, K. M. and A. M. Thomas (2009). *The Science Fiction Handbook*, Oxford: Wiley Blackwell.
Bottomley, K. A. and C. Coleman (1981). *Understanding Crime Rates: Police and Public Roles in the Production of Official Statistics*, Aldershot: Gower.
Boym, S. (2001). *The Future of Nostalgia*, New York: Basic.
Brain, T. (2010). *A History of Policing in England and Wales from 1974: The Turbulent Years*, Oxford: Oxford University Press.
Brown, G. (2006). Budget speech, 22 March, House of Commons, London.
Brunsdon, C. (2000). 'The structure of anxiety: Recent British television crime fiction', in E. Buscombe (ed.). *British Television: A Reader*, Oxford: Clarendon Press, pp. 195–217.
Brunsdon, C. (2001). 'London films: From private gardens to utopian moments', *Cineaste*, 26.4: 43–46.
Brunsdon, C. (2010). *Law and Order*, BFI TV Classics, London: British Film Institute.
Brunsdon, C. (2016). 'Bad sex, target culture, and the anti-terror state: New contexts for the twenty-first century British television police series', in R. McElroy (ed.), *Cops on the Box: Contemporary British Television Crime Drama*, London: Routledge, pp. 27–39.
Brunsdon, C., J. D'Acci, and L. Spigel (eds) (1997a). *Feminist Television Criticism: A Reader*, Oxford: Oxford University Press.
Brunsdon, C., J. D'Acci, and L. Spigel (1997b). 'Introduction', in C. Brunsdon, J. D'Acci, and L. Spigel (eds), *Feminist Television Criticism: A Reader*, Oxford: Oxford University Press, pp. 1–16.

References

Brunsdon, C., J. D'Acci, and L. Spigel (eds) (2008). *Feminist Television Criticism: A Reader*, 2nd edn. Oxford: Oxford University Press.

Bryson, V. and T. Heppell (2010). 'Conservatism and feminism: The case of the British Conservative Party', *Journal of Political Ideologies*, 15.1: 31–50.

Buscombe, E. (1976). '*The Sweeney*: Better than nothing?', *Screen Education*, 20: 66–69.

Buscombe, E. (ed.) (2000). *British Television: A Reader*, Oxford: Clarendon Press.

Cardwell, S. (2007). 'Is quality television any good? Generic distinctions, evaluations, and the troubling matter of critical judgement', in J. McCabe and K. Akass (eds), *Quality TV: Contemporary American Television and Beyond*, London; New York: I.B. Tauris, pp. 19–34.

Caughie, J. (2000). *Television Drama: Realism, Modernism, and British Culture*, Oxford: Oxford University Press.

Cavadino, M. and J. Dignan (2006). 'Penal policy and political economy', *Criminology and Criminal Justice*, 6.4: 435–456.

Chapman, J. (2002). *Saints and Avengers: British Adventure Series of the 1960s*, London: I.B. Tauris.

Chapman J. (2009). 'Not "another bloody cop show": *Life on Mars* and British television drama', *Film International*, 7.2: 6–19.

Chappell, L. (2012). 'Review: *Prime Suspect*, Series 3', https://thiswastv.com/2012/08/29/review-prime-suspect-series-3/ (accessed 26 October 2018).

Chilton, L. (2021). '*Line of Duty* named UK's most-watched tv drama of the 21st century', Independent, 11 May, www.independent.co.uk/arts-entertainment/tv/line-of-duty/line-of-duty-ratings-bbc-b1845404.html (accessed 1 May 2020).

Chipping, T. (2012). 'An interview with the writer of *The Killing*, Søren Sveistrup', Holy Moly, 11 December, www.holymoly.com/tv/interviews/interview-writer-killing-s%C3%B8ren-sveistrup65350 (accessed 12 November 2018).

Clark, D. (ed.) (1991). *Marriage, Domestic Life and Social Change: Writings for Jacqueline Burgoyne (1944–88)*, London: Routledge.

Clarke, A. (1992). '"You're nicked": TV police series and the fictional representation of law and order', in D. Strinatic and S. Wagg (eds), *Come on Down? Popular Media Culture in Post-War Britain*, London: Routledge, pp. 232–253.

Clarke, R. V. G. (1987). 'Rational choice theory and prison psychology', in B. J. McGurk, D. Thornton, and M. Williams (eds), *Applying Psychology to Imprisonment: Theory and Practice*, London: HMSO.

Clover, C. J. (1992). *Men, Women and Chainsaws: Gender in the Modern Horror Film*, Princeton: Princeton University Press.

Cloward R. A. and L. E. Ohlin (1998 [1960]). *Delinquency and Opportunity: A Theory of Delinquent Gangs*, London: Routledge.

Cohen, A. K. (1955). *Delinquent Boys: The Culture of the Gang*, New York: Free Press.

Cohen, E. L. and M. Felson (1979). 'Social change and crime rate trends: A routine activity approach', *American Sociological Review*, 44.4: 588–608.
Connell, R. W. (2005). *Masculinities*, 2nd edn. Cambridge: Polity.
Cooke, L. (2005). 'Style, technology and innovation in British television drama', *Journal of British Cinema and Television*, 2.1: 82–99.
Cooke, L. (2012). *Troy Kennedy Martin*, Television Series, Manchester: Manchester University Press.
Cooke, L. (2013). *Style in British Television Drama*, Basingstoke: Palgrave Macmillan.
Cooke, L. (2015a). *British Television Drama: A History*, 2nd edn. London: British Film Institute.
Cooke, L. (2015b). 'The police procedural', in G. Creeber (ed.), *The Television Genre Book*, London: British Film Institute, pp. 26–27.
Cooke, L. (2020). 'Ben Lamb, *You're Nicked: Investigating British Television Police Series*' book review, *Screen*, 61:4: 655–658.
Coote, A. and B. Campbell (1987). *Sweet Freedom: The Struggle for Women's Liberation*, 2nd edn. Oxford: Basil Blackwell.
Copping, J. (2014). 'Police told to avoid saying "evenin' all"', *Daily Telegraph*, 24 October, www.telegraph.co.uk/news/uknews/law-and-order/6423899/Police-told-to-avoid-saying-evenin-all.html (accessed 11 October 2018).
Corner, J. (ed.) (1991). *Popular Television in Britain: Studies in Cultural History*, London: British Film Institute.
Cornish, C. B and R. V. G. Clarke (1987). 'Understanding crime displacement: An application of rational choice theory', *Criminology*, 25.4: 933–947.
Cowley, R. (2011). *A History of the British Police: From the Earliest Beginnings to the Present Day*, Stroud: History Press.
Creeber, G. (2002). 'Old sleuth or new man? Investigations into rape, murder and masculinity in *Cracker* (1993–1996)', *Continuum Journal of Media & Cultural Studies*, 16.2: 169–183.
Creeber, G. (2004). *Serial Television: Big Drama on the Small Screen*, London: British Film Institute.
Creeber, G. (2015a). 'Killing us softly: Investigating the aesthetics, philosophy and influence of Nordic noir television', *Journal of Popular Television*, 3.1: 21–35.
Creeber, G. (2015b). *The Television Genre Book*, 3rd edn. London: British Film Institute.
Creed, B. (2003). *The Monstrous-Feminine: Film, Feminism, Psychoanalysis*, London: Routledge.
Crest (2020). *Understanding the Lessons of Policing the COVID-19 Pandemic*. London: Crest Advisory.
Crewe, Q. (1974). 'Time to spring a surprise', *The Times*, 27 July.
Crozier, D. (2013). Interview with the author.
D'Acci, J. (2004). 'Television, representation and gender', in R. C. Allen and A. Hill (eds), *The Television Studies Reader*, London: Routledge.

D'Arcy, G. (2018). *Critical Approaches to TV and Film Set Design*, London: Routledge.
Dave, P. (2017). 'Contemporary British social realist film: *Bypass*, obscure forces and ontological unrest', in E. Mazierska and L. Kristensen (eds), *Contemporary Cinema and Neoliberal Ideology*, London: Routledge, pp. 121–136.
De Beauvoir, S. (1993 [1953]). *The Second Sex*, London: David Campbell.
Deane Potter, J. (1976). 'Potato poaching is just one more burden for the village bobby', *TV Times*, 29 May–4 June.
Dennington, J., and J. Tulloch (1976). 'Cops, consensus and coherence', *Screen Education*, 20: 47–53.
Devine, F. (2004). *Class Practices: How Parents Help Their Children Get Good Jobs*, Cambridge: Cambridge University Press.
Diamond, J. (2005). *Collapse: How Societies Choose to Fail or Succeed*, New York: Viking.
Donald, J. (1985). 'Anxious moments: *The Sweeney* in 1975', in M. Alvarado and J. Stewart (eds), *Made for Television: Euston Films Ltd*, London: British Film Institute, pp. 117–135.
Douglas, S. and M. Michaels (2004). *The Mommy Myth: The Idealization of Motherhood and How It Has Undermined Women*, London: Free Press.
Dowland, P., S. Furnell, H. Illingworth, and P. Reynolds (1999). 'Computer crime and abuse: A survey of public attitudes and awareness', *Computers and Security*, 18.8: 715–26.
Drummond, P. (1976). 'Structural and narrative constraints in *The Sweeney*', *Screen Education*, 20: 15–36.
Duguid, M. (2009). *Cracker*, BFI TV Classics, London: British Film Institute.
Dyer, G. and H. Baehr (eds) (1987). *Boxed In: Women and Television*, New York; London: Pandora Press.
Dyer, R. (1980). 'Introduction', in R. Dyer, M. Jordan, T. Lovell, R. Paterson, J. Stewart, and C. Geraghty (eds), *Coronation Street*, BFI TV Monographs, London: British Film Institute, pp. 1–8.
Dyer, R., M. Jordan, T. Lovell, R. Paterson, J. Stewart, and C. Geraghty (eds) (1980). *Coronation Street*, BFI TV Monographs, London: British Film Institute.
Edwards, S. (1989). *Policing 'Domestic' Violence: Women, the Law and the State*, London: SAGE.
Elam, K. (1980). *The Semiotics of Theatre and Drama*, London: Methuen.
Erickson, C. L. (1999). 'Neo-environmental determinism and agrarian "collapse" in Andean prehistory', *Antiquity*, 73: 634–642.
Evans, D. T. (1993). *Sexual Citizenship: The Material Construction of Sexualities*, New York: Routledge.
Feuer, J. (1992). 'Genre study and television', in R. Allen (ed.), *Channels of Discourse, Reassembled*, London: Routledge, pp. 138–160.
Fichtelberg, A. and A. Kupchik (2011). 'Democratic criminology: The place of criminological expertise in the public sphere', *Journal of Theoretical and Philosophical Criminology*, 3.1: 57–88.

Finch, J. and D. Morgan (1991). 'Marriage in the 1980s: A new sense of realism?', in D. Clark (ed.), *Marriage, Domestic Life and Social Change: Writings for Jacqueline Burgoyne (1944–88)*, London: Routledge, pp. 55–82.

Fisher, M. (2014). *Ghosts of My Life: Writings on Depression, Hauntology and Lost Futures*, Winchester: Zero.

Fiske, J. (2003). *Reading Television*, 2nd edn. London: Routledge

Franklin, B. (ed.) (2005). *Television Policy: The MacTaggart Lectures*, Edinburgh: Edinburgh University Press.

Fraser, D. (2009). *The Evolution of the British Welfare State*, 4th edn. Basingstoke: Palgrave Macmillan.

Freud, S. (2003 [1919]). *The Uncanny*, trans. D. McLintock, London: Penguin.

Friedan, B. (2010 [1963]). *The Feminine Mystique*, London: Penguin.

Frith, S. (2000). 'The black box: The value of television and the future of television research', *Screen*, 41.1: 33–50.

Fukuyama, F. (1989). 'The End of History?', *The National Interest*, 16: 1–18.

Gallix, A. (2011). 'Hauntology: A not-so-new critical manifestation', *Guardian*, 17 June, www.theguardian.com/books/booksblog/2011/jun/17/hauntology-critical (accessed 8 November 2018).

Gambaccini, P. and R. Taylor (1993). *Television's Greatest Hits: Every Hit Television Programme since 1960*, London: Network.

Gamman, L. (1988). 'Watching the detectives: The enigma of the female gaze', in L. Gamman and M. Marshment (eds), *The Female Gaze: Women as Viewers of Popular Culture*, London: Women's Press, pp. 8–26.

Gamman, L. and M. Marshment (eds) (1988). *The Female Gaze: Women as Viewers of Popular Culture*, London: Women's Press.

Garland, D. and R. Sparks (eds) (2000a). *Criminology and Social Theory*, Oxford: Oxford University Press.

Garland, D. and R. Sparks (2000b). 'Criminology, social theory, and the challenge of our times', in D. Garland and R. Sparks (eds), *Criminology and Social Theory*, Oxford: Oxford University Press, pp. 1–22.

Garnett, T. (1998). '"Trojan horses" and "bad apples": Tony Garnett discusses *The Cops*'. Unpublished transcript of a seminar held in the Department of Film and Drama, University of Reading, November 1998, plus material incorporated from an interview by Madeline Macmurraugh-Kavanagh, 5 January 1998.

Garnett, T. (2008). 'Criminal minds documentary', *Law and Order*, BBC DVD.

Genz, S. (2009). '"I'm not a housewife but ...": Postfeminism and the rise of domesticity' in Stacy Gillis and Joanne Hollows (eds), *Feminism, Domesticity and Popular Culture*, New York; London: Routledge, pp. 49–62.

Genz, S. and A. Brabon (2018). *Postfeminism: Cultural Texts and Theories*, Edinburgh: Edinburgh University Press.

Geraghty, C. (1991). *Women and Soap Opera: A Study of Prime Time Soaps*, Cambridge: Polity Press.
Gibbs, J. (1975). *Crime, Punishment, and Deterrence*, New York: Elsevier.
Giddens, A. (1991). *Modernity and Self-Identity: Self and Society in the Late Modern Age*, Cambridge: Polity Press.
Giddens, A. (1992). *The Transformation of Intimacy: Sexuality, Love and Eroticism in New Societies*, Cambridge: Polity Press.
Gifford, T. (1986). *The Broadwater Farm Inquiry*, London: Karia Press.
Gilbert, G. (2013). 'David Tennant: From time traveller to crime unraveller', 20 February, www.independent.co.uk/arts-entertainment/tv/features/david-tennant-from-time-traveller-to-crime-unraveller-8501554.html (accessed 11 November 2018).
Gillis, S. and J. Hollows (eds) (2009). *Feminism, Domesticity and Popular Culture*, New York; London: Routledge.
Glaser, D. (1971). *Social Deviance*, Chicago: Markham.
Gledhill, C. (1987). *Home Is where the Heart Is: Studies in Melodrama and the Woman's Film*, London: British Film Institute.
Glover, M. (2003). 'The Thriller', in M. Priestman (ed.), *The Cambridge Companion to Crime Fiction*. Cambridge: Cambridge University Press, pp. 135–154.
Goodwin, A. and G. Whannel (eds) (1990). *Understanding Television*, London: Routledge.
Goodwin, T. (2007). 'Cops and clobber: What I learned from 24 years in *The Bill*', *Guardian*, 8 March, www.theguardian.com/media/2007/mar/08/broadcasting.tvandradio (accessed 19 October 2018).
Gorton, K. (2016). 'Feeling northern: "Heroic women" in Sally Wainwright's *Happy Valley* (BBC One, 2014–)', *Journal for Cultural Research*, 20.1: 73–85.
Grabosky, P. and R. Smith (2001). 'Telecommunication fraud in the digital age: The convergence of technologies', in D. Wall (ed.), *Crime and the Internet*, London: Routledge.
Graham, A. (2013). '*Broadchurch*: Alison Graham interviews Chris Chibnall on making a perfect TV murder drama', *Radio Times* (13–19 April), www.david-tennant-news.com/blog/broadchurch-alison-grahaminterviews-chris-chibnall-on-what-makes-a-perfect-tv-murder-dramavia-radio-times/ (accessed 11 November 2018).
Graham, M. (2008). '*Life on Mars*: Your Questions,' www.bbc.co.uk/lifeonmars/backstage/questions_inspiration.shtml (accessed 8 November 2018).
Grainge, P. (2002). *Monochrome Memories: Nostalgia and Style in Retro America*, Connecticut: Praeger.
Gray, R. (ed.) (1962). *Kafka: A Collection of Critical Essays*, Englewood Cliffs: Prentice Hall.
Green, D. G. (1996). 'Foreword: The emerging British underclass', in R. Lister (ed.), *Charles Murray and the Underclass: The Developing Debate*, London: Institute of Economic Affairs Health and Welfare Unit, pp. 19–22.

References

Green, R. (2007). 'Forensic investigation in the UK', in T. Newburn, T. Williamson, and A. Wright (eds), *Handbook of Criminal Investigation*, Cullompton: Willan, pp. 338–356.

Greer, A. (2017). '"I'm not your mother!": Maternal ambivalence and the female investigator in contemporary crime television', *New Review of Film and Television Studies*, 15.3: 327–347.

Greer, G. (2008 [1970]). *The Female Eunuch*, London: Harper Perennial.

Home Affairs Committee (HAC) (2016). *Police and Crime Commissioners: Here to Stay*, House of Commons Home Affairs Committee, Seventh Report of Session 2015–16, HC844.

Hall, E. (1966). *The Hidden Dimension*, New York: Doubleday.

Hall, S. (1973). 'Encoding and decoding in the television discourse', paper for the Council of Europe Colloquy on 'Training in the critical reading of television language', organised by the Council and the Centre for Mass Communication Research, University of Leicester, September, Centre for Contemporary Cultural Studies, stencilled paper no. 7.

Hall, S., C. Critcher, T. Jefferson, J. N. Clarke, and B. Roberts (1978). *Policing the Crisis: Mugging, the State, and Law and Order*, London: Macmillan.

Hallam, J. (2000). 'Power plays: Gender, genre, and Lynda La Plante', in J. Bignell, S. Lacey, and M. MacMurraugh-Kavanagh (eds), *British Television Drama: Past, Present and Future*, Basingstoke: Palgrave, pp. 140–149.

Hallam, J. (2005). *Lynda La Plante*, Television Series, Manchester: Manchester University Press.

Hallam, J. and M. Marshment (2000). *Realism and Popular Cinema*, Manchester: Manchester University Press.

Hanmer, J. (1989). 'Women and policing in Britain', in J. Hanmer, J. Radford, and E. Stanko (eds), *Women, Policing, and Male Violence: International Perspectives*, London: Routledge, pp. 90–124.

Hanmer, J., J. Radford, and E. Stanko (eds) (1989). *Women, Policing, and Male Violence: International Perspectives*, London: Routledge.

Harvey, D. (2005). *A Brief History of Neoliberalism*, Oxford: Oxford University Press.

Hay, J. and L. Ouellette (2008). *Better Living through Reality TV: Television and Post-Welfare Citizenship*, Oxford: Blackwell.

Heath, S. (1981). *Questions of Cinema*, London: Macmillan.

Hennessy, P. (2010). 'Labour's *Ashes to Ashes* poster scores own goal', *Daily Telegraph*, 3 April, www.telegraph.co.uk/news/election-2010/7550214/Labours-Ashes-to-Ashes-poster-scores-own-goal.html (accessed 27 November 2018).

Her Majesty's Stationery Office (HMSO) (1998). *Human Rights Act*, Chapter 42.

Hewitt, R. (2021). 'Street protest sees "Ted Hastings" take on Downing Street party claims', *Belfast Telegraph*, 15 December, www.belfasttelegraph.co.uk/news/northern-ireland/street-protest-sees-ted-hastings-take-on-downing-street-party-claims-41154300.html (accessed 1 May 2020).

Higgins, A. (2021). *Police in Place: Why the Police Need to Reconnect Locally*, Police Federation, www.police-foundation.org.uk/publication/perspectives-on-policing-police-in-place-why-the-police-need-to-reconnect-locally (accessed 1 May 2020).
Higson, A. (ed.) (1996a). *Dissolving Views: Key Writings on British Cinema*, London: Cassell.
Higson, A. (1996b). 'Space, place, spectacle: Landscape and townscape in the "kitchen sink" film', in A. Higson (ed.), *Dissolving Views: Key Writings on British Cinema*, London: Cassell, pp. 133–156.
Hill, C. P. (1985). *British Economic and Social History 1700–1982*, 5th edn. London: Edward Arnold.
Hill, J. (1986). *Sex, Class and Realism: British Cinema 1956–1963*, London: British Film Institute.
Hill, J. (2000). 'Failure and utopianism: Representations of the working class in British cinema of the 1990s', in R. Murphy (ed.), *British Cinema of the 90s*, London: British Film Institute, pp. 178–187.
Hills, M. (2002). *Fan Cultures*, London: Routledge.
Hobbes, G. (1980). '*The Gentle Touch*', *Daily Mail*, 11 April, p. 27.
Hobbs, D. (1988). *Doing the Business: Entrepreneurship, the Working Class and Detectives in the East End of London*, Oxford: Clarendon Press.
Hockenhull, S. (2009). 'An aesthetic approach to contemporary British social realism: London to Brighton', *Film International*, 7.6: 65–74.
Hogarth, R. (2020). 'The government must draw a clear line between law and guidance during the coronavirus crisis'm *Institute for Government*. Available from: www.instituteforgovernment.org.uk/blog/government-law-and-guidancecoronavirus-crisis (accessed 1 May 2022).
Hoggart, R. (2009 [1957]). *The Uses of Literacy: Aspects of Working-Class Life*, London: Penguin.
Holdsworth, A. (2011). *Television, Memory and Nostalgia*, Basingstoke: Palgrave Macmillan.
Holmes, S. (2008). *The Quiz Show*, Edinburgh: Edinburgh University Press.
Home Office (2001). *Policing a New Century: A Blueprint for Reform*, Cm 5326.
Home Office (2018). *Crime Outcomes in England and Wales: Year Ending March 2018*, Statistical Bulletin HOSB 10/18.
Hopkins, J. and A. Prior (1963). 'Allan Prior and John Hopkins talking about the *Z Cars* series', *Screen Education*, 21: 8–21.
Hopkins Burke, R. (2013). *An Introduction to Criminological Theory*, 4th edn. Cullompton: Willan.
Hurd, G. (1976). '*The Sweeney*: Contradiction and coherence', *Screen Education*, 20: 47–53.
Intergenerational Commission (2018). *A New Generational Contract: The Final Report of the Intergenerational Commission*, London: Resolution Foundation.

Ipsos MORI Social Research Institute (2017). *Public Perceptions of Policing in England and Wales 2017*, report for Her Majesty's Inspectorate of Constabulary and Fire & Rescue Services.

Irving, B. (1986). 'The interrogation process', in J. Beynon and C. Bourn (eds), *The Police: Powers, Procedures and Properties*, Oxford: Pergamon, pp. 136–149.

Irving, B. and I. McKenzie (1989). *Police Interrogation: The Effects of the Police and Criminal Evidence Act 1984*, London: Police Foundation.

ITV (2017). 'Report: Final *Broadchurch* episode pulls in biggest ever audience', www.itv.com/news/westcountry/2017-04-18/final-broadchurch-episode-pulls-in-biggest-ever-audience/ (accessed 27 September 2018).

Jachimiak, P. H. (2012). 'Time travel, childhood, and the uncanny home in *Life on Mars* and *Ashes to Ashes*', in S. Lacey and R. McElroy (eds), *'Life on Mars': From Manchester to New York*, Cardiff, University of Wales Press, pp. 91–104.

James, A. (2013). *Examining Intelligence-Led Policing*, Basingstoke: Palgrave Macmillan.

Jancovich, M. (ed.) (2001). *Horror: The Film Reader*, London: Routledge.

Jenkins, H. (2012). *Textual Poachers: Television Fans and Participatory Culture*, 2nd edn. London; New York: Routledge.

Jenner, M. (2017). 'Binge-watching: Video-on-demand, quality TV and mainstreaming fandom', *International Journal of Cultural Studies*, 20.3: 304–320.

Jermyn, D. (2008). 'Women with a mission: Lynda La Plante, DCI Jane Tennison and the Reconfiguration of Crime Drama', in C. Brunsdon, J. D'Acci, and L. Spigel (eds), *Feminist Television Criticism: A Reader*, 2nd edn. Oxford: Oxford University Press, pp. 57–71.

Jermyn, D. (2010). *Prime Suspect*, BFI TV Classics, London: British Film Institute.

Jermyn, D. (2013). 'Labs and slabs: Television crime drama and the quest for forensic realism', *Studies in History and Philosophy of Science Part C: Studies in History and Philosophy of Biological and Biomedical Sciences*, 44.1: 103–109.

John, T. and M. Maguire (2004). *The National Intelligence Model: Key Lessons from Early Research*, Home Office Online Report 30/04, http://citeseerx.ist.psu.edu/viewdoc/download?doi=10.1.1.625.4738&rep=rep1&type=pdf (accessed 8 November 2018).

Johnson, C. and R. Turnock (eds) (2005). *ITV Cultures: Independent Television over Fifty Years*, Maidenhead: Open University.

Jones, E. (2003). *The European Miracle: Environments, Economies and Geopolitics in the History of Europe and Asia*, 3rd edn. Cambridge: Cambridge University Press.

Kantis, C., S. Kiernan, J. Socrates Bardi, and L. Posner (2022). 'Timeline of the Coronavirus', *Think Global Health*, 29 April, www.thinkglobalhealth.org/article/updated-timeline-coronavirus (accessed 1 May 2022).

References

Keay, D. (1987). 'No such thing as society', interview for *Woman's Own*, 23 September, pp. 3–45, www.margaretthatcher.org/document/106689 (accessed 19 October 2018).
Kennedy Martin, I. (2008). *Juliet Bravo*, www.iankennedymartin.com/page6.htm (accessed 19 October 2018).
Kennedy Martin, T. (1961). '*Z Cars*', BBC WAC T5/ 2, 506/1.
Kennedy Martin, T., T. Childs, and T. Clegg (2007). 'Thin ice' episode commentary, *The Sweeney: Series One*, Network DVD.
Kenny, M. (1981). 'A policewoman's lot is such a happy one', *Daily Mail*, 7 November, pp. 18–19.
Keynes, J. M. (1949). *The General Theory of Employment, Interest, and Money*, London: Macmillan.
Kingston, A. (2004). *The Meaning of Wife*, London: Piatkus.
Kingsley, H. (1994). '*The Bill*': *The First Ten Years*, London: Boxtree.
Kingsley Kent, S. (1999). *Gender and Power in Britain, 1640–1990*. London; New York: Routledge.
Kinsey, R. (1985). *Survey of Merseyside Police Officers: First Report*, Liverpool: Merseyside County Council.
Koestler, A. (2015 [1941]). *Darkness at Noon*, New York: Simon and Schuster.
Kovacich, G. (1999). 'Hackers: Freedom fighters of the 21st century', *Computers and Security*, 18.7: 573–576.
Kristeva, J. (1982). *Powers of Horror: An Essay on Abjection*, trans. L. S. Roudiez, Columbia: Columbia University Press.
Kupers, T. A. (2005). 'Toxic masculinity as a barrier to mental health treatment in prison', *Journal of Clinical Psychology*, 61.6: 713–724.
Lacey, S. (2005). 'Becoming popular: Some reflections on the relationship between television and theatre', in J. Bignell and S. Lacey (eds), *Popular Television Drama: Critical Perspectives*, Manchester: Manchester University Press, pp. 198–214.
Lacey, S. (2007). *Tony Garnett*, Television Series, Manchester: Manchester University Press.
Lacey, S. and M. MacMurraugh-Kavanagh (1999). 'Who framed theatre?', *New Theatre Quarterly*, 57: 58–74.
Lacey, S. and R. McElroy (eds) (2012). *'Life on Mars': From Manchester to New York*, Cardiff: University of Wales Press.
Laing, S. (1991). 'Banging in some reality: The original *Z Cars*', in J. Corner (ed.), *Popular Television in Britain: Studies in Cultural History*, London: British Film Institute, pp. 125–144.
Lamb, B. (2014). '"Ah! Our very own *Juliet Bravo*, or is it Jill Gascoine?" *Ashes to Ashes* and Representations of Gender', in J. Bignell and S. Lacey (eds), *British Television Drama: Past, Present and Future*, 2nd edn. Basingstoke: Palgrave, pp. 203–213.
Lea, J. (2010). 'Left Realism, Community and State-Building', *Crime, Law and Change*, 54: 141–158.
Lea, J. and J. Young (1993). *What Is to Be Done about Law and Order? Crisis in the Nineties*, London: Pluto Press.

Lefebvre, M. (2011). 'On landscape in narrative cinema', *Canadian Journal of Film Studies*, 21.1: 61–78.
Levitas, R. (1990). *The Concept of Utopia*, London: Philip Allan.
Lewis, J. (ed.) (1997). *Lone Mothers in European Welfare Regimes: Shifting Policy Logics*, London: Jessica Kingsley.
Lewis, J. and B. Hobson (1997). 'Introduction', in J. Lewis (ed.), *Lone Mothers in European Welfare Regimes: Shifting Policy Logics*, London: Jessica Kingsley, pp, 1–20.
Lewis, P. (1962). '*Z Cars*', *Contrast* 1.4: 301–315.
Lister, R. (ed.) (1996). *Charles Murray and the Underclass: The Developing Debate*, London: Institute of Economic Affairs, Health and Welfare Unit.
Logan, E. (2016). '"Quality television" as a critical obstacle: Explanation and aesthetics in television studies', *Screen*, 57.2: 144–162.
Lopate, C. (1977). 'Daytime television: You'll never want to leave home', *Radical America*, 11.1: 32–51.
Loveday, B. and A. Reid (2003). *Going Local: Who Should Run Britain's Police?*, London: Policy Exchange.
Lynch, T. (1991). '*The Bill': The Inside Story of British Television's Most Successful Police Series*, London: Boxtree.
Lyon, D. (2007). *Surveillance Studies: An Overview*, Cambridge: Polity Press.
Lyons, J. and M. Jancovich (2003). *Quality Popular Television: Cult TV, the Industry and Fans*, London: British Film Institute.
Lyotard, J. F. (1984). *The Postmodern Condition: A Report on Knowledge*, Manchester: Manchester University Press.
MacDonald, K. (2021). *BBC Breakfast*, BBC One, 26 April.
MacInnes, J. (1998). *The End of Masculinity: The Confusion of Sexual Genesis and Sexual Difference in Modern Society*, Buckingham: Open University Press.
Maguire, M. and R. Morgan (eds). *The Oxford Handbook of Criminology*, 4th edn. Oxford: Oxford University Press.
Mahase, E. (2021). 'Calling out liars: five minutes with ... Jed Mercurio', *British Medical Journal*, 10 December, p. 375.
Mann, S. (2013). 'Veillance and reciprocal transparency: Surveillance versus sousveillance, AR glass, lifelogging, and wearable computing', in *2013 IEEE International Symposium on Technology and Society (ISTAS 2013): Social Implications of Wearable Computing and Augmediated Reality in Everyday Life, Toronto, Ontario, Canada, 27–29 June 2013*, Piscataway, NJ: IEEE, pp. 1–12.
Mays, J. (1954). *Growing Up in the City: A Study of Juvenile Delinquency in an Urban Neighbourhood*, Liverpool: Liverpool University Press.
Mazierska, E. and L. Kristensen (eds) (2017). *Contemporary Cinema and Neoliberal Ideology*, London: Routledge.
McCabe, J. and K. Akass (2007). *Quality TV: Contemporary American Television and Beyond*, London; New York: I.B. Tauris.

McCahill, M. (2002). *The Surveillance Web: The Rise of Visual Surveillance in an English City*, Cullompton: Willan.
McDaniel, J. L. M. (2018). 'Evaluating the ability and desire of police and crime commissioners (PCCs) to deliver community-oriented policing', in G. Leventakis and M. R. Haberfeld (eds), *Societal Implications of Community-Oriented Policing and Technology Practice*, London: Springer.
McElroy, R. (ed.) (2016). *Contemporary British Television Crime Drama: Cops on the Box*, New York: Routledge.
McGrath, J. (2005 [1976]). 'Television drama: The case against naturalism', in B. Franklin (ed.), *Television Policy: The MacTaggart Lectures*, Edinburgh: Edinburgh University Press, pp. 35–44.
McGuigan, J. (ed.) (2013). *Raymond Williams on Culture and Society: Essential Writings*, Los Angeles: SAGE.
McGuire, B. and A. Wraith (2000). 'Legal and psychological aspects of stalking: A review', *Journal of Forensic Psychiatry*, 11.2: 316–327.
McLean, G. (2012). 'The no. 1 ladies' detective agency', *Radio Times* (10–16 March): 10–13.
McRae, S. (1999). *Changing Britain: Families and Households in the 1990s*, Oxford: Oxford University Press.
McRobbie, A. (2007). 'Postfeminism and popular culture: *Bridget Jones* and the new gender regime', in A. McRobbie, Y. Tasker, and D. Negra (eds), *Interrogating Postfeminism: Gender and the Politics of Popular Culture*, Durham, NC: Duke University Press, pp. 27–39.
McRobbie, A., Y. Tasker, and D. Negra (2007) (eds). *Interrogating Postfeminism: Gender and the Politics of Popular Culture*, Durham, NC: Duke University Press.
Meggers, B. J. (2010). *Prehistoric America: An Ecological Perspective*, 3rd edn. New Brunswick: Aldine Transaction.
Mellencamp, P. (1986). 'Situation comedy, feminism and Freud: Discourses of Gracie and Lucy', in T. Modleski (ed.), *Studies in Entertainment: Critical Approaches to Mass Culture*, Bloomington: Indiana University Press, pp. 80–95.
Mercurio, J. and V. McClure (2017). '*Line of Duty* Masterclass' in *Edinburgh TV Festival*, 24 August, www.youtube.com/watch?v=pAKaXfNvfpE (accessed 1 May 2022).
Merton, R. K. (1938). 'Social structure and anomie', *American Sociological Review*, 3: 672–682.
Messner, S. and R. Rosenfeld (2013). *Crime and the American Dream*, Belmont: Wadsworth Cengage Learning.
Metropolitan Police (2008). 'Flying Squad', http://webarchive.nationalarchives.gov.uk/20081107220129/http:/www.met.police.uk/history/flying_squad.htm (accessed 17 October 2018).
Meyer, W. B. and D. M. T. Guss (2017). *Neo-Environmental Determinism: Geographical Critiques*, Basingstoke: Palgrave Macmillan.
Millington, B. and R. Nelson (1986). '*Boys from the Blackstuff*': *The Making of TV Drama*, London: Comedia.

Mittell, J. (2008). 'A cultural approach to television genre theory', in G. R. Edgerton and B. G. Rose (eds). *Thinking Outside the Box*, Lexington: University Press of Kentucky, pp. 37–64.

Modleski, T. (1979). 'In search of tomorrow in today's soap operas: Notes on a feminine narrative form', *Film Quarterly*, 33.1: 12–21.

Modleski, T. (ed.) (1986). *Studies in Entertainment: Critical Approaches to Mass Culture*, Bloomington: Indiana University Press.

Moffit, B. and S. Tormey (2014). 'Rethinking Populism: Politics, Mediatisation and Political Style', *Political Studies*, 62:2, pp. 381–397.

Moodie, D. (1957). Memo, 13 November, BBC WAC T12/75/3.

More, J. (2017). 'Budget 2017: Chancellor tries *Dixon of Dock Green* act but it can't last', *Independent*, 8 March, www.independent.co.uk/news/business/comment/budget-2017-chancellor-tries-dixon-of-dock-green-act-but-it-cant-last-a7619001.html (accessed 11 October 2018).

Morris, T. (1998 [1957]). *The Criminal Area: A Study in Social Ecology*, London: Routledge & Kegan Paul.

Morris, W. (1993 [1890]). *News from Nowhere*, London: Penguin.

Mort, F. (1996). *Cultures of Consumption: Masculinities and Social Space in Late Twentieth-Century Britain*, London: Routledge.

Mudde, C. (2007). *Populist Radical Right Parties in Europe*, Cambridge: Cambridge University Press.

Mulvey, L. (1989 [1975]). 'Visual pleasure and narrative cinema', in L. Mulvey (ed.), *Visual and Other Pleasures*, Basingstoke: Macmillan, pp. 14–30.

Munt, S. R. (1994). *Murder by the Book: Feminism and the Crime Novel*, London; New York: Routledge.

Murphy, R. (ed.) (2000). *British Cinema of the 90s*, London: British Film Institute.

Murray, C. (1996 [1989]). 'The emerging British underclass', in R. Lister (ed.), *Charles Murray and the Underclass: The Developing Debate*, London: Institute of Economic Affairs, Health and Welfare Unit, pp. 23–52.

Naughton, J. (2006). 'The most original cop show ... since the 70s', *Radio Times* (7–13 January), p. 9.

Neale, S. (1986). 'Melodrama and tears', *Screen*, 27.6: 6–23.

Neale, S. (2015). 'Television and genre', in G. Creeber (ed.), *The Television Genre Book*, London: British Film Institute, pp. 4–6.

Negra, D. (2009). *What a Girl Wants? Fantasizing the Reclamation of Self in Postfeminism*, Abingdon: Routledge.

Nelson, R. (2007). *State of Play: Contemporary 'High-End' TV Drama*, Manchester: Manchester University Press.

Newcomb, H. (ed.) (2000). *Television: The Critical View*, 6th edn. Oxford: Oxford University Press.

Newcomb, H. and P. Hirsch (2000). 'Television as a cultural forum', in H. Newcomb (ed.), *Television: The Critical View*, 6th edn. Oxford: Oxford University Press.

Newman, S. (1962). 'My policy for archair theatre', *Television Mail*, 27 April, 1–6.

Nolan, M. P. (1995). *The Seven Principles of Public Life*, www.gov.uk/government/publications/the-7-principles-of-public-life (accessed 1 May 2022).
Oborne, P. (2021). 'Mission statement', *The lies, falsehoods and misrepresentations of Boris Johnson and his government*, 23 November, https://boris-johnson-lies.com/mission-statement (accessed 1 May 2022).
Office for National Statistics (2017). 'Overview of the UK population', www.ons.gov.uk/peoplepopulationandcommunity/populationandmigration/populationestimates/articles/overviewoftheukpopulation/july2017 (accessed 28 September 2018).
Orwell, G. (2008 [1949]). *1984*, London: Penguin.
Osgerby, B. (1998). *Youth in Britain since 1945*, Oxford: Blackwell.
Oxford English Dictionary (2011). Oxford: Oxford University Press.
Parker, S. (ed.) (2013a). *The Squeezed Middle: The Pressure on Ordinary Workers in America and Britain*. Bristol: Policy Press.
Parker, S. (2013b). 'Introduction', in S. Parker (ed.), *The Squeezed Middle: The Pressure on Ordinary Workers in America and Britain*. Bristol: Policy Press, pp. 1–14.
Paterson, E. (1991). 'Gritty Woman', *Time Out*, 10 April.
Paterson, R. (1976). '*The Sweeney*: A Euston Films Product', *Screen Education*, 20: 5–14.
Paterson, R. (1980). 'The production context of *Coronation Street*', in R. Dyer, C. Geraghty, M. Jordan, T. Lovell, R. Paterson, and J. Stewart (eds), *Coronation Street*, BFI TV Monographs, London: British Film Institute, pp. 53–66.
Perks, L. G. (2015). *Media Marathoning: Immersions in Morality*, New York: Lexington.
Perry, G. (2016). *The Descent of Man*, London: Penguin.
Perryman, M. (ed.). *Altered States: Postmodern Politics and Culture*, London: Lawrence Wishart.
Phillips, M. (1980). 'Hartley's heroine', *Radio Times* (30 August–5 September), p. 9.
Pickering, M. and E. Keightley (2006). 'The modalities of nostalgia', *Current Sociology*, 54.6: 919–941.
Pickett, K. and R. Wilkinson (2010). *The Spirit Level: Why Equality Is Better for Everyone*. London: Penguin.
Pilkington Committee (1962). *Broadcasting Policy: The Pilkington Report*, Cmnd 1753.
Piper, H. (2015). *The TV Detective: Voices of Dissent in Contemporary Television*, New York; London: I.B. Tauris.
Piper, H. (2016). 'Broadcast drama and the problem of television aesthetics: Home, nation, universe', *Screen*, 57.2: 163–183.
Piper, H. (2017). '*Happy Valley*: Compassion, evil and exploitation in an ordinary "trouble town"', in D. Forrest and B. Johnson (eds), *Social Class and Television Drama in Contemporary Britain*, Basingstoke: Palgrave Macmillan, pp. 181–200.
Porter, A. (2011). 'UK riots: Michael Gove pledges to tackle the underclass',

References

Daily Telegraph, 2 September, https://www.telegraph.co.uk/news/politics/8736640/UK-riots-Michael-Gove-pledges-to-tackle-underclass.html (accessed 11 November 2018).
Potter, J. (1990). *Independent Television in Britain, Vol. IV: Companies and Programmes, 1968–80*, London: Macmillan.
Priestman, M. (ed.) (2003). *The Cambridge Companion to Crime Fiction*, Cambridge: Cambridge University Press.
Probyn, E. (1990). 'New traditionalism and post-feminism: TV does the home', *Screen*, 31.2: 147–159.
Pugh, M. (2017). *State and Society: A Social and Political History of Britain since 1870*, 5th edn. London: Bloomsbury.
Rawlings, P. (2002). *Policing: A Short History*, Cullompton: Willan.
Redvall, E. N. (2013). '"Dogmas" for television drama: The ideas of "one vision", "double storytelling", "crossover" and "producer's choice" in drama series from the Danish public service broadcaster DR', *Journal of Popular Television*, 1.2: 227–234.
Reiner, R. (2007). 'Political economy, crime and criminal justice', in M. Maguire and R. Morgan (eds), *The Oxford Handbook of Criminology*, 4th edn. Oxford: Oxford University Press, pp. 341–380.
Reiner, R., S. Livingstone and J. Allen (2001). 'Casino culture, media, and crime in a winner–loser society', in K. Stenson and R. R. Sullivan (eds), *Crime, Risk and Justice: The Politics of Crime Control in Liberal Democracies*, Cullompton: Willan, pp. 194–213.
Reith, J. (1925). 'Memorandum of information on the scope and conduct of the Broadcasting Service', Reading: BBC Written Archive.
Richards, M. and B. J. Elliot (1991). 'Sex and marriage in the 1960s and 1970s', in D. Clark (ed.), *Marriage, Domestic Life and Social Change: Writings for Jacqueline Burgoyne (1944–88)*, London: Routledge, pp. 33–54.
Ridgman, J. (2012). 'Duty of care: Crime drama and the medical encounter', *Critical Studies in Television*, 7.1: 1–12.
Roberts, K. (2011). *Class in Contemporary Britain*, 2nd edn. Basingstoke: Palgrave Macmillan.
Roberts, L. (2016). 'Landscapes in the frame: Exploring the hinterlands of the British procedural drama', *New Review of Film and Television Studies*, 14.3: 364–385.
Rogers, M. (2009). 'The Bill 1984–2009: Genre, production, redefinition', *Refractory*, 15, refractory.unimelb.edu.au/2009/06/25/the-bill-1984-%E2%80%93-2009-genre-production-redefinition-margaret-rogers/ (accessed 19 October 2018).
Rolinson, D. (2011). 'Small screens and big voices: Televisual social realism and the popular', in D. Tucker (ed.), *British Social Realism in the Arts since 1940*, Basingstoke: Palgrave Macmillan, pp. 172–211.
Sachs, J. D. (2008). *Common Wealth: Economics for a Crowded Planet*, New York: Penguin.
Sampson, H. O. (1958). Memo, 1 November, BBC WAC T12/75/2.

Sartre, J.-P. (2000 [1938]). *Nausea*, London: Penguin
Sartre, J.-P. (2007 [1945]). *Existentialism Is a Humanism*, New Haven: Yale University Press.
Scannell, P. (1990). 'Public service broadcasting: The history of a concept', in A. Goodwin and G. Whannel (eds), *Understanding Television*, London: Routledge, pp. 11–29.
Scarman, L. R. (1982). *The Scarman Report. The Brixton Disorders, 10–12 April 1981: Report of an Inquiry. Presented to Parliament by the Secretary of State for the Home Department by Command of Her Majesty, November 1981*, London: Penguin.
Seiter, E. (1982). 'Promise and contradiction: The daytime television serials', *Screen*, 23 (Winter): 150–163.
Sherry, T. (2009). 'Cops like us,' *Radio Times* (11–17 July), p. 10.
Shubik, I. (1975). *Play for Today: The Evolution of Television Drama*, Manchester: Manchester University Press.
Skirrow, G. (1987). 'Women/acting/power', in G. Dyer and H. Baehr (eds), *Boxed In: Women and Television*, New York; London: Pandora Press, pp. 164–183.
Smart, B. (2015). 'Producing classics on outside broadcast in the 1970s: *The Little Minister* (1975), *As You Like It* (1978), and *Henry VIII* (1979)', *Critical Studies in Television*, 10.3: 67–82.
Smith, M. (2022). 'Public opinion of Boris Johnson's competence and trustworthiness reach new lows', *YouGov*, https://yougov.co.uk/topics/politics/articles-reports/2022/02/22/public-opinion-boris-johnsons-competence-and-trust (accessed 1 May 2022).
Soen, H. (2021). '*Line of Duty* viewing figures: how many people watched each series of the show', *The Tab*, https://thetab.com/uk/2021/04/23/line-of-duty-viewing-figures-each-series-statistics-203184 (accessed 1 May 2020).
Sparks, R. (1992). *Television and the Drama of Crime: Moral Tales and the Place of Crime in Public Life*, Buckingham: Open University Press.
Stenson, K. and R. R. Sullivan (eds) (2001). *Crime, Risk and Justice: The Politics of Crime Control in Liberal Democracies*, Cullompton: Willan.
Stott, C. (2020). 'The challenges of change: policing, legitimacy and the liberalisation of government guidance', *Policing insight*. Available from: https://policinginsight.com/features/analysis/the-challenges-of-change-policing-legitimacyand-the-liberalisation-of-government-guidance (accessed 1 May 2022).
Stott, C., O. West, and M. Harrison (2020). 'A turning point, securitization, and policing in the context of COVID-19: building a new social contract between state and nation?', *Policing*, 14.3: 574–578.
Strinatic, D. and S. Wagg (eds) (1992). *Come on Down? Popular Media Culture in Post-War Britain*, London: Routledge.
Sutcliffe, T. (2003). 'Last night's television', *Independent*, 28 March, p. 19.
Suvin, D. (1988). *Positions and Presuppositions in Science Fiction*, Kent, OH: Kent State University Press.

References

Sydney-Smith, S. (2002). *Beyond 'Dixon of Dock Green': Early British Police Series*, New York; London: I.B. Tauris.

Sylvester, R. and A. Thomson (2016). 'Beat bobbies are failing to cut crime rates', *The Times*, 24 March, www.thetimes.co.uk/article/beat-bobbies-are-failing-to-cut-crime-rates-n9v9xf7l5 (accessed 11 October 2018).

Tannock, S. (1995). 'Nostalgia critique', *Cultural Studies*, 9.3: 453–464.

Taylor, J. R. (1962). *Anatomy of a Television Play*, London: Weidenfeld & Nicolson.

Telotte, J. P. (1980). 'Faith and idolatry in the horror film', *Literature/Film Quarterly*, 8: 143–155.

Thomas, D. and B. Loader (eds) (2000a). *Cybercrime: Law Enforcement, Security and Surveillance in the Information Age*, London: Routledge.

Thomas, D. and B. Loader (2000b). 'Introduction – cybercrime: Law enforcement, security and surveillance in the information age', in D. Thomas and B. Loader (eds), *Cybercrime: Law Enforcement, Security and Surveillance in the Information Age*, London: Routledge, pp. 1–14.

Thomas, L. (1997 [1995]). 'In love with *Inspector Morse*', in C. Brunsdon, J. D'Acci, and L. Spigel (eds), *Feminist Television Criticism: A Reader*, Oxford: Oxford University Press, pp. 184–204.

Thompson, R. J. (1997). Television's Second Golden Age: From *Hill Street Blues* to *ER*, New York: Syracuse University Press.

Travis, A. (2018). 'Rise in recorded crime is accelerating in England and Wales', *Guardian*, 25 January, www.theguardian.com/uk-news/2018/jan/25/knife-and-gun-rises-sharply-in-england-and-wales (accessed 11 November 2018).

Trouleau, W., A. Ashkan, D. Weicong, and B. Eriksson (2016). 'Just one more: modeling binge watching behavior', in *KDD '16: Proceedings of the 22nd ACM SIGKDD International Conference on Knowledge Discovery and Data Mining* (KDD San Francisco August 13–17), pp. 1215–1224.

Tucker, D. (ed.) (2011). *British Social Realism in the Arts since 1940*, Basingstoke: Palgrave Macmillan.

Tulloch, J. (1990). *Television Drama: Agency, Audience, Myth*, London: Routledge.

Turnbull, S. (2014). *The TV Crime Drama*, Edinburgh: Edinburgh University Press.

Turnbull, S. (2015). 'Trafficking in TV crime: Remaking *Broadchurch*', *Continuum: Journal of Media & Cultural Studies*, 29.5: 706–717.

Urwin, J. (2016). *Man Up: Surviving Modern Masculinity*, London: Icon.

Voiskounsky, A., J. Babeva, and O. Smyslova (2000). 'Attitudes towards computer hacking in Russia', in D. Thomas and B. Loader (eds), *Cybercrime: Law Enforcement, Security and Surveillance in the Information Age*. London: Routledge.

Wacquant, L. (2009). *Punishing the Poor: The Neoliberal Government of Social Insecurity*. Durham, NC: Duke University Press.

Walker, C. and S. Roberts (2017a). 'Masculinity, labour, and neoliberalism: Reviewing the field', in C. Walker and S. Roberts (eds),

234 References

Masculinity, Labour, and Neoliberalism: Working-Class Men in International Perspective, Basingstoke: Palgrave Macmillan, pp. 1–28.
Walker, C. and S. Roberts (2017b). *Masculinity, Labour, and Neoliberalism: Working-Class Men in International Perspective*, Basingstoke: Palgrave Macmillan.
Wall, D. (ed.) (2001). *Crime and the Internet*, London: Routledge.
Wall, D. S. (1998). *The Chief Constables of England and Wales: The Socio-Legal History of a Criminal Justice Elite*, Aldershot: Ashgate.
Walton-Pattison, E., S. U. Dombrowski, and J. Presseau (2018). '"Just one more episode": frequency and theoretical correlates of television binge watching', *Journal of Health Psychology*, 23:1, 17–24.
Webb, R. (2018). *How Not to Be a Boy*, Edinburgh: Canongate.
Wells, H. G. (2006 [1905]). *A Modern Utopia*, London: Penguin.
Wheatley, H. (2005). 'Rooms within rooms: *Upstairs Downstairs* and the studio costume drama of the 1970s', in C. Johnson and R. Turnock (eds), *ITV Cultures: Independent Television over Fifty Years*, Maidenhead: Open University, pp. 143–158.
Wheatley, H. (2006). *Gothic Television*, Manchester: Manchester University Press.
Wheatley, H. (2016). *Spectacular Television: Exploring Televisual Pleasure*, London: I.B. Tauris.
Wheeler, W. (1994). 'Nostalgia isn't nasty: The postmodernising of parliamentary democracy', in M. Perryman (ed.), *Altered States: Postmodern Politics and Culture*, London: Lawrence Wishart, pp. 94–107.
White, L. (2003). *'Armchair Theatre': The Lost Years*, Tiverton: Kelly.
White, M. (1992). 'Ideological analysis and television', in R. Allen (ed.), *Channels of Discourse, Reassembled*, London: Routledge, pp. 161–202.
Wickham, P. (2010). '*New Tricks* and the invisible audience', *Critical Studies in Television*, 5.1: 69–81.
Williams, R. (1990). *What I Came to Say*, London: Hutchinson Radius.
Williams, R. (2013). 'The idea of a common culture', in J. McGuigan (ed.), *Raymond Williams on Culture and Society: Essential Writings*, Los Angeles: SAGE, pp. 93–100.
Willis, A. (2012). 'Memory banks failing! *Life on Mars* and the politics of re-imagining the police and the seventies', in S. Lacey and R. McElroy (eds), *'Life on Mars': From Manchester to New York*, Cardiff: University of Wales Press, pp. 57–68.
Willis, M. (2016). 'Unlocking the mechanism of murder: Forensic humanism and contemporary crime drama', in R. McElroy (ed.), *Contemporary British Television Crime Drama: Cops on the Box*, New York: Routledge, pp. 40–53.
Willis, T. (1964). 'Dock Green through the years', *Radio Times* (12–18 September), p. 7.
Wilson, E. (1987). 'Thatcherism and women: After seven years', *Socialist Register*, 23: 199–235.

References

Wilson, J. Q. (1975). *Thinking about Crime*, New York: Basic.

Winkler, R. O. C. (1962). 'The novels', in R. Gray (ed.), *Kafka: A Collection of Critical Essays*, Englewood Cliffs: Prentice Hall, pp. 45–52.

Wood, R. (2001 [1979]). 'The American nightmare: Horror in the 70s', in M. Jancovich (ed.), *Horror: The Film Reader*, London: Routledge, pp. 25–32.

Wyllie, C., S. Platt, J. Brownlie, A. Chandler, S. Connolly, R. Evans, *et al.* (2012). *Men, Suicide, and Society: Why Disadvantaged Men in Mid-Life Die by Suicide*, London: Samaritans Research Report.

Yar, M. (2013). *Cybercrime and Society*, Los Angeles: SAGE.

Young, J. (1992). 'Ten points of realism', in R. Matthews and J. Young (eds), *Rethinking Criminology: The Realist Debate*, London: SAGE, pp. 24–68.

Young, J. (2003). 'Merton with energy, Katz with structure', *Theoretical Criminology*, 7.3: 389–414.

Young, J. and R. Matthews (eds) (1992). *Rethinking Criminology: The Realist Debate*, London: SAGE.

Zimring, F. and G. Hawkins (1973). *Deterrence*, Chicago: University of Chicago Press.

Index

Note: 'n.' after a page reference indicates the number of a note on that page.

A10 42–43
ABC (Associated British
    Corporation) 14–17,
    35–36
abject, the 93–95, 97–98, 100,
    103, 105–106, 110, 116,
    160–161, 183
    see also horror film; monstrous
    feminine
angry young men 24
    see also British new wave; social
    realism
anomie theory 23–35, 27, 29,
    32, 34, 50
    see also deviant subculture theory;
    predestined actor model
Armchair Theatre 14, 15, 17
ASBO (anti-social behaviour order)
    138, 139
Ashes to Ashes 190
Associated Rediffusion 36
ATV (Associated Television) 35–37
austerity 11, 149, 152–154,
    158–167, 169, 171, 176,
    178–179, 184

BAFTA 92, 94, 96, 111, 130, 152
Barlow at Large 33
Barr, Robert 5, 17, 181
Barry, Michael 14, 17, 182

BBC (British Broadcasting
    Corporation) 6, 9, 14–17,
    19, 29, 32–33, 41, 62–63,
    72, 79, 91, 111, 119, 120–121,
    122, 126, 129, 144, 149,
    152, 182
Between the Lines 111
Beveridge, William 2, 25
Bill, The 9–10, 61, 62, 79–88, 89,
    90, 119, 183, 184, 185, 191
binge watching 149
Blair, Tony 90, 99, 113, 138
Blue Lamp, The 14
Blunkett, David 134
bourgeois 99–103, 105–108, 111, 119,
    173, 187
Brexit 192
Bridge, The 151, 155
British new wave 11, 24, 162,
    163–166, 171, 186
    see also angry young men; social
    realism
British Police Force 8, 9, 10, 14,
    17, 18–19, 21, 22, 29, 34,
    38, 39, 41, 49, 50, 61, 65,
    66, 68, 80–82, 84–86,
    88–89, 90, 91–92, 110, 113,
    121–122, 134, 153–154, 182
Brixton riots (1981) 65, 71
Broadcasting Act (1990) 91

Index   237

Broadcasting Act (2003) 128
Broadchurch 1, 11, 149, 151–152, 154, 160–164, 169–173, 176–180, 183, 186, 187, 192
Broadwater Farm 85
Brown, Gordon 138

Cameron, David 170, 190
Carleton Greene, Hugh 17
Carlton Television 91, 121
CCTV (closed circuit television) 123, 130, 134–135, 140
see also sousveillance; surveillance
Channel 4 91, 96, 115, 121, 151, 152
chav 138–139
Chibnall, Steve 149, 151, 152
Childs, Ted 35, 41–45, 53, 57, 182
CID (Criminal Investigation Department) 19–22, 29–30, 37–38, 88
Citizen's Charter 92, 96
coalition government 153
common culture 11, 172–176, 178–179
Communications Act (2003) 121
Conservative Party, the 50, 134, 171, 190
Cops, The 5, 10, 90, 111–119
Coronation Street 18, 27, 90, 126
Cracker 90, 91, 92, 96–98, 103–105, 109–111, 118–119, 183, 185, 188, 190, 192
Crime and Disorder Act (1998) 114, 116
Cross, Neil 150
CSI: Crime Scene Investigation 123
cybercrime 137–138, 142, 148

deindustrialisation 33, 115, 142, 183
see also masculinity, in crisis; working class, masculinity
democratic criminology 175
deterrence doctrine 51–52, 73, 184

see also rational actor model
deviant subculture theory 9, 13, 23, 25, 28, 29, 184
see also anomie theory; predestined actor model
Dixon of Dock Green 4, 5, 9, 13–18, 23, 27, 28, 30, 32–33, 37, 76, 182, 187
DNA 122–123, 127–128, 152
see also forensics
docusoap 10, 119, 111–112, 115–117
Domestic Proceedings and Magistrates' Courts Act (1978) 48
Domestic Violence and Matrimonial Proceedings Act (1976) 48
drone aerial photography 148, 172, 178, 183
see also landscape documentaries
dystopia 183, 130–134, 148
see also sci-fi

Elstree Studios 36
Endeavour 190
Euston Films 36, 41, 44
see also Thames Television
existentialism 107–111, 118
see also new individualism

Fabian of the Yard 33n.2
fandom 191
feminism 3, 7, 9, 35, 45–50, 56, 58–59, 70–73, 89, 103, 107, 110, 189
see also middle class, femininity; postfeminism; upper class, femininity
Flying Squad 9, 41–43, 50, 57
forensic humanism 124–126, 135
forensics 95, 106, 122–124, 125, 127, 148, 160
see also DNA
freeview 149

Garnett, Tony 5, 6, 61, 111, 114, 115, 183
Gentle Touch, The 9, 61–63, 66–68, 70–71, 73–75, 77–79, 82, 83, 87, 88–89, 182, 184, 189, 191
Gideon's Way 3
gothic, the 102–103, 118, 185
  see also horror film
Graham, Matthew 120, 130
Granada 92, 96, 121
Greater Manchester Police 96, 130, 134, 150, 183, 189, 190

Happy Valley 11, 149, 151–152, 158–162, 164–169, 171–176, 178–180, 184, 186, 192
Harris, Richard (writer) 94, 108
hauntology 133–134
  see also postmodernism
HD (high definition) 149, 171, 172, 178, 183, 186
Heath, Edward 2, 50, 189
  law and order campaign 50
Highway Patrol 19
Hinterland 151
Hooper, Ewan 37
horror film 3, 10, 90–91, 93, 97–108, 110, 118, 120, 183, 185
  see also abject, the; gothic, the; monstrous feminine
Howard, Michael 92
Hunter's Walk 9, 35, 37–41, 45–50, 52, 53–56, 58–59, 64, 76, 77, 78, 94, 108, 171, 182, 184, 189, 191
hyperreal 124, 125, 148
  see also postmodernism; utopia

Inspector George Gently 190
Inspector Morse 58, 91, 94, 96, 121, 135
intelligence-led policing 3, 121–122, 123–124, 126, 128–129, 132–133, 134, 136, 147–148, 183
  see also smart policing

interdependence 151, 154, 155–156, 160–161, 169, 171–172, 176, 179, 184
interrogation methods 53, 66–67, 98, 123–124, 130–131, 183
ITA (Independent Television Authority) 14, 36
ITC (Incorporated Television Company) 36
ITV (Independent Television) 11, 14–18, 59, 91, 111, 121, 122, 151

Jack and Knaves 33n.2
Juliet Bravo 4, 9, 61–70, 71–79, 182, 184, 189, 191

Kennedy Martin, Ian 4, 41, 43, 62, 66, 191
Kennedy Martin, Troy 6, 17, 21–22, 44, 60n.5, 191
Killing, The 151, 152, 155

La Plante, Lynda 6, 58, 62, 71, 92
Labour Party, the 3, 10, 104, 113, 114, 129, 134, 138–139, 140, 152, 153, 190, 192
  see also New Labour
Lancashire Constabulary 21
landscape documentaries 11, 162–166, 186
Law and Order 6, 61
Left Realism 10, 91, 114
Liberal Democrats 153
Life on Mars 10, 120, 129–134, 140–148, 183, 185, 188, 190
Line of Duty 150, 192
Loach, Ken 115, 119
Luther 150, 192
LWT (London Weekend Television) 63

Macready, Sir Nevil 41
Major, John 92
male gaze 56–57, 62, 187
Mark, Robert 5, 38, 41, 182

Index

masculinity 3, 43, 58
　in crisis 10, 90, 103–105,
　　109–111, 119
　see also deindustrialisation; toxic
　　masculinity; working
　　class, masculinity
May, Theresa 153
Maynard Keynes, John 2, 138
McGovern, Jimmy 6, 96, 103
McGrath, John 13, 17, 19
Mecurio, Jed 150
melodrama 63, 78, 88, 110, 182
Menaul, Christopher 91
Merseyside Police 22, 34
Metropolitan Police 5, 38, 41, 63,
　　84, 92, 110, 126, 127, 153,
　　182, 187
middle class
　femininity 10, 45–48, 57, 71–73,
　　100, 105, 118, 169–172,
　　185–187
　professionalism 57, 109, 138,
　　140–143, 185 187
　values 24, 28, 30, 31, 43, 101,
　　107–109, 138, 163–166, 173,
　　175–176, 185–186, 192
　see also bourgeois;
　　squeezed middle
Mirren, Helen 92
monstrous feminine 93–94, 97,
　　106, 111, 183
　see also abject, the; gothic, the;
　　horror film
Moodie, Douglas 15, 16
Murder One 152

Neal, Gub 96
neo-environmental determinism
　　163–164, 169, 171, 172,
　　179, 186
neoliberalism 2, 71, 74, 75, 89,
　　138, 141, 148 151, 152, 155,
　　161, 169, 172, 176, 186,
　　188, 192
Netflix 151
new individualism 10, 91, 117–119

New Labour 10, 91, 111, 113–114,
　　129, 134, 138–140,
　　152, 185
　see also Labour Party, the
New Scotland Yard 59
New Tricks 10, 120, 126–129, 134,
　　138–140, 142, 143, 146–148,
　　183, 185
Newman, Kenneth 85
Newman, Sydney 16, 17, 33
Nordic Noir 11, 151, 152, 154,
　　157, 162
nostalgia 9, 10, 129, 133, 143,
　　144–148
　nostalgia mode 129, 133
　reflective nostalgia 143, 146
　see also postmodernism

OB (outside broadcasting) 10
Ofcom (Office of
　　Communications) 121
offender profiling 97, 190
Osborne, George 153

Parkin's Patch 59
Pilgrim Street 5
Pinewood studios 35, 36
Play for Today 33, 61, 115
　see also social realism;
　　Wednesday Play
Police 79
Police Act (1964) 92
Police Act (1996) 92
police and crime commissioners 153
Police and Criminal Evidence
　　Act (PACE) (1984) 66,
　　80–82, 88
Police and Magistrates Court Act
　　(1994) 91–92
Police Authority, the 92
Police Federation 153
postfeminism 10, 11, 73, 83, 88–89,
　　171–172, 178
　new traditionalism 11, 171, 178
　new momism 178
　see also feminism

Index

postmodernism 120, 124–125, 129–130, 133, 143, 147–148, 186, 188, 192
  see also hyperreal; nostalgia, nostalgia mode
postwar settlement 2, 7–9, 13, 23, 25–27, 29, 32, 35, 59, 68, 85, 91, 143, 175, 184, 188
  see also Welfare State
predestined actor model 23, 50, 73, 114, 138
  see also anomie theory; deviant subculture theory
Prime Suspect 10, 58, 62, 71, 90–94, 96, 97, 98, 99–101, 103, 105–107, 110, 115, 118–119, 121, 131, 147–148, 183, 185, 187, 190
Professionals, The 3
proletariat, the 99–101, 105–106
  see also working class, culture; working class, masculinity
proxemics 30

quality television 11, 149, 191

rational actor model 10, 35, 50–53, 59, 61, 73, 75, 90, 111, 114, 138, 166
  see also deterrence doctrine
rational choice theory 73–75, 87–88, 184
Reith, John 14, 16, 32
Ripper Street 190
routine activity approach 87–88
Royal Commission on Criminal Procedure (1979) 66
Rutherford, Norman 17

Scarman Report (1981) 9, 65 86, 87, 89
sci-fi 3, 10, 125, 130, 147, 183
Scotland Yard 41, 44, 59
Scott & Bailey 150–151

semiotics 7, 187
sexual division of labour 3, 54, 58, 70–71, 74, 77–78
Sexual Offences Act (1956) 66
Sherlock 3
Shirley, Lloyd 36
Shubik, Irene 40
Silent Witness 122
sitcom 15, 187
smart policing 126–129
  see also intelligence-led policing
soap opera 3, 11n.4, 9, 28, 50, 58, 76, 78–79, 88, 96, 110, 117, 150–151, 182, 187
social class relations 2–3, 6–8, 11, 14, 35, 59, 61, 68, 90, 137, 178–180, 184–186, 191
  see also wealth gap
social realism 3, 13, 18–19, 22–23, 28, 33, 91, 115–158, 119, 120, 130, 162, 164–165, 171, 176, 182, 184
  horizontality 91, 116–118, 119
  see also angry young men; British new wave; Loach, Ken
Social Security Act (1973) 11n.2
Social Security Act (1986) 11n.2
Social Security and Housing Benefit Act (1982) 11n.2, 85
Softly Softly 5, 33, 61
sousveillance 135–137, 140, 142
South Yorkshire Police 153
Southcliffe 151
Special Branch 61
Special Branch 139
Spooks 3, 129
squeezed middle 11, 166–169
  see also middle class, professionalism; middle class, values
Storyboard 79
super-rich, the 139–140, 142, 148, 185

Index

Supplementary Benefit Act (1966) 11n.2
surveillance 99, 120, 135, 140
   see also CCTV
Sweeney, The 1, 4–5, 9, 35–36, 41–45, 50–53, 56–57, 59, 61, 62, 131, 182, 184, 189

Target 61
Tearaway 33n.2
technological utopianism 125–126, 147, 183
   see also utopia
Teddington Studios 79
Telecrimes 5, 181
Television Act (1954) 13
Thames Television 36, 91
   see also Euston Films
Thatcher, Margaret 2, 68, 70, 78, 83
   Thatcherism 68–70
Touch of Frost, A 10, 90–92, 94–95, 98, 101–103, 105, 107–109, 110, 111, 118, 119, 183, 185, 190
toxic masculinity 167–169, 172, 175, 177, 179, 186
   see also masculinity, in crisis; working class, masculinity
Trial and Retribution 122
Tunnel, The 151
Turner, Stephanie 189
Twin Peaks 152

uncanny, the 143–146
underclass 10, 90, 98–102, 103, 105, 110, 114–116, 118–119, 142, 164–166, 171–173, 179, 185–186
upper class 52
   femininity 70–71, 75, 77
Upstairs Downstairs 7, 187
utopia 125, 134, 137
   see also forensic humanism; sci-fi; technological utopianism

Wainwright, Sally 150
Waking the Dead 10, 120, 122–126, 128, 129, 130, 133, 134–138, 140, 142, 147, 183, 185, 191–192
wealth gap 29, 140, 142, 162, 164, 166, 169
   see also social class relations
Wednesday Play 33, 115
   see also Play for Today; social realism
Welfare State 2, 13, 29, 54, 84–85, 89, 98, 104, 151, 161–162
   see also postwar settlement, Beveridge, William
Wessex Police 154–155
West Yorkshire Police 49, 159
western influence 3
Whitechapel 190
Who, Me? 33n.2
Widows 62, 71
Willis, Ted 14, 37
Wilsher, J. C. 111
Wilson, Harold 2
working class
   culture 18, 22, 25, 28, 31–34, 114, 139, 140–144, 148, 163, 173, 182, 185, 192
   masculinity 9, 10, 13–14, 18, 23–34, 43, 52, 59, 69–70, 74, 75, 88, 109–111, 131, 185, 188, 192
   see also deindustrialisation; proletariat, the; social class relations; underclass
World Productions 111

Yorkshire Ripper, the 49

Z Cars 5, 9, 13, 17–34, 38, 39, 40, 44, 45, 56, 64, 76, 77, 78, 81, 115, 165, 172, 179, 182, 184, 187, 188

EU authorised representative for GPSR:
Easy Access System Europe, Mustamäe tee 50,
10621 Tallinn, Estonia
gpsr.requests@easproject.com

www.ingramcontent.com/pod-product-compliance
Lightning Source LLC
Chambersburg PA
CBHW070326240426
43671CB00013BA/2375